THE COMMUNIST CHASM:

How the Dreams of a Better Life Became a Terrible Nightmare

THE COMMUNIST CHASM:
How the Dreams of a Better Life Became a Terrible Nightmare

by

Nan Wisherd

Brule, Wisconsin

THE COMMUNIST CHASM:
How the Dreams of a Better Life Became a Terrible Nightmare

First Edition

Published by:
  Cable Publishing, Inc.
  14090 E Keinenen Rd
  Brule, WI 54820
  Website: cablepublishing.com
  E-mail: nan@cablepublishing.com

No part of this book may be reproduced or transmitted in any form or by any means, electronic or mechanical, including photocopying, recording, or by any information storage or retrieval system without the written permission of the publisher, except for the inclusion of brief quotations in a review.

© 2022 by Nan Wisherd
All rights reserved. Published in 2022.

Hardcover: ISBN 978-1-934980-83-5
Soft cover: ISBN 978-1-934980-84-2

Library of Congress Control Number: 2022935633

Cover design by Larry at lverkeyn@gmail.com
Layout by Jackie at barebonz@gmail.com

Front cover: The swirling colors of the Karelian flag symbolize the dreams of the Communist Finns going up in smoke.

Printed in the United States of America

To my precious relatives – my dad Herb Aho, my grandma Jennie Maki Johnson, my cousin Viola Wentela Palo, and my cousin Gene "Boots" Tuura – who, through their stories, kept the past alive for me. And to my husband Scott, who never seems to tire of joining me on my endless searches for the keys that unlock the past.

Translation:

PROGRAM FOR THE BATTLE

Platform for (Communist) Workers Party in the year 1928.
For our Battle.

Published by [the] Finnish Bureau of (Communist) Workers Party and Finnish Labor Movement at the hands of the Central Committee in 1000 Belmont Ave., Chicago, Ill.

This booklet was found in Oulu, Wisconsin, and outlines the various communist grievances against capitalists. It was distributed by the three newspapers of the Finnish Workers Federation which, in 1928, was a communist-leaning organization. *Oulu Cultural & Heritage Center*

A PREAMBLE

In 1947 my father, Major Albin L. Fortney, resigned his commission, having served for 10 years during World War II as a chaplain in the U.S. Army. As a civilian minister, one of his calls was to a Lutheran Church in Ishpeming, Michigan. I was looking at old photos of the area one day when I saw one that looked to me very much like the Bible camps that are sponsored by the Lutheran Church, but then I noticed the flag flying proudly over the recreation area. On it was stitched the Hammer and Sickle, the emblem of the communist party! I was actually looking at a summer camp for young American communists.

After graduating from college in 1928, my father taught in Comertown, Montana, five miles from the Canadian and North Dakota borders. He often told us that many of the ranchers in that area were Red–communists. During the Great Depression, they had organized themselves into cells, armed themselves to the teeth, and were seriously contemplating a revolution against the United States government.

Oulu Township of Bayfield County in far Northwestern Wisconsin is a Finnish settlement. Many of the older Finns still speak – often in hushed tones – of the days when the Communist Finns, the Reds, tore apart their community's harmony.

What is one to make of the growth of the communist party in these icy northern areas of America? The Depression was a bitter one. Many were desperate. The economic disaster was complete. Is it any wonder that from the late '20s into the '30s so many Americans were flirting with the idea of a Red takeover?

Enter recruiters hired by Soviet Russia who began to preach the Red gospel, particularly to the Finnish settlements in Michigan, Wisconsin, and Minnesota. They promised a Workers' Paradise in Karelia, a Russian province that bordered Finland. *Come to the Workers' Paradise*, they preached, and in the '30s many desperate Finnish Americans did just that – as many as 10,000 of them.

The conditions promised them, however, turned out to be shabby and desperate. The quality of their food was terrible. Farming was difficult if not impossible. The discontent of these new soviet citizens was deep. And then Joseph Stalin became paranoid. He did not trust these Americans. They were enemies of his state. He began to round them up. The men, even the Karelian recruiters, disappeared one by one.

In *The Communist Chasm*, Nan Wisherd tells this story, which includes little-known details of the early American Labor Movement and the growth of the American Communist Movement. She tells of the communist missionaries to the American Finn communities, which led to the reverse migration of thousands who sought a nonexistent Workers' Paradise.

Beginning in hope and ending in tragedy, this story is a sad one but one of importance. Nan Wisherd's skillful telling of it creates a story that few know very much about but one that all should know and understand.

Steven Fortney
Author of *The Cabin* and
Kraby: The Dark Secrets behind a True-Crime Murder

GLOSSARY

Bolshevik: The majority.

CCE: Cooperative Central Exchange.

Central Executive Committee or **Central Committee of the Communist Party:** The one-party legislature of the Soviet Union from 1922-1938.

Citizen's Alliance: An anti-union organization formed about 1900 by businesses and individuals, which believed that organized labor was Un-American.

Comintern: Communist International, also known as the Third International.

Council of Peoples Representatives or **People's Delegates:** Name given to the Red Finn leaders of the FSWR.

CPUSA: Communist Party of the United States.

Dacha: A Russian summer cottage.

Eduskunta: The Finnish Parliament.

Finnish Federation or **Yhdysvaltain Suomalainen Sosialistijärjestö:** A Finnish American organization dedicated to helping the working class during the Labor Movement.

FSWR or **Finnish Socialist Workers' Republic:** Name given by the Red Finns to the newly independent Grand Duchy of Finland at the start of Finland's Civil War.

FWF or **Finnish Workers Federation:** Organized in 1927 after the Finnish Federation was disbanded, it was strongly affiliated with the Comintern.

First Category Arrests: People slated for execution during the Great Terror.

First International or **International Workingmen's Association:** Founded in 1864 with the organizational papers written by Karl Marx. It dissolved in 1876.

Grand Duchy of Finland: Became known as the Republic of Finland, or Finland, after the 1918 Civil War.

Gulags: Russian forced labor camps established in the 1920s by Joseph Stalin

Insnab stores: "Supplies for Foreigners" stores in Karelia provided fresh fruit, white bread, butter, and sweets for immigrants only.

International Workingmen's Association: Also known as the First International.

IWW: International Workers of the World.

Karelia or **Karelian Autonomous Soviet Socialist Republic:** A northwestern province of Soviet Russia beginning on June 27, 1923. Its capital is Petrozavodsk.

KTA or **Karelian Technical Aid:** Organized on May 1, 1931 with Matti Tenhunen as its first manager.

Kulaks: Prosperous Russian peasants.

NKVD or the **People's Commissariat of Internal Affairs (state secret police):** During the Great Terror, the NKVD had almost limitless power. The NKVD eventually became the KGB.

People's Commissariats: Commissions of finance, internal affairs, agriculture, etc. were given the title to "emphasize the importance of the people's role in government affairs." Later, the People's Commissariats titles were changed to Ministers.

Raivaaja ("The Pioneer"): Newspaper of the Finnish Federation's Eastern District that began in 1905. Its first editor was a fugitive wanted by the Czar of Russia.

Red Guard or *Punakaarti*: The military unit of the Grand Duchy of Finland's SDP. It participated on the Red Finn side during the Finnish Civil War.

SDP: The Grand Duchy of Finland's Labour Party became the *Suomen sosialidemokraattinen puolue*, or SDP, in 1903. It was a Marxist-leaning labor-based organization.

Second International: Formed in 1889 to unite the various labor groups worldwide that adhered to Marxism. It dissolved in 1916 during WWI.

Soviet Russia or **Russia** or the **Russian Federation:** An independent state from 1917-1922 before becoming the largest of the 15 republics comprising the Soviet Union. Moscow, the capital of the Soviet Union, was in Soviet Russia.

Soviet Union or **Union of Soviet Socialist Republics** or **USSR:** Organized on December 30, 1922, it unified 15 republics including of Russia, Transcaucasia, Ukraine, and Byelorussia. The Soviet Union spanned 11 time zones and was an approximate area of 6200 miles east to west and 4500 miles north to south. Vladimir Lenin, the first premier, was succeeded by Joseph Stalin.

Third International: Formed in 1919 and also known as the Communist International or Comintern.

Toveri ("The Comrade"): Newspaper of the Finnish Federation's Western District that began in 1907. Aku Kissonen, a fugitive wanted by the Czar of Russia, was the first editor.

Twin Ports: The adjacent cities of Superior, WI and Duluth, MN in the westernmost tip of Lake Superior.

Työmies ("The Worker"): Newspaper of the Finnish Federation's most radical district, the Midwest District. Moved to Hancock, MI from the East Coast in 1904 to serve the largest concentration of Finns in America. Editor was Kaapo Murros, who was exiled from the Grand Duchy of Finland for his political protests.

WFM: Western Federation of Miners.

WPC or **Work People's College** or *Työväen Opisto*: Founded in 1907 near Duluth in Smithville, MN.

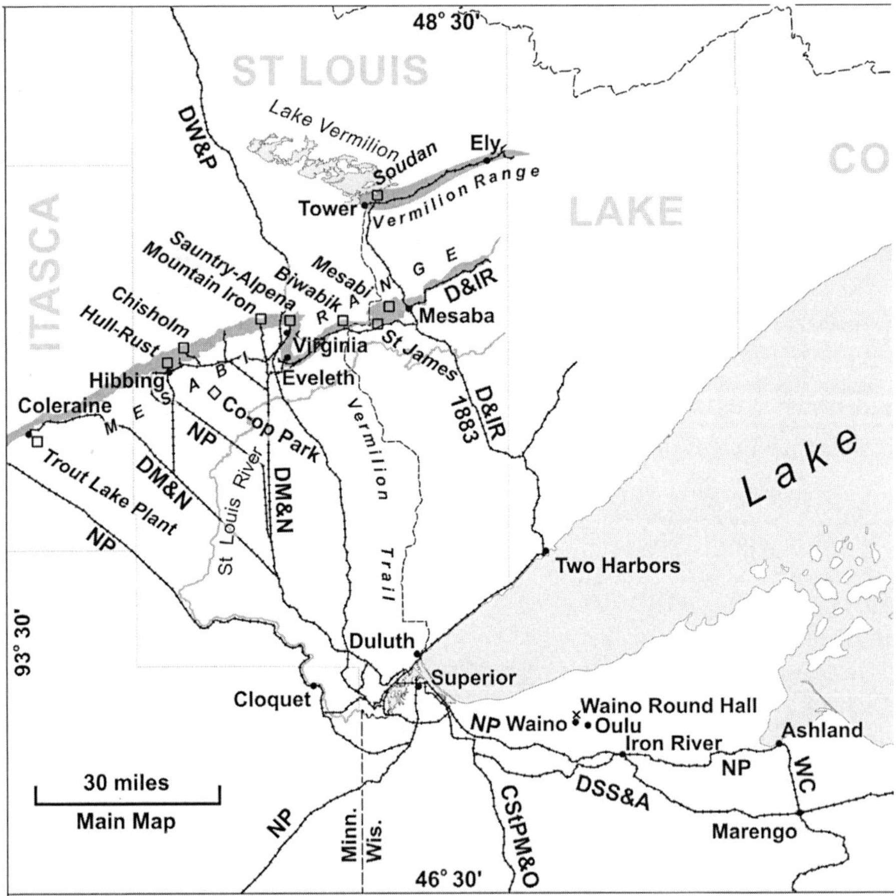

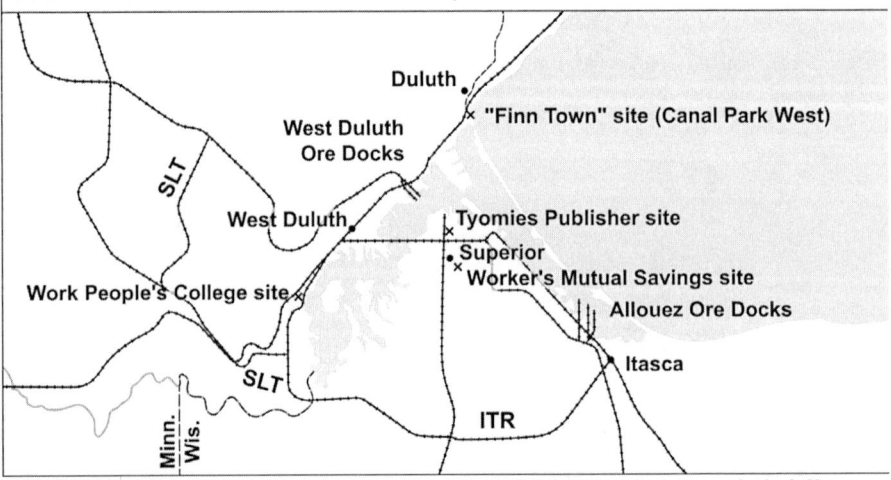

Above Left: The Vermilion and Mesabi Ranges in the 1920s. The Trout Lake Concentration plant opened in 1909 to process lesser-grade ores. This accelerated the shift from underground to open pit mining. Taconite was not yet a viable product.
Below Left: Ore Docks were built first at Allouez, then in West Duluth.

Map by R. Jerrard. References: The Duluth, South Shore & Atlantic Railway 2009 John Gaertner. Geologic Map Ghost Plants: The Trout Lake Concentrator 2015 www.industriallandscapes.org/ghost-plants. Missabe Railroad Leading Out of Duluth to the Vermilion Range Before 1869. Not credited. Minnesota digital library collections.

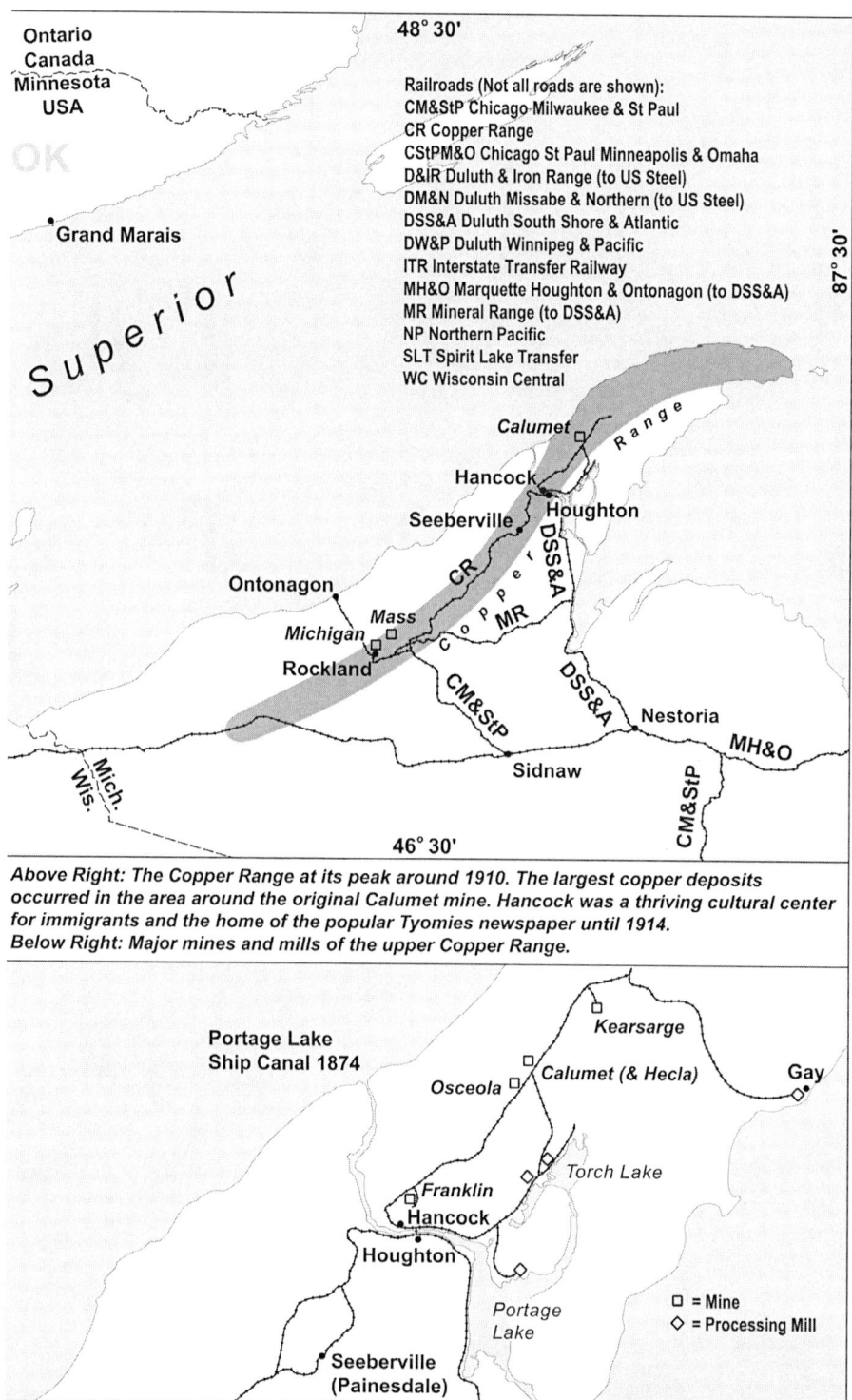

Above Right: The Copper Range at its peak around 1910. The largest copper deposits occurred in the area around the original Calumet mine. Hancock was a thriving cultural center for immigrants and the home of the popular Tyomies newspaper until 1914.
Below Right: Major mines and mills of the upper Copper Range.

Mesabi Iron Range, Minnesota, 2nd ed. 1999 D.G. Meineke, R.L. Buchheit, E.H. Dahlberg, G.B. Morey, L.E. Warren. Historical Society, 1930 System Maps Vol. 1 and 2. www.missabe.com/maps. Map of Duluth: Roads and Trails

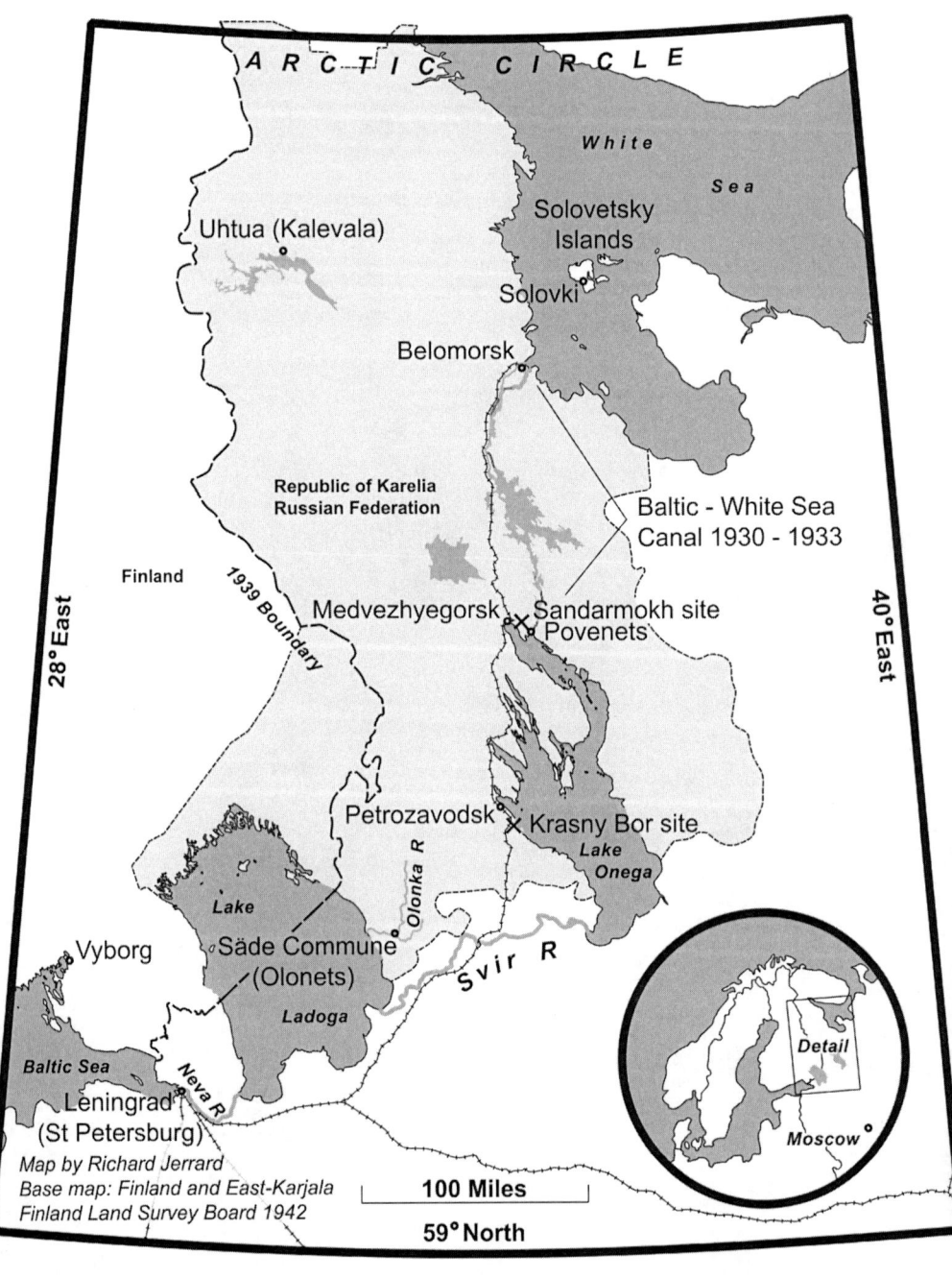

TABLE OF CONTENTS

Repercussions 1
Where do I Begin? 3
The Influential Red Finn Activists 6
Who Were the Influential Red Finn Activists? 9
Karl Marx & the International Workingmen's Association . . . 14

PART I: THE LABOR MOVEMENT
1: The Late 1800s: Migrants & Mines 19
2: Land Ownership & Labor Struggles 35
3: Evolving Towns & Organizations 63
4: Where Were the Activists in 1916? 71

PART I: THE COOPERATIVE & COMMUNIST MOVEMENTS
5: The Year 1917: A Time of Change 77
6: The 1917 Aftermath 89
7: The Roaring '20s 105
8: Joseph Stalin's Dictates 113
9: The Battle for the CCE 127

PART III: KARELIAN FEVER & THE GREAT TERROR
10: KTA: Promoting Karelian Fever 139
11: The Door Closed 151
12: The Journey to Karelia 165
13: Life in Karelia 173
14: Stalin's Great Terror 185
15: The Truth be Told 197

What Happened to the Influential Red Finn Activists? . . . 205
Epilogue 209
With Thanks 211
Source Notes 212
Bibliography 216
Index 220

REPERCUSSIONS

"There will be repercussions if you write a book about the Communist Movement."

I HEARD THAT OMINOUS warning a few years ago, spoken by the daughter of a Communist Finn. She wanted to bury an extremely contentious time in our local history that is known as the Communist Movement. It began in the first half of the 1900s and caused a bitterness among the non-Communist Finnish Americans and the Communist Finns that lasted for decades. There are descendants of the Communist Finns who refuse to discuss those times even today, hoping that as time passes no one will remember that the Communist Movement ever existed.

The Communist Movement and Karelian Fever really did happen, and they shouldn't be forgotten. They drove a wedge between families and friends – at first by differing ideologies and then, for some, by thousands of miles and decades in time. Because two of the top communist promoters lived in northwestern Wisconsin, and 41% of the Karelian immigrants left the states bordering Lake Superior, Karelian Fever and Joseph Stalin's Great Terror affected a larger-than-normal percentage of residents in the area where I grew up. It impacted many of my ancestors, and I've focused the story leading up to Karelian Fever on the Lake Superior region.

The Communist Chasm is the story of thousands of very idealistic people who believed – or were manipulated to believe – that the capitalist governments in America and Canada were terribly wrong and absolutely evil, but there was a Workers' Paradise in the Soviet Russia's province of Karelia where life was far better than what they currently had, where they were wanted, where there was work for everyone, and where everyone worked for the common good.

The Workers' Paradise where thousands dreamed of beginning a new and better life was actually a workers' deadly hell but, for many, that reality came much too late.

"Where do I Begin?"

I ASKED MYSELF THAT more than once as I began writing this book. At first the story seemed very clear-cut: Many years ago in northwestern Wisconsin, there were Finns and Communist-leaning Finns. In the early 1900s, the Communist Finns had "stolen" two Finn halls and had attempted a hostile takeover of a large distribution center before many moved to Soviet Russia and disappeared. The Finns' bitterness over losing the halls they had helped build was long-lasting, even after many decades. End of story, or so it seemed.

But as I began researching the Communist Movement, there were increasingly unanswered questions. What, or who, had compelled so many Communist Finns to leave America and move to Soviet Russia? Where did they go? When did this mass exodus begin, and when did it end? What happened to the emigrants? What was Karelian Fever? Why do most American historians never mention the thousands of North Americans who moved to Soviet Russia before the start of World War II? And why are so many Finns who are aware of Karelian Fever unwilling to discuss or even acknowledge that it happened?

For many weeks and months I found myself floundering mentally, wondering if I could adequately write the story I thought needed to be written. I felt like I was beginning a very difficult jigsaw puzzle that could be pieced together in only one way. *The Communist Chasm* spans two continents and four countries – America, Canada, Finland, and Soviet Russia. Romanovs, Marxists, Bolsheviks, Russians, Finns, Americans, Canadians, communists, and capitalists along with ever-changing organizations and acronyms that made my head spin were mixed into the widely varying theories and opinions of some very educated, knowledgeable historians as well as many people who had actually lived during the events of the early 1900s. It was hard to find two people sharing the same opinions about the who, what, when, where, why, and how of the Communist Movement. (The story comes to mind of the blind people describing an elephant by touching different parts of it.)

I felt there had to be something that tied the two continents and the groups together, and I felt I found the clue I needed in a 1917 newspaper article about the organization of the Workers' Mutual Bank in Superior, Wisconsin. In that article, Matti Tenhunen (who turned out to be a very important individual in the Communist Movement and Karelian Fever) mentioned that "his group" already had a bank in Fitchburg, Massachusetts, but the distance was a problem. *Fitchburg, Massachusetts?!* How and why was a group in the far northwestern corner of Wisconsin affiliated with people in Massachusetts? Tenhunen's brief reference, however, led me to understand the Finnish Federation's impact on many American Finns nationwide.

But there still remained a question: *What was the common thread that connected so many people in so many countries in the early 1900s when communication was slow at best?* Even in America, that same connection was a cohesive force that bound people living throughout the country together. *What was it?*

Part of the answer was the Comintern (the shortened term for Communist International). The Comintern was comprised of communist parties and their members from many countries worldwide. I felt I was on the right track, but I needed more information. Many of the influential Finnish leaders who were instrumental in America's Labor Movement and Communist Movement arrived in America before World War I, and the Comintern was organized *after* World War I. There was still a missing piece to the puzzle.

I believe the answer begins with the revolutionary, Karl Marx, in the mid-1800s. His ideologies and the formation of the First International (or International Workingmen's Association) united labor leaders and workers in many countries who had struggled for untold years against horrific working conditions with minimal compensation. Their international conventions forged ties that, years later, allowed the seeds of communism to spread and flare into what had begun as a worldwide Labor Movement.

Karl Marx's First International (of the International Workingmen's Association) ended in 1876, and it was 13 years before the Second International began. During the Second International, many radical Finnish labor leaders met, associated with, and aided Vladimir Lenin before many of those Finns were forced to flee the

Grand Duchy of Finland. The bonds they forged with the Russian revolutionary remained strong as many fled to North America and became involved in the American Labor Movement.

For many radical Finns, the Labor Movement evolved first into the Communist Movement after World War I and finally into Karelian Fever. Today, many people living in "America's hotbeds" of the Communist Movement – mainly the Upper Midwest and Pacific Northwest – have no idea that families, friends, and entire communities were once ripped apart by differing ideologies that, I believe, began with Karl Marx.

The Communist Movement and Karelian Fever are little known but fascinating slices of American history that cannot be forgotten. There are still many untold stories about Karelian Fever, but I hope you will be interested in the accounts I have included in *The Communist Chasm*.

Nan Wisherd

The Influential Red Finn Activists

AS I BEGAN THE research for *The Communist Chasm*, I knew a Communist Finn named Oscar Corgan had traveled throughout the Upper Midwest, giving speeches in the Communist Finn halls and encouraging the Communist Finns to leave America for the "Workers' Paradise" in Soviet Russia's Karelian province. Oscar Corgan had briefly managed the Co-op Store in Brule, Wisconsin – the town where I live. Corgan's daughter, Mayme, was even born in Brule.

At that time, I had no idea that Corgan was just one member of a large network of men coordinating their efforts in North America and Soviet Russia. I didn't know anything about the group of Finnish ideologues who maintained communications and controlled thousands of Finnish immigrants through various means, but I did wonder how just one man (Corgan) could encourage thousands of people to move overseas.

Unfamiliar names kept reappearing in what I was reading. Santeri Nuorteva…Yrjö Sirola…Leo Laukki – all Finnish men who fled to America in the early 1900s **because they were wanted for treason against the Czar of Russia.** *What was this all about? What were they doing in America?* Similar affiliations began appearing – members of the Finnish SDP… Finnish Parliament members… and newspaper affiliations – with these men and others, like Otto Kuusinen and Edvard Gylling, who lived in Russia after fleeing, **not from the Czar of Russia but from their Finnish countrymen.** *What?!* That didn't seem to make any sense at all.

Further research showed that these men were initially linked in Finland through their political ties and friendships. Whether living in Europe or North America, Marxist ideologies, the Labor Movement, and the International Workingmen's Association had firmly bonded these men and many others. Though the Atlantic Ocean and thousands of miles separated these influential leaders and their associates, their staunch Marxist beliefs remained unchanged: A revolutionary overthrow of capitalist governments by workers worldwide was imminent. And these powerful, radical political activists impacted thousands of lives on two continents.

In the late 1800s and early 1900s, a worldwide Labor Movement pitted workers against wealthy businessmen and land owners, the *bourgeoisie*, for better wages and working conditions. At the time, The Grand Duchy of Finland was ruled by Nicholas II, the Czar of Russia. The General Strike in 1905 – also known as the Russian Revolution of 1905 – created fugitives of many Finnish SDP* leaders to America and European countries in order to avoid incarceration or execution for instigating, aiding, and encouraging the unrest, which had become increasingly violent.

Remaining in the Old Country were additional influential, radical SDP members – many of whom were serving in the Finnish Parliament – who maintained communications with their exiled Finnish comrades. Known as the Red Finns, they were prepared to activate the Red Guard, the paramilitary unit of Finland's SDP, and assume control of the Finnish government when they felt the time was right.

The Grand Duchy of Finland gained its independence from Russia in late 1917. In early 1918, the newly independent Finland fell into a short but brutal Civil War after the radical SDP leaders, who believed the time was finally right for a Bolshevik-style revolution in Finland, declared southern Finland to be the Marxist-leaning Workers' Republic of Finland.

The decisive White Finn victory in Finland's Civil War sent thousands of Red Finns, the Red Guard, and their leaders who hadn't been killed or captured fleeing for their lives. This time, however, Czar Nicholas II of Russia had been executed in 1917 during the Bolshevik Revolution, and they were welcomed to Russia by its new leader and their long-time acquaintance, Vladimir Lenin. Among the fleeing Red Finns were Otto Kuusinen and Edvard Gylling, whom the White Finns had vowed to execute if they were captured. Over time, both men rose to positions of power in Soviet Russia along with fellow Red Finn Yrjö Sirola, who had

---

*Many European countries had SDP associations that were organized in the late 1800s and early 1900s. They all belonged to the Marxist-leaning International Workingmen's Association (the Second International).

once been a director of the Work People's College (WPC) near Duluth, Minnesota.

The violent labor strikes of the early 1900s subsided after World War I as the American economy boomed. Yet as the Labor Movement weakened in the 1920s, the Communist Movement strengthened. The influential Finnish ideologues in America were now Communist Party members. Their radical faction had split from the moderate members of America's Finnish Federation, taking the *Työmies* and *Raivaaja* newspapers and their large readerships with them.

Charismatic Communist Finn speakers kept the communist-leaning Finns energized, speaking passionately at Finn halls in heavily populated Finnish communities throughout America and Canada. Speaking against the capitalist system, they urged their audiences to contribute what they could and help their comrades in Karelia. *Työmies* and *Raivaaja* repeatedly emphasized the urgent need for overseas aid. Both the speakers and newspapers extolled the Workers' Paradise as a land free of capitalistic repressions where the Communist Finns were both needed and wanted.

The Great Depression began in 1929 and ended America's postwar booming economy. Banks failed and savings evaporated. Unemployment spiraled up as the economy spiraled down with no bottom in sight. The communist speakers and newspapers continued their praise of the Workers' Paradise to Finnish families now struggling in debilitating poverty, unemployed and unable to pay their bills or provide for their families. Suddenly, Karelia with its need for skilled workers and its promise of workers being wanted and valued shone like a beacon of hope for those who had no hope. Many Finns, who had listened with interest to the communist speakers and read the *Työmies* and *Raivaaja* newspapers for years, now listened with a growing excitement. For many it was a lifeline out of crushing poverty and despair. For others it was a place where their beliefs would not be scorned or criticized.

The former SDP Finn leaders, now firmly committed to the Communist Movement, probably knew at some point that there would never be a worldwide communist revolution as Karl Marx had wholeheartedly believed. But they did know that their ideologies were still very much alive. And in a Russian province named Karelia, led by their fellow fugitive friend Edvard Gylling, help was needed by like-minded Communist Finns to develop what Gylling hoped would be the Red Finland of Russia. The result was called Karelian Fever, and it was the culmination of the Red Finn ideologues' work.

WHO WERE THE INFLUENTIAL RED FINN ACTIVISTS?

FINLAND IS LOCATED IN Northwestern Europe and is 130,559 square miles in size – about the same size as the combined states of New Mexico and Connecticut. From this relatively small country in the early 1900s, a number of very experienced Marxist-leaning labor leaders, many of them members of the Finnish Parliament, fled the Grand Duchy of Finland and arrived in America. With a few exceptions, these men did not immigrate to America because they wanted to work in the mines or rail and shipping industries: They fled to avoid incarceration or even execution by the Czar of Russia. What they found in America was a vast country nearly 24 times larger than the Old Country with a fledgling Labor Movement, but one whose exploited workers were enduring the same horrific conditions and pitifully low wages in a booming capitalistic society as the workers throughout Europe.

The labor leaders quickly became active in the Finnish Federation, a nationwide organization that began in Hibbing, Minnesota, in 1906 and that, through the years, included various degrees of affiliations with the IWW (International Workers of the World), the WFM (Western Federation of Miners) and – after the Bolshevik Revolution – the CPUSA (Communist Party of the U.S.A.). The labor leaders became editors of the Finnish Federation newspapers – the *Työmies, Toveri,* and *Raivaaja* – that were a vital means of communication before the days of radios, televisions, and telephones. They became eloquent, impassioned speakers. And they became teachers at the Work People's College in Smithville, Minnesota, and promoted their radical Marxist ideologies. Their impact on the Labor Movement in communities largely populated by Finns was immeasurable.

The fugitive Finn labor leaders wrote and spoke mostly to the Finnish immigrants scattered throughout America. Many of the immigrants did not speak English and relied heavily on what was said in the Finnish community halls or was written in Finnish language newspapers. The newspapers were a connection with the relatives and friends they had left behind in the Old Country, but it also connected them with fellow immigrants living in their new homeland. A centralized Finnish Federation news committee controlled much of what was printed in every paper. Along with news from Finland and from the various regions in America, the newspapers also included stories of human interest and news about the ongoing Labor Movement in the early 1900s. They included chapter books and humor... There was a wide variety of news and interesting information for every subscriber. But the centralized newspaper committee was also able to influence their readers with subtle or sometimes not-so-subtle propaganda.

Joining the radical exiled labor leaders were young men who, as young adults, had also arrived in America during the early 1900s but had found employment in the extractive, transportation, and retail industries before being drawn into the Labor Movement. Three of them – Oscar Corgan, Matti Tenhunen, and John Wiita – eventually joined many others in the struggle for workers' rights by becoming newspaper editors, teachers, speakers, and activists working for the Finnish Federation.

When the Marxist Finnish labor leaders fled the Grand Duchy of Finland in the early 1900s, their homeland was controlled by the Czar of the Russian Empire – a condition they abhorred. At that time, Soviet Russia, free of czarist rule, did not exist. There was not a Comintern (Third International) bonding communists throughout the world. And there were certainly no plans for creating a Red

Finland in a Soviet Russian province named Karelia. But as a kaleidoscope of world events unexpectedly turned in the early 1900s and changed the economic, political, cultural, and social landscapes forever, the focus of the exiled Finnish leaders living in America became directed toward Karelia and a vision of that province filled with like-minded Communist Finns who fervently believed their endeavors would ultimately create a Workers' Paradise.

No one knows how many Finnish SDP members fled to America in the early 1900s, and no one knows how many Finns they influenced in the Labor, Cooperative, and Communist movements in North America. Their fellow Finnish SDP members remaining in Europe but maintaining communications with them also played an important role in the North American Finnish communities where everyone was striving for a better life.

The Communist Chasm highlights eight Finnish men who worked together, coordinating their efforts in several important ways. During the Labor Movement, their efforts as members of the International Workingmen's Association (Second International) remained focused on fighting for improving the wages and working conditions of miners, dock workers, and other labor-intensive occupations. During the Cooperative and Communist Movements, however, their focus as members of the Comintern (Third International) shifted in subtle degrees to an emphasis geared more toward the needs of the Communist Party and events in Soviet Russia. The men I have chosen to follow, I feel, represent just a few of the leaders who controlled the lives of innumerable Finnish families.

The eight men were very talented motivational speakers, writers, educators, and leaders. Although history shows that their efforts and beliefs were not always the best choices, their expertise in swaying fellow Communist Finns is unquestioned.

In 1905, two events happened in the Grand Duchy of Finland that had a tremendous impact on North American Finnish immigrants, although no one could have foreseen it at the time. The first was the General Strike, which was organized by the SDP and included the Viapori Military Revolt. The second event was Czar Nicholas II's law that all males 18 years and older were to serve in the Russian Army.

YRJÖ SIROLA, at 29 years old, was the Secretary of the SDP in 1905 when he first met Vladimir Lenin. He had joined the SDP in 1903 while working for *Kansan Lehti* (where Leo Laukki also worked) and was later the managing editor of the *Työmies*, the major organ of the SDP. Sirola served in the Finnish Parliament from 1907 to 1909 and worked with Edvard Gylling, Otto Kuusinen, and Santeri Nuorteva during that time. He was considered to be a formidable force in both the SDP and Finnish Parliament. Sirola left the Finnish Parliament in 1909 after Leo Laukki asked him to move to America and join him at the Work People's College in Smithville, Minnesota.

Two years after Yrjö Sirola left the Grand Duchy of Finland, he was joined in America by his friend and fellow SDP member of the Finnish Parliament, **SANTERI NUORTEVA**. Nuorteva, who was born in 1881 and named Alexander Nyberg, had changed his name in 1905 during the Finnish General Strike in order to evade the Czar Nicholas II's police. In 1907, he helped Vladimir Lenin avoid capture by czarist forces and make his escape through the Grand Duchy of Finland as he headed into exile for the next 10 years. Nuorteva served in the Finnish Parliament from 1907 to 1910 as a member of the SDP and often had differences of opinion with fellow member Otto Kuusinen. He was known as a radical revolutionary and was imprisoned for six months in 1909 for conspiracy against the czar. Nuorteva fled the Grand Duchy of Finland with his family two years later to avoid further imprisonment. The Nuorteva family immigrated to America in 1911.

Born Leo Lindqvist in 1880, **LEO LAUKKI** started working at an early age to support himself and help his impoverished family. He was an editor at the Finnish newspaper *Kansan Lehti* – where Yrjö Sirola also worked. After attending the Helsinki University and a military academy, he joined a Russian cavalry regiment and became an anti-czar revolutionary while serving in the Russian military. After participating in the Viapori Military Revolt in 1905 and changing his name, Laukki fled the czar's police force and in 1907 moved to Hancock, Michigan, where he became an editor for the *Työmies* newspaper.

JOHN WIITA avoided being drafted into the Russian military when he arrived in America in 1905 at the age of 17. He found work in Superior, Wisconsin, as a rail car repairman and longshoreman as he gradually became more politically active.

MATTI TENHUNEN also avoided being drafted into the Russian military when he emigrated from the Grand Duchy of Finland in 1905. Matti was born in 1887 and worked in various jobs including as a grocery clerk in Ironwood, Michigan, before moving to Wentworth, Wisconsin, in Douglas County.

Like Matti Tenhunen, **OSCAR CORGAN** was born in 1887 and moved to America in 1905. After working in Upper Michigan's copper mines, he moved to Superior, Wisconsin. Oscar gradually became active in the Labor Movement while living in Superior, where he initially met John Wiita and Matti Tenhunen. Through the years, the three men became friends and co-workers.

Remaining in the Grand Duchy of Finland were **EDVARD GYLLING** and **OTTO KUUSINEN**, who were both born in 1881 and met as schoolmates in 1892. Gylling and Kuusinen both began serving in the Finnish Parliament in 1908 as members of the SDP.

Otto Kuusinen became active in politics and anti-capitalistic at an early age and graduated from Helsinki University in 1905. In 1906, Kuusinen, then only in his mid-20s, was instrumental in toppling the chairman of the relatively moderate SDP and became a dominant figure in its increasingly Marxist ideologies. Beginning in 1906, he also wrote for and edited the Helsinki-based Finnish newspaper *Työmies* (Worker), where he worked with fellow Parliament member Yrjö Sirola.

Five of the Red Finn activists – Edvard Gylling, Otto Kuusinen, Leo Laukki, Santeri Nuorteva, and Yrjö Sirola – were contemporaries whose mutual friendships, political beliefs, and business associations in the Grand Duchy of Finland created the strong bonds that ultimately influenced thousands of American Finns. By the end of 1920, all five were working together again as citizens of Soviet Russia.

The remaining three men – Oscar Corgan, Matti Tenhunen, and John Wiita – immigrated to America as teenagers in 1905 and were unknown to one another until their work in the Labor Movement brought them together in the Twin Ports (Superior, Wisconsin and Duluth, Minnesota). Corgan, Tenhunen, and Wiita continued working together in America for the Communist Party after the others fled or were deported to Soviet Russia.

All of these radical activists eventually removed themselves from their work in America. One of them left the Communist Party and remained in America. Everyone else lived in Soviet Russia and worked faithfully for the Party for the rest of their lives. Of the seven living in Soviet Russia, only two died of natural causes. The remaining five died violently because of a paranoid madman named Joseph Stalin.

Karl Marx & the International Workingmen's Association

KARL MARX, THE PHILOSOPHER, historian, and passionate revolutionary, said to be the most influential thinker of the 1800s, was born in Germany on May 5, 1818. His father was a free-thinking, well-respected Jewish lawyer.

Karl attended universities in Bonn and Berlin and met theologian Bruno Bauer while in Berlin. Bauer's radical anti-Christian, anti-autocracy ideologies were a great influence on Marx. Karl and Bruno were known to scandalize their classmates by laughing in church, frequently becoming inebriated, and galloping drunkenly through Berlin on donkeys.

Marx moved to Paris at the end of 1843. He became a communist in 1844. (Communism during that time called for a working-class revolution that would destroy the capitalist world.) In 1845, he was expelled from France and moved to Brussels, Belgium. During the remainder of the 1840s, Marx studied political economics and met with groups of revolutionary-leaning workers while waiting for the coming revolution that would topple capitalism. In 1847, he was a founding member of the Communist League, an organization that rejected capitalism morally, economically, and philosophically. Marx co-authored *The Communist Manifesto*, which was published in 1848.

The Communist Manifesto begins with, "*A spectre is haunting Europe – the spectre of communism*" and ends with, "*The proletarians have nothing to lose but their chains. They have a world to win. Workers of the world, unite!*" His prediction of a "haunting spectre of communism" eventually came true, but not for nearly seventy years.

Marx stated that, "The history of all hitherto existing society is the history of class struggles." He believed that the proletariat (working class) produced everything, but the bourgeoisie (capitalists and members of the upper class) controlled everything. He felt that struggles between the proletariat and bourgeoisie would ultimately end in communism.

After a very brief time back in Germany, the country of his birth, Marx was considered a political threat and fled from the country in 1849. In the early 1850s, Karl and his wife Jenny lived with their children in a three-room flat in London. The family was completely poverty-stricken, and their income came from the help of acquaintances and from weekly articles Karl wrote for the *New York Daily Tribune*.

On September 28, 1864, the International Workingmen's Association was organized at St. Martin's Hall in London. Among those in attendance were 46-year-old Karl Marx. The Association's aim was uniting various communist, anarchist, and trade union groups in their common working class and class struggles.* Their goals

---

* Also known as the First International, the organization claimed a membership of eight million members at its peak. Marxism slowly became the primary ideology of the First International, and its color was red. It dissolved in 1876. The Second International was formed in 1889 in Paris and continued the ideologies of Karl Marx. It dissolved in 1916 during WWI. The Third International, organized in Moscow in 1919 by Vladimir Lenin, is better known as the Communist International, or Comintern. Joseph Stalin dissolved it during WWII.

Karl Marx (1818–1883)
H.F. Helmolt, (Contributor). University of Texas Libraries Collections.

included staying in contact and sharing labor information from each country.

One week after the first meeting of the First International (the International Workingmen's Association), a second meeting took place in Marx's home. It was decided that the wording for the organization should be written by one author, and Karl Marx was chosen as its author and elected to the First International's General Council. Marx's influence was greatly felt in future years with the founding of numerous Marxist-leaning organizations, such as the SDPs in numerous countries, which supported labor groups and their struggles against capitalism.

In the last years of his life, Marx remained interested in contemporary politics, especially in Russia and Germany. Karl Marx was preceded in death by his beloved wife Jenny and three of their six children. He died on March 14, 1883, at age 64 and is buried in London. Three days after his death, his close friend and fellow revolutionary, Friedrich Engels, delivered Marx's eulogy. It read, in part: "*An immeasurable loss has been sustained both by the militant proletariat of Europe and America, and by historical science, in the death of this man. The gap that has been left by the departure of this mighty spirit will soon enough make itself felt.*

"*Marx was before all else a revolutionary. His real mission in life was to contribute, in one way or another, to the overthrow of capitalist society and of the state institutions which it had brought into being, to contribute to the liberation of the modern proletariat, which he was the first to make conscious of its own position and its needs, conscious of the conditions of its emancipation. Fighting was his element, and he fought with a passion, a tenacity, and a success such as few could rival...*

"*In addition to a host of militant pamphlets, work in organizations in Paris, Brussels, and London, and finally, crowning all, the formation of the great International Workingmen's Association – this was indeed an achievement of which its founder might well have been proud even if he had done nothing else.*

"*And consequently, Marx was the best hated and most calumniated man of his time. Governments deported him from their territories. Bourgeois, whether conservative or ultra-democratic, vied with one another in heaping slanders upon him... And he died beloved, revered, and mourned by millions of revolutionary fellow workers – from the mines of Siberia to California, in all parts of Europe and America...*

"*His name will surely endure through the ages, and so also will his work.*"

Karl Marx's economic and radical political ideologies were ignored for the most part during his lifetime but became increasingly accepted after his death. The worldwide revolutionary movement he predicted failed to materialize, but his contribution to the Labor Movement and, later, the Communist Movement in world history was immeasurable. When the Second International was formed in 1889, years after his death, the philosophies of Karl Marx, known as Marxism, were widely accepted throughout Europe.

WE ARE A NATION OF IMMIGRANTS

Since Native Americans willingly walked across the Bering Strait on a land bridge from Asia over 10,000 years ago, and African Americans unwillingly arrived in ships over 400 years ago, immigrants have made their homes in America. At no time, however, have there been more immigrants than in the late 1800s and early 1900s.

During that time, the great Westward Expansion and America's industrialization created a critical shortage of workers in mining and logging – America's extractive industries. Workers were needed to build the ships and railroads for transporting the natural resources to mills and factories. Workers were needed to load and unload the millions of logs and tons of ore. Domestic and retail workers were also needed to cook, clean, house, and provide goods for the laborers. Carpenters and brick layers – specialty trades – were needed for building cities, and employers knew that they wouldn't need to pay $3 per day for a carpenter or $4 per day for a mason if they hired immigrants. Immigrants who had fished or farmed in their home country were unskilled workers in the mines, or on the docks and railroads, and could be hired for far less than unskilled Americans demanded.

The need for workers was great, and America was touted as the Land of Opportunity for those living in abject poverty across the ocean. Agents were dispersed, mainly to the Northern European countries, and extolled the great wealth and opportunities possible for those who were willing to work. And thousands of Finns, Swedes, Norwegians, Poles, Italians, and many, many other nationalities came to America hoping for a better life.

But in reality, the greatest opportunities lay with those who bought the heavily forested lands or properties rich in ore. The corporations they formed made astronomical fortunes for themselves, their friends and families, and their shareholders. The stark contrast between the wealthy owners and their struggling laborers inevitably created conditions very similar to those the immigrants had left behind. The Labor Movement – the bitter and sometimes violent clash for better wages and working conditions that began in Europe – moved to America.

1 THE LATE 1800s: MIGRANTS & MINES

"I remember just how beautiful that ore was, glinting blue there under the green of the pines. It was a dream come true, a satisfying fact that nature had yielded to us the great secret she had guarded through the ages."

JOHN MERRITT
One of the Seven Iron Men

MINING ON MICHIGAN'S KEWEENAW PENINSULA IN THE 1800S

In Upper Michigan is a 70-mile-long peninsula jutting into eastern Lake Superior called the Keweenaw Peninsula, and within the Keweenaw Peninsula lie formations once laced with veins of the world's largest copper deposits. Native Americans knew about the copper for centuries and used it for things like cooking pots and ornaments. Europeans became very interested in the metal in 1766 after an expedition discovered a two-ton piece of copper on the peninsula.

On the Keweenaw Peninsula in 1858, a surveyor named Edwin Hulbert found a pit with a cache of copper in the bottom. Assuming it had been mined on the nearby lands by Native Americans, Hulbert began buying land in the area and discovered a large vein of copper in 1864. Hulbert's discovery became the Calumet Company in 1865, which then spun off the Hecla Company the following year. The Calumet and Hecla mines began operating in the late 1860s, becoming the most profitable mines on the Keweenaw Peninsula. They merged into the Calumet and Hecla Mining Company (C & H) in 1871 and during the next nine years extracted more than half of America's copper.

Because most of the owners and shareholders lived in the Boston area, a well-known phrase at the time was, "The four greatest words in the New England annals are Concord and Lexington, Calumet and Hecla. The first two made New England history; the second two made New England fortunes." In the last two decades of the 1800s, the Calumet and Hecla mines paid 57 percent in dividends, or $72 million, to their shareholders and was the most profitable mining company in the country during that time.

Soon after they formed, the mining companies built boardinghouses and hundreds of homes near the mines for their workers, initially charging monthly rent of one dollar for each room. Many had gardens in the backyard or on a nearby rented lot. Dolores Capello remembered, "Dad rented extra lots. There he would plant potatoes, pole beans, cucumbers, and raspberry bushes. In the garden behind the house he had lettuce, tomatoes, carrots, rutabagas, and onions. Mother slaughtered chickens in our backyard. Backyards could include gardens, outhouses, saunas, barns, clotheslines, and perhaps room to play."

For a small fee, the mining companies rented small plots of land for pastures, and cows were walked out of the mining towns daily to the pastures. Children could earn a little money by walking the cows to and from the pastures every day. The mining companies also built schools and churches. In addition, about a thousand houses were built by the miners themselves on C & H land with the stipulation that the homeowners might need to vacate the land on short notice.

The C & H was the Peninsula's preferred mining employer, enabling them to hire the best workers. The mining supervisors, called captains, were usually Cornish miners. Finns, Norwegians, Irish, Poles, and Italians made up the majority of the laborers, but at one time there were 32 ethnic groups on the Keweenaw Peninsula. During the late 1800s, over half of all Finnish immigrants moved from Finland directly to the Keweenaw Peninsula. In the 1890s, Calumet was said to have the largest Finnish community in America with 6,000 Finnish immigrants.[1]

Until 1893 when the first rail line was completed, the Keweenaw Peninsula was isolated after Lake Superior froze and shipping ended until the next spring. Because of the Keweenaw's remote location and lack of transportation, the mine workers and their families were dependent on the mining companies for the food they couldn't produce, all supplies, and even the tools they needed for their jobs. The company charged the miners wholesale prices for necessities like coal and firewood. The cost of everything they had to buy was deducted from their wages, keeping them subservient to the mining companies.

The land around the mines had to be cleared before the shafts could be drilled into the solid rock, and several hundred feet usually separated the individual shafts. The shafts were connected by underground openings called drifts, which were typically only five feet wide and six feet tall. Through the drifts and shafts moved hundreds of men carrying the shovels, picks, drills, fuses, black powder, and all other supplies needed in a typical working day. Squeezing into the tight passages were also the timber crews carrying the giant logs needed to stabilize the shafts and drifts.

In the earliest years, miners descended into the mining shafts on ladders. The time spent in reaching their work site each day wasn't included in their nine- or ten-hour work shifts and, as time went on and the shafts became deeper, as much as an hour was spent descending underground before they could begin working. Later, side-by-side ladders moved the men more quickly, and man engines gradually replaced the side-by-side ladders. The man engines were abandoned when the shafts exceeded four thousand feet below the ground.*

The earliest source of light for the miners was a tallow candle affixed to their helmets with a ball of clay or placed in the rock wall. Stearine candles replaced the tallow candles beginning in the mid 1870s. Stearine candles, made with vegetable and animal fat, burned brighter and lasted longer than tallow candles. Local businesses on the Keweenaw Peninsula made the candles, and the mining companies purchased them by the ton.

Many miners spent their days working two-man drills that slowly pierced the rock. At the end of their shift, the miners cleared pieces of rock from the holes and filled the holes with black powder. Fuses were set and lit while the men scrambled to safety. Two hours after the blast, the air in the mine was deemed safe to breathe, and

---

* In the late 1890s, C & H's Red Jacket shaft was the deepest mine in the world with a vertical shaft of 4,900 feet.

The #5 shaft of the Tamarack Mine was owned by the C & H. The horses are pulling timbers to be used in the mine shaft. *MI Technological University Archives & Copper Country Historical Collections*

Man cars allowed the miners to ascend and descend quickly with no physical exertion.
MI Technological University Archives & Copper Country Historical Collections

the trammers moved in to clear the ore and rock before the next crew arrived. Silicosis, a lung disease, was caused by the dust of the underground blasting. It was a common disease in the mining towns.

Trammers loaded the rock and copper ore into tram cars that were pushed out of the area so more drillers could continue their work or timbers could be strategically placed to avoid cave-ins. Because of the lifting, pushing, loading, and unloading of tons of rock and ore, trammers had the most physically taxing job in the mining industry. The trammers' average working career was just seven years.

At shift's end, the underground workers could finally begin their ascent "to get to grass." Whether it took ten minutes or an hour, the miners were not paid for their "commuting" time.

Through the years, wages of contract workers gradually increased from $1 per day to $2.50 per day. However, inexperienced workers (usually recently arrived immigrants) began working for the mining companies at a significantly lower wage. Drill boys were hired at $1 per day to deliver water, tools, and other supplies to the drillers. The mines operated 24 hours a day except for Sundays and holidays. The contract miners worked fifty- to sixty-hour weeks.[2]

In 1881, twenty-year-old N.P. (Nils Peter) Johnson was one of many who immigrated to the Keweenaw Peninsula. N.P.'s parents, John and Britta, and his brother Mark joined him in 1882. N.P.'s first job was as a general helper at the Osceola Mine, and he was paid $35 per month. The Osceola Mine later became part of the C & H.*

There were always some mine workers who were paid daily. These men substituted for miners unable to work because of injuries, or they might be hired for a job lasting only a few days. Most men hired by the mining companies, though, were contract workers who were paid monthly or every three months. There was usually little left of their wages after rent and the other needed purchases were deducted.

---

* On September 7, 1895, the Osceola Mine was the site of the deadliest fire in the Keweenaw Peninsula mining history when a fire of unknown origin began on Level 27. At the time there were 200 miners underground. Four boys were among the thirty who died.

Some companies even charged their workers for the doctors they employed. At least one company charged fifty cents per month for the changing area where the men donned their work clothes. Necessary tools like ladders, picks, shovels, and ropes were deducted from wages. Shifting expenses to the workers meant more profits – and higher dividends – for the mining company's shareholders.

The mining companies were able to manipulate the contract workers' pay as the price of copper and availability of labor fluctuated. This was one reason the mining companies preferred the contract system. Occasionally, the workers pushed back at what they perceived to be lower than expected wages, but the mining companies always had the option of not renewing the contracts of the troublesome workers. Most of the mine workers were immigrants who didn't speak English and had little or no negotiating power. There was usually little hope of improvement.

The last two decades of the 1800s were profitable years for the copper mines on the Keweenaw Peninsula when the price of copper held steady at 10 to 12 cents per pound. In the late 1890s, copper prices jumped to 16.5 to 17.5 cents per pound, and shareholder dividends soared with nearly $10 million paid in dividends each year for four years beginning in 1898. The pounds of copper found in each ton of rock was decreasing during this time on the Keweenaw Peninsula, and the mining equipment was becoming increasingly outdated, but they were masked by the roaring seller's market.[3]

As the years passed, the mine shafts on the Keweenaw Peninsula grew deeper and yielded less copper at the same time the production costs were increasing. The C & H, which had been the Keweenaw's dominant mining company, suddenly faced competition from companies with new, more cost-efficient equipment and methods.

The mines on the Keweenaw Peninsula had dominated the American copper industry for most of the 1800s but faced competition from new mines in Arizona and Montana as the nineteenth century ended. The new Western mines had more modern equipment, better technology, and employed college-educated men armed with the latest techniques. In the 1800s, hiring unskilled migrants did not pose many problems, but as mining operations needed to become more efficient and keep profits high for themselves and their shareholders, unskilled labor was in less demand. Unskilled mining workers lucky enough to have a job experienced increased pressure to work more for the same pay…or less.

Mining on Minnesota's Vermilion Range in the 1800s

In 1865, geologist George Stuntz was seeking gold on the Vermilion Range (a rock formation approximately 25 miles in length and up to two miles wide in northeastern Minnesota) when he discovered the presence of iron ore in several locations. Stuntz returned to Duluth with 60 pounds of iron ore samples but couldn't garner much interest in his find. People wanted to hear about gold strikes, not iron ore, and Stuntz was unable to find any financial backers.

Traveling to the East Coast four years later, Stuntz interested a wealthy and influential banker named Jay Cooke about his discovery of the potential wealth in iron ore hidden in northeastern Minnesota's wilderness. Cooke passed the information to a fellow banker named George Stone, who arrived in Duluth in May 1869.

The Panic of 1873 financially ruined both Jay Cooke and George Stone, but both men rose to wealth and prominence again in the years following the Panic. In 1875 George Stone, with iron ore samples in hand, was searching for a wealthy financial backer to invest in the mineral-rich Vermilion Range. In Philadelphia, he approached and piqued the interest of Charlemagne Tower.

On July 13, 1875, an expedition to the Vermilion Range included a geologist named Albert Chester, who had been hired by Charlemagne Tower, and lead guide George Stuntz. Soon after realizing Stuntz's vast knowledge of the area's natural resources, Chester allowed Stuntz to choose the site for setting off a charge of explosives. The astonishing quantity of iron ore exposed by the blast launched the start of mining on the Vermilion Range.

In July 1880, Albert Chester and George Stuntz were again on the Vermilion Range. Chester returned to Duluth in August and reported to his employer, Charlemagne Tower, that the iron ore samples he had examined were 50 to 75 percent in purity. Tower immediately directed his financial resources to the Vermilion Range. Simultaneously, George Stone, who was then a Minnesota state legislator, quickly and successfully promoted the passage of a law guaranteeing the taxation of iron ore at one penny per ton.

Stuntz, who had been hired by the State of Minnesota as a surveyor, reported to Minnesota that the Lake Vermilion area contained very little swampland, because swampland could not be sold by the state. To Charlemagne Tower, Stuntz enthusiastically noted eight thousand acres of potentially rich iron-ore deposits.

Tower purchased 17,000 acres of land on the Vermilion Range for about $40,000 in 1881. The following year, he purchased 3,000 additional acres. In June 1882 and overseen by George Stone, three men with hand drills dug the first test pits on Tower's land. The test pits yielded very encouraging results and on December 1, 1882, the Minnesota Iron Mining Company was incorporated.

With Charlemagne Tower as president of the company and owner of 60 percent of the stock, Tower then quit-claimed the Vermilion Range land as well as land in Two Harbors, Minnesota, to the corporation. Ore docks were later constructed on the Two Harbors land.

In 1882, Minnesota Legislator George Stone obtained the charter of the defunct Duluth and Iron Range Company, reorganized it, and arranged for Charlemagne Tower to primarily finance the purchase of the railway company. Stone also arranged for the construction of the 68-mile rail line between the Vermilion Range and Two Harbors. Six hundred men began constructing the rail line in June 1883.

Edward Prince was hired by Tower to oversee the opening of the first mine. By September 1883 men had cleared a large area of trees and shrubs. A sawmill produced 10,000 feet of lumber each day. A dozen houses for mine workers were constructed by year's end.

For each mile of track laid, the Duluth and Iron Range Railway Company received ten sections of swampland within ten miles of the tracks. Thus, Tower became the owner of an additional 435,200 acres of land in northeastern Minnesota. Train engines arrived in Two Harbors by ship, and the first train pulling ore cars arrived on the Vermilion Range in July 1884. By the end of 1884, eighty-two thousand tons of the highest grade of iron ore ever mined in

America had arrived in Two Harbors from the Vermilion Range.* The early mines were open pit mines but, by 1890, most area mines were underground.[4]

George Stone hired Elisha Morcum as the mine's first supervisor. Morcum had worked in the copper mines on the Keweenaw Peninsula before becoming a supervisor in Michigan's iron mines. He left Michigan in March 1884 with 120 miners and their families. The group traveled from Michigan to Superior, Wisconsin, on the Northern Pacific Railroad and then by wagon for the 110-mile, three-day trip north on the Vermilion Trail.

Three months later, 400 copper miners left the Keweenaw Peninsula and followed the same route to northeastern Minnesota. The miners had been hand-picked and were said to be the best hard-rock miners ever assembled. N.P. Johnson was a member of the second group and worked on the Vermilion Range for over two years. (He returned to the Keweenaw Peninsula in August 1886 and worked as a timber foreman until moving a few years later to northwestern Wisconsin.)

In 1887 and at the age of 78, Charlemagne Tower sold his land on the Vermilion Range, his docks in Two Harbors, and the Duluth and Iron Range Railroad Company for $8.5 million, doubling his investment. The buyers were a syndicate including Cyrus McCormick, Marshall Field, and John D. Rockefeller. The syndicate, which had learned of Tower's questionable acquisition of the northeastern Minnesota "swampland," threatened him with years of litigation. They also threatened to directly compete with his rail line between the Vermilion Range and Two Harbors, where Rockefeller controlled most of the shipping. Feeling he had no choice but to sell, Charlemagne Tower capitulated and lived his remaining years in relative peace.

By 1888, nearly two thousand people lived near the mines on the Vermilion Range. Most of the single men lived in two-story boarding houses, but cottages – built on company land – could be rented or purchased. The cottages each had a fenced-in yard, outhouse,

---

*Thanks to the legislation promoted by Charlemagne Tower's associate, George Stone, the state tax paid to Minnesota by the Minnesota Iron Mining Company for the 82,000 tons of mined high-grade iron ore was $820.

kerosene lamps, and wood stoves. The cottages faced unpaved streets. Behind the cottages was a network of boardwalks ending in stairways that descended into the mines. Cows wandered freely through the mining towns, and water was drawn from community wells. Single and married women living near the mines worked as teachers, seamstresses, or in boardinghouses.

MINING ON MINNESOTA'S MESABI RANGE IN THE 1800S

Minnesota's Mesabi Range lies north of Duluth and west of the Vermilion Range. It is approximately one hundred ten miles long and up to three miles in width. During the mid- to late-1880s, several sons of Lewis Merritt, a hotel owner and millwright, were employed by the logging companies as timber cruisers. While walking the vast tracts of land, two of the brothers found iron ore samples that looked promising.

Even though the mining experts all believed that no large iron-ore deposits existed, the Merritts began a concerted effort to prove the experts wrong. In 1889, the Seven Iron Men began walking one forty-acre parcel after another and searching for iron ore deposits. The Seven Iron Men were four Merritt brothers who, as timber cruisers, knew the area well, and their three nephews.

During the next four years, the Seven Iron Men walked an estimated five hundred square miles, mapping much of Itasca, Cook, Lake, and St. Louis counties. Within that vast area, they discovered iron ore of 64 percent purity. Later, John Merritt stated, "I remember just how beautiful that ore was, glinting blue there under the green of the pines. It was a dream come true, a satisfying fact that nature had yielded to us the great secret she had guarded through the ages."[5]

The Merritt family incorporated the Mountain Iron Company on July 10, 1890, and just a few months later discovered a large iron-ore deposit that eventually became the Mountain Iron Mine. Mining experts from Michigan arrived on the Mesabi Range, not believing the area could possibly be rich in iron ore. The Michigan experts were used to working with hard, solid ore and not the soft, granular ore the Seven Iron Men had discovered. Labeling the Merritts as farmers, not miners, the experts returned to Michigan after having a good laugh.

Undeterred, the Seven Iron Men met with Andrew Carnegie, who was then America's largest steel manufacturer. Carnegie sent his expert to northern Minnesota and was uninterested when his expert called the soft ore "a sample of dirt."

But Carnegie's chief competitor, Henry Oliver, heard the stories and traveled to Minnesota where he met with the Merritts and viewed their discoveries. A very impressed Oliver bought one of their land parcels with the ore deposits for $75,000 plus 65 cents for each ton his company mined.

Henry Oliver retained Chester Congdon of Duluth as his legal counsel. Congdon formed the Oliver Mining Company on September 30, 1892, and Henry Oliver began mining soon after. In November 1892, two thousand tons of ore arrived at the Allouez docks in Superior, Wisconsin, and were loaded into Alexander McDougall's whaleback ships.

The Seven Iron Men, who owned several mines and retained interest in others, experienced difficulties in transporting their ore to the Twin Ports docks. To solve their problem, they formed and incorporated the Duluth, Missabe, and Northern Railway Company and decided to build their own ore docks in the Twin Ports, where their railway company would transport the ore. The Panic of 1893 struck before the Seven Iron Men's dream of a mining empire was realized. Financially strapped and in debt to John D. Rockefeller for millions of dollars, they were forced to sell most of their property to him.

John D. Rockefeller bought the remainder of the Seven Iron Men's holdings in February 1894. Two months later, Andrew Carnegie, who now believed the Merritts had owned more than a sample of dirt, bought a half ownership of the Oliver Iron Mining Company in order to compete with Rockefeller. Since Carnegie controlled the nation's steel mills, Rockefeller was forced to sell his iron ore to Carnegie.

In 1896, a compromise was reached by Oliver, Carnegie, and Rockefeller. Oliver mined the iron ore, and Rockefeller transported it on his rail system to the ore docks on Lake Superior. The iron ore was then shipped to Carnegie's steel mills. The company organized by the three men was named U.S. Steel, and it was the world's largest corporation. Soon after its formation, U.S. Steel agents were encouraging Europeans struggling to survive in horrific economic conditions to immigrate to the Twin Ports and northeastern Minnesota.

By 1900, 13,900,000 tons of iron ore had been mined on the Mesabi Range and shipped from the Twin Ports.

Formation of the Second International

On July 14, 1889, delegates from 20 countries met in Paris and formed the Second International (also called the International Workingmen's Association). The delegates represented labor organizations and trade unions in their respective countries and followed the philosophies of Karl Marx. During the last decade of the 1800s, their coalition greatly influenced the policies, methods, and ideologies in the European Labor Movement's struggles against capitalism.* The Second International rejected the gradual achievement of workers' rights and concluded that only a revolution would accomplish the goals of the working class.

The Second International met three more times during the 1890s in different European cities. Members of each country had their own labor organizations and pledged to contest elections, build and support trade unions, and involve themselves in their country's working class and Labor Movement.

In Finland, the Second International's labor organization was originally named the Labour Party but later became the *Suomen sosialidemokraattinen puolue*, or SDP. Members of the Finnish SDP included Yrjö Sirola, Santeri Nuorteva, Otto Kuusinen, and Edvard Gyyling – all of whom later became internationally well known.

It was almost preordained that the Second International's fight for better wages and working conditions would find its way into the relatively young American Labor Movement because of America's exploding demands for ores, lumber, and the transportation of them.

---

* By 1912, the Second International's membership totaled over 8 million members from Europe, America, Canada, and Japan. (www.britanica.2nd.intl)

LABOR STRUGGLES IN THE 1800S

Labor conflicts began almost as soon as mines opened in the Upper Midwest, but there were initially no organizing forces. An early strike on the Keweenaw Peninsula in 1872 ended in the copper-mine owners' favor. On the Mesabi Range, there were nearly 50 walk-outs and strikes between 1883 and 1900. They all failed.

Trade unions in the Upper Midwest for the most part ignored the immigrants working in the iron and copper mines or on the docks shipping the ore. Unions during this time included the Licensed Lake Tugmen and the Amalgamated Association of Iron and Steel Workers, but U.S. Steel was very anti-union, and employees were fired if they showed any interest in unionizing.

There were many small iron-mining companies on Minnesota's Iron Range (which included the Vermilion and Mesabi ranges) but, by the beginning of the twentieth century, 41 of those companies were controlled by the Oliver Mining Company, a subsidiary of U.S. Steel. The power of U.S. Steel was unquestioned, and income from the iron ore extracted on the Iron Range created the world's first billion-dollar corporation.

In addition to controlling most of the mines on the Iron Range, U.S. Steel owned the railroads bringing ore from the mines to the ore docks. The ore docks in Superior, Wisconsin, and West Duluth and Two Harbors in Minnesota were affiliated with U.S. Steel. And the majority of ships transporting ore to the steel mills in Cleveland, Pittsburgh, and Chicago were controlled by the powerful corporation and its subsidiaries.

U.S. Steel was the indisputable giant the immigrants had to fight if they wanted better pay or working conditions. The most dangerous jobs were given to the immigrants, who usually received the lowest pay. In 1889, the average wage of an unskilled immigrant worker on the Iron Range was $1 per day. With the majority unable to speak English, their pay or horrendous working conditions were unlikely to improve without unification and representation.

Mine managers posted signs on the Iron Range in 1896* that forbade workers to join unions. The workers who the managers believed might belong to unions or were thinking of joining a union were fired immediately. No proof was necessary. Ore trimmers, hired to evenly spread ore in the holds of ships to make the loads more stable, were not allowed on docks owned by John D. Rockefeller if they belonged to any union.

Escape from the Mines

The permanent settling of northwestern Wisconsin began in the late 1880s with most settlers arriving by train on the Northern Pacific Railroad to booming logging towns like Maple, Brule, or Iron River. From there they began their journeys on rough trails or logging spurs to the land they had purchased or were homesteading. Walking for miles with all the supplies and provisions they could carry, their journey usually ended at the cutover land or in the thick forests where they would carve their new lives. There were no roads, no electricity, and no way to communicate with whatever neighbors they might have. Water was plentiful, not from wells, but from nearby crystal-clear streams. The trees provided wood for heat, for building furniture, and lumber for the buildings that needed to be constructed before the long winter began. Game was plentiful for those lucky enough to own a rifle and bullets.

The communities of Waino and Oulu no longer exist on most maps, but they once rang with the sounds of hand saws and hammers. Both communities were predominantly Finnish, and many early settlers had fled the oppression of the mining industry. In Waino and Oulu, there was no danger of mine explosions and cave-ins, and no mine captains urged them to work faster or risk getting fired.

---

* Also in 1896, the first issue of the *Labor World* newspaper in Duluth began with the promise that laborers would be treated fairly in its publication. Sabrie Akin, founder of *Labor World* and obviously not a proponent of capitalism stated, "The monopolist...and the slimy capitalist robber will sink into an oblivion deeper and darker than hell itself, there to remain till the crack of doom."[6]

Lydia Tuura wrote about the late 1800s and life in Waino: "There were no roads, no stores, nothing but wilderness. All provisions had to be gotten from Brule where there was a store... It was the men folks who walked to Brule [about six miles one way] and brought back provisions. The country store [after it was finally built in Waino] was within walking distance so the women folks could see what they were buying. The store also gave them an outlet for the only product they had for sale – homemade butter. Butter was packed in crocks or molds. The storekeeper stored it in the cellar until he could [get it to the Brule rail station and] ship it to Superior."[7]

The country store owners typically bought supplies and provisions from wholesale houses in Duluth and Superior and picked them up at the train station nearest them. The owners of Ludvala's store, which was north of Brule on the west side of the Brule River, drove their horse and wagon to the Blueberry station west of Brule. Harju's store [north of Brule on the east side of the Brule River] received their shipments at the Brule station. Lanterns, milk pails, skidding chains, sugar barrels, cracker barrels, bologna barrels and many other essentials filled the store.

In 1898, a post office opened in the community of Waino. Matt Harju was the first postmaster, and the first post office was in his store. John Oja had the first horse in Waino and was hired to haul the mail from the Brule station three times a week. Men worked in logging camps during the winter. Men too old to work in the camps stayed home and made skis, sleds, and furniture. The old men helped the women and children with the chores on the farms.

The life of the early settlers in northwestern Wisconsin was not easy but, for those who had come to America hoping for a better life only to spend years working underground in horrific conditions while barely making enough to provide for their family, it was a new beginning filled with sunshine and hope.

THE NEW CENTURY

Immigrant struggles in the Upper Midwest continued as the new century began. Land was offered by the government for homesteading. Land was also sold by the government, agents for the logging and railroad companies, and by individuals and businesses. Miners left their subterranean work places for an equally hard life, but one in which they reaped the benefits of their hard work. The American immigrants who arrived in the 1800s and early 1900s, however, had a better chance for land ownership than immigrants who arrived later.

Thousands of men, though, continued working long hours in the extraction and transportation industries in dangerous working conditions for pitiful wages and no benefits. Attempts to improve their lives were largely unsuccessful. The beginning of the twentieth century saw many attempts to unify workers into a stronger Labor Movement through the organization of unions, outreach by media outlets, and by improving their education.

The 1900 federal census showed half of all Finnish immigrants lived in Wisconsin, Minnesota, and Michigan. Most of them lived near the copper and iron mines. In 1905, 85 percent of Mesabi Range residents were foreign born, mainly from Finland, Italy, and the Slavic countries. In some of Upper Michigan's small mining towns, Finns constituted up to 80 percent of the population.

In the early 1900s, events in Finland and Russia reverberated as far as North America, affecting Finnish communities in ways no one could have foreseen.

2 LAND OWNERSHIP & LABOR STRUGGLES

"I was small when I came along with thousands to the Land of the Free at the turn of the century, my mother holding me up to see the Statue of Liberty! We rode the train with others going to the North Country, and I looked out the window and saw what I would never forget – the red Mesabi! Everything was red – the roads, the water in the ditch, the miners' clothes, the big open pit, the sidewalks, the skin of the people. The red ore seemed to penetrate, to drive into everything. I came to know it stood for U.S. Steel, which claimed our lives, our thoughts, and our allegiance. Father worked in the red mine; my mother would cry when she tried to wash off the red dirt from my father's clothes and body. The neighbors around us spoke a strange language – my mother would wash the clothes and cry for Finland." [1]

Finnish immigrant IRENE PAULL

BUILDING FINNISH COMMUNITIES IN NORTHWESTERN WISCONSIN

The Beck School was the first school built north of Brule in the predominantly Finnish community of Waino. The school was built on land donated by Matt Ulvila. South of the school was Harju's store. The National Lutheran Church, the Waino Evangelical Lutheran Church and the Eternal Rest Cemetery were close by – just east of the school and store. This was the center of Waino and where the annual *Juhannus Juhla*, the Mid-summer Festival, was celebrated. The area was about six miles north of the village of Brule.

About one mile west of Waino's center was the area known as Riverside, and Riverside was where N.P. Johnson and his family

The Waino Pioneer Chapel is the oldest building still in use in Waino, Wisconsin. Completed in 1895, its bell tolled the age of an early settler after their passing, spreading the news to everyone for miles around. Mary Koski Wentela was the first baby christened in the chapel in 1895.
Scott Wisherd collection

lived after leaving the mines in Michigan and Minnesota. Before there was a store in Riverside, N.P. took orders from his neighbors and picked them up in Brule. He donated land for a school saying, "Education is the key to the world." He helped build and organize a church. He built a two-mile telephone line for the residents of Waino. N.P. and his two brothers-in-law, John Tuura and August Wentela, strongly believed in being active in community affairs. In 1902, N.P. became the second postmaster and store manager of the United Farmers' Store Company after Matt Harju left the area.

At that time, eggs and butter were traded for groceries and farm supplies. A dozen eggs cost 10 cents, and a pound of butter ranged in value from 12 to 15 cents.

N.P.'s nearest neighbor in Riverside was the Henry Aho family. Duane Westfield, Henry's oldest grandson, later shared: "My grandfather played an important role in my earliest years. Standing a mere 5'6", he was nevertheless a 'giant of a man' as those close to him described him. Grandpa Henry had been left an "orphan," the word used to characterize his situation in Finland at the time, since his father, Matti, had died when Grandpa was 14. It was a sad enough experience and could well have become a tragedy in the Finland of those days except for two very important considerations.

"First, as an *orpho*, or orphan, he was entitled to receive a thorough vocational education in a school run by the Russian Army for children who had lost one or both parents. [Finland at that time was ruled by the Russian Empire.]

"Second, and this is far more significant, in addition to sharing with his sons his rudimentary knowledge of farming and woodwork, his father [Matti] had also introduced him to the skills needed for carpentry, leather crafting, and metal work. He had not only the basic skills in these areas, which were highly valued in his day, but he developed them to the point where he was recognized as a master craftsman.

"Grandpa came to America when he was 18 after serving or studying in the school – I'm not sure of the distinction – for three years. He worked, first in Hancock, Michigan [in the copper mines] and later in Wakefield [in the iron mines] to save money to buy land. In the latter town, he met a woman [Alexandra Laulaja] who would later become his wife and my grandmother. She was working in the boardinghouse where he was staying. Together they combined their savings and purchased 80 acres of land in what was frontier property in Brule, Wisconsin. They were among only a handful of settlers to move to that area at the time [in 1904].

"I take great pride in driving through the countryside where they built up their working farm. There they also used their imagination and energies in helping to build a community around them. The level of culture they attained was far in excessw of what one would imagine their primary needs to have been at the time.

"Grandpa, together with a few neighboring men, was responsible for the planning, design, and construction of the first elementary school in the area, the N.P. Johnson School, named for a friend of his who donated the land. Together they helped incorporate the first Dairy Co-operative east of Superior [in Oulu] and one of the early cooperative stores, which was built in Brule. They were also responsible for the construction of a community hall [the Waino Round Hall] out of the conviction that one should not live by work alone, vital and fulfilling that it proves, but that he or she needed social activities as well for a full life experience.

"He shared his carpentering skills with all male members of the family, including myself. It was his conviction that we should all be fully prepared to take care of our needs as well as those of our families."

South of Waino's center lived the Oscar Maki family. Oscar had immigrated to America in 1890 as a teenager and worked in a copper mine on the Keweenaw Peninsula until the mines began laying off their workers. After traveling around America for several years, he joined his brother Isaac in Hanna, Wyoming. The Union Pacific had a coal mine there, and workers were in great demand. In 1902, Oscar's sister and her husband were moving back to Finland and sold their farm in Waino to Oscar and his wife Mary.* Like N.P. and Henry, Oscar believed in being an active member of the community and served on the Brule Town Board and as a Douglas County Supervisor. Oscar and Mary lived in Waino for the rest of their lives.

East of Waino, settlers began arriving in the neighboring township of Oulu in the late 1880s after trudging on the primitive trails north of Brule. Among the earliest homesteaders were John Kangas, Henry Maryland, and Fred Johnson. In 1891, the Little Red School became the first school built in the town of Oulu on land sold by homesteader Fred Johnson for one dollar. In 1904, Oulu saw its first store when Herman Koski opened a small grocery store in a portion of the Fred Johnson home.

In the earliest years, Henry Maryland drove his team of oxen to Brule, bought the supplies needed by the area's settlers, and collected Oulu's mail. When Matt Harju opened his store in Waino, the Oulu settlers began buying what they needed at the closer store and also picked up their mail. Oulu's first post office opened in 1903 in a lean-to at Andrew Lauri's home. The mail was then carried on horseback north to Oulu three days a week from Iron River.

Most of Oulu's earliest settlers were homesteaders who were required to construct a building – which was usually a sauna – and clear at least an acre of land after filing their first papers for ownership. In addition, the homesteaders were required to file papers toward becoming U.S. citizens.

After the land available for homesteading was claimed, the settlers had to barter for or buy land. Charles Silvola traded his horse for twenty acres of land. In 1907, Fred Kopplin and his son, Harry, began selling cutover land in Oulu, and many of the buyers came from mining towns in northern Minnesota and Upper Michigan.

In the earliest days, there were no town or county governments

---

* On June 30, 1903, there was an explosion in the Union Pacific Coal Company's mine #1. The explosion and resulting cave-in killed 169 miners with 46 miners barely escaping. Among those killed was Oscar Maki's brother, Isaac.[2]

Built in 1899, the original Pudas house was 24' X 40'. Before any area Finn halls, schools, or churches were built, the large home was often used for town meetings, Sunday services, and funerals. The second photo shows the Pudas family farm. The Pudas house was later disassembled and moved to its permanent location at the Oulu Cultural & Heritage Center.
Pudas family collection

funding the construction of fledgling communities like Waino and Oulu. If the settlers wanted a community hall, school, or church, they needed to work together and pool their resources to build it. If a neighbor needed a new barn, everyone helped with the barn-raising gatherings that always culminated with a barn dance. The pride in their community was strong as they watched it spring from a few scattered farms in the wilderness to a community large enough to justify its own post office, stores, schools, churches, and halls.

Many of Waino and Oulu's earliest settlers emigrated from Finland and found their first work in America's mines. Through the long hazardous six-day weeks spent underground and the pitiful wages, they managed to persevere until the reprieve of land ownership arrived. Gone were the walk-outs and strikes, and the fruitless battles against the mine owners who hired armed guards or bought politicians who passed laws in the mining company's favor. As they cleared their land for fields and pastures, and built their homes using the most basic tools, the work was equally hard and the hours long. But they were their own boss. There was no regular paycheck, but their compensation were the green fields filled with grazing livestock, the gardens bursting with produce, and the family welcoming them home after a long day.

Together, the early settlers in Waino and Oulu worked together in harmony and with pride in their communities.

THE BOLSHEVIKS & THE SECOND INTERNATIONAL

The Labor Movement that swept across Europe as the 1800s drew to a close continued into the new century. Better pay and working conditions were demanded, and labor parties affiliated with the Second International (the Marxist-leaning International Workingmen's Association) that had formed in 1889 were organized in numerous countries in their common battle against capitalism.

In 1903, the Russian Labour Party split into the Bolsheviks (the majority) and the Mensheviks (the minority). With Vladimir Lenin increasingly gaining control in the Bolshevik Party, he was described during this time as "there being no other man who is

VLADIMIR LENIN: THE FATHER OF REVOLUTION

Vladimir Lenin was a radical political and revolutionary figure whose actions started the ripple effect of the Communist Movement from Russia to North America and far beyond. Without Lenin's obsession with revolution, the overthrow of the Czarist Russian Empire, Finnish independence and its subsequent Civil War, the international proliferation of Communism, and the rise of Joseph Stalin may have never happened.

Vladimir Ilich Ulyanov was born to a wealthy middle-class family in the Russian Empire on April 22, 1870. He was the third of six children. His mother was a physician, and his father was a teacher. Vladimir was a bright student and graduated from high school at the top of his class. Except for becoming an atheist when he was 16, there was nothing unusual in his upbringing to suggest that he would later lead revolutionaries in a newly toppled Russian Empire and start a Communist Movement that reverberated around the world.

When Vladimir was 17, two events changed his life. His father passed away prematurely, and his oldest brother, Alexandr, who was a student at the Kazan University, was hanged for conspiring with a terrorist group planning to assassinate Russian Emperor Alexander III. At age 17, Lenin suddenly became the male head of the family.

Following in his brother's footsteps to Kazan University, Vladimir was expelled after just three months for participating in an illegal student assembly against the Russian Empire's czarist government. During his banishment, he read the philosophies of Karl Marx, becoming a Marxist in January 1889 at the age of 18.

As a revolutionary activist, Vladimir worked against capitalism, writing articles and distributing pamphlets to workers and peasants. His activities led to his arrest in December 1895, after which he was imprisoned for 15 months followed by a three-year exile in Siberia. During his exile, he maintained contact with fellow exiled revolutionaries.

Vladimir moved to Munich, Germany, after his exile and continued his anti-capitalist activities after changing his last name to Lenin in 1901. By then, he fervently believed in the violent overthrow of what he saw as the bourgeoisie-controlled government, which would then be followed by the replacement of the dictatorship by the proletariat, or people.

In Munich, Lenin wrote and distributed pamphlets aimed at Russian peasants and workers, attempting to change their pro-czar attitudes by showing them that their miserable existence was directly linked to the Russian czar. During this time, Lenin and his fellow comrades began to believe that it was the right time to organize a radical, revolutionary Marxist party. Their First Congress in 1898 ended when most attending members were arrested for conspiring against the Czar.

In 1903, the organization Vladimir Lenin helped found was known as the Bolsheviks, or Communists.

absorbed by the revolution twenty-four hours a day, who has no other thoughts but the thought of revolution, and who even when he sleeps, dreams of nothing but revolution."

Long before the Bolshevik Revolution, Lenin's dream was of forming an international organization that would carry out revolutions and overthrow capitalist governments – one country at a time – then replacing them with communist governments. His dream began in 1905 when he joined the Second International.

In 1907, Vladimir Lenin's revolutionary activities forced him into exile for the second time in his life but, before he left Russia, he helped draft a Second International resolution that stated its members would use a crisis, such as war, to promote their revolution.

THE EARLY 1900S IN THE GRAND DUCHY OF FINLAND

In 1901, the Czar of Russia decreed that all Finnish men over the age of 18 must serve in the Russian Army. There was massive resistance to this new law and, in 1902, the greatest number of Finnish immigrants – a total of 23,152 – arrived in America.

Finnish people immigrated to America because of several factors in addition to the mandatory service in the Russian Army. Jobs were hard to find in Finland, and many rural men moved to cities seeking jobs because they were not the first-born males on the family farms and therefore had no chance of inheriting the land. At the same time, American agents sent to Europe began promoting the "Promised Land" where there was a great need for workers in mines, logging camps, building railroads, or as dock workers. Women were needed as maids and cooks.

Finnish immigrants were often helped by family members who had previously immigrated to America. They often moved to heavily Finnish communities – especially in the Upper Midwest – where the land and climate was similar to what they'd left behind. Still, many missed their family, friends, and homeland. Learning to speak English was difficult for many, and some refused to learn the new language.

Unrest and a growing feeling of discontent and revolution continued in Finland. The Viapori Military Revolt began on July 30, 1905, on an island near Helsinki with an attempted uprising instigated by three junior Russian officers. One officer, Sergei Tsion, was a secret Bolshevik sympathizer and had contacted a few hundred men from the Finnish SDP's military unit – also known as the Red Guard – for help. The Red Guard was an anti-czarist group favoring a Finnish social revolution, but they were ill-equipped and untrained, and the uprising lasted just 60 hours. The fate of Tsion is unknown, but the other two officers involved were executed. A total of 43 involved were executed, and 127 insurgents were sentenced to hard labor. Over 700 revolutionaries were jailed but later released. One who successfully escaped imprisonment was a young Russian Cavalry lieutenant named Leo Lindqvist,* who fled to America and became a leader in the American Labor Movement.

On October 30, 1905, the Finnish SDP's Red Guard participated in the General Labor Strike. The strike against the Russian regime included mostly Finnish citizens whose demands were in part met on November 4 when the Russian czar promised a new constitution for Finland and equal suffrage. The Labor Movement ended the strike on November 6, even though their demands were not fully met.

The SDP, as many members leaned more heavily toward Marxism, played an increasingly major role in Finnish politics. Every laborer belonged to the SDP, and the SDP was closely affiliated with the Finnish Trade Union Federation. As time went on, the SDP became more revolutionary and less willing to compromise with the Russian Empire.

In 1906, SDP member Otto Kuusinen** toppled the moderate chairman of the SDP and became a dominant leader in the SDP when he was only in his mid-20s. It came as a great surprise to many

---

* Leo Lindqvist changed his name to Leo Laukki in order to avoid capture by the czar's police force. He arrived in America in 1907 and first settled in Hancock, Michigan.

** In 1906, the same year Otto Kuusinen toppled the SDP chairman, he also began working as an editor for the Helsinki-based Finnish newspaper *Työmies* (Worker), a publication of the SDP.

when the SDP gained 80 of the 200 Finnish Parliament seats in 1907 and became the largest political party in the Parliament. Otto Kuusinen began serving in the Finnish Parliament in 1908 with fellow SDP member Yrjö Sirola.

Czarist Russia moved aggressively to stop the new workers' militant activities by repressing workers' rights and stamping out any acts of rebellion. After the Russian czar began demanding jail sentences for the treasonous leaders of the Grand Duchy of Finland's Labor Movement, many of those leaders fled the country. Two of the leaders, Santeri Nuorteva and Yrjö Sirola, escaped to America where they found working conditions very similar to what they had left behind with little or no organization to fight capitalism.

WESTERN FEDERATION OF MINERS & THE INDUSTRIAL WORKERS OF THE WORLD: UNIONS OF THE LABOR MOVEMENT

The Western Federation of Miners (WFM), a militant labor union, was formed in 1893 by several smaller mining unions in the Western states. The miners joining WFM felt themselves to be "wage slaves" to the "back-east" absentee owners who were willing to run them out of town, hire armed guards and strikebreakers, and jail them without a right to a trial or bail rather than accede to their demands. "Big Bill" Haywood, a silver miner, derisively said of the mine owners, "They did not find the gold, they did not mine the gold, they did not mill the gold, but by some weird alchemy all the gold belonged to them!"[3]

The Industrial Workers of the World (IWW, also known as the "Wobblies") was formed by the WFM in Chicago on June 27, 1905, and Big Bill Haywood became IWW's first chairman. He defined the IWW as "socialism with its working clothes on." At the time, the WFM felt there was a need for a national union that would unite industrial and immigrant workers. They wanted all workers to belong to a national union while also being members of smaller organizations according to their occupations.

The IWW was soon seen as a radical, revolutionary segment of America's Labor Movement. The Wobblies believed that all workers should organize as one class and included in the Preamble to its Constitution: "The working class and the employing class have nothing in common. There can be no peace so long as hunger and want are found among millions of the working people and the few, who make up the employing class, have all the good things of life." The Wobblies motto was, "An injury to one is an injury to all." They strongly promoted solidarity in the coming revolutionary struggles that, they believed, would ultimately lead to the overthrow of the employing class. The IWW believed in forms of direct action such as boycotts and strikes.

Factional differences led to a split of the WFM and IWW in 1905.

In 1905, a Help Wanted ad was asking for 500 men needed to work on building and maintaining the rail lines. The wage was $2.25 per day less $4.00 per week for meals and lodging.

Citizens' Alliance & the Anti-Union Pushback

Citizens' Alliance was organized in Dayton, Ohio, about 1900. It was formed as a group aggressively opposed to unions, and its membership was all anti-union individuals and businesses with anti-union policies. It consisted mainly of small, local associations believing that organized labor was "un-American and evil" and that the Labor Movement was "a war between the owners of American industry and the working class."

Members of Citizens' Alliance visited businesses that favored the Labor Movement and were pro-union, encouraging them to break their labor contracts and threatening boycotts of the business if they didn't. These tactics prompted the *Denver Post* in 1903 to print: "The Citizens' Alliance and other employers' associations have adopted one of the very methods of unionism that they condemn so vehemently – the submit or be destroyed method – to bring offending employers in line. They certainly can no longer wonder where laboring men get their ideas for pushing strikes and boycotts. If these steps had been taken by unions, all the so-called better class in the city would be loud in denouncing them."

In Minnesota, businesses belonging to Citizens' Alliance worked on their anti-union policies by passing legislation on the state and local levels. They also formed the Minnesota Employers' Association.

Establishing the *Työmies* Newspaper

Antero F. Tanner, a Marxist devotee and Finnish SDP member, was exiled from the Grand Duchy of Finland in 1899 for his extremist beliefs. Tanner remarked that, "For only one year had I time to take part in the Labor Movement in Finland before I had to leave to become an apostle overseas." He was one of the earliest "Apostles of Socialism."* Tanner was a gifted agitator and established the first Marxist club in America. He was joined by Finnish immigrant Martin Hendrickson in 1900. Together, they established the *Työmies* newspaper and traveled to hundreds of Finnish communities throughout the country, energizing crowds in the Finnish halls. During one nine-month tour, Hendrickson claims he traveled 13,000 miles in 28 states and spoke to 45,000 Finns.

On July 20, 1903, the *Työmies* was first printed as a four-page weekly newspaper in Worchester, Massachusetts. The first editor, Vihtori Kosonen, stated that the principle purpose of the publication was to support the "human dignity and justice for the oppressed peoples." The mission statement** read in part: "The *Työmies* shall be the voice of the Finnish Working People in America. It will devote what strength it may have to become the most ardent promoter of the spiritual and physical endeavors of the Finnish working people...

"Our dearest obligation is to make clear the problems of the working people. In clarifying these important social problems we will adhere to the staunch principles of the international working people's movement [The Second International]...

---

*Tanner was given the title by the late Dr. Michael G. Karni, a former Research Associate at the University of Minnesota.

**Translated by Donald Wirtanen in the June 1991 *Finnish-American Reporter*. Wirtanen also stated: "Our Finnish forebears acted through their newspapers and organizations."

Above photo: Delivery of the *Työmies* newspapers to the post office in Hancock, Michigan, circa 1910.

Top photo, previous page: The *Työmies* press room in Hancock, Michigan, was a bustling place during the Copper Strike in 1913, bringing the latest news as the strike wore on. By 1914, the Copper Strike of 1913 had forced the Työmies Society, which had firmly sided with the striking copper miners, to shut down its newspaper on the Keweenaw Peninsula due to a massive loss of business advertising. Deeply in debt, the Society relocated to Superior, Wisconsin – another hotbed of unrest during the Labor Movement.

Bottom photo, previous page: Shown in the photo is the back of the Työmies building in Hancock, Michigan, circa 1910. In May 1904, the *Työmies* began serving what was then the largest Finnish community in America. It was in Hancock that Leo Laukki, after successfully evading the Russian czar's police and fleeing the Grand Duchy of Finland, first found work as an editor of the *Työmies* in 1907.

Credit for all three photos: IHRCA, Anderson Library, U of MN

"Let it be briefly stated: We demand human dignity and justice for the oppressed peoples...

"Briefly put: We will monitor the interests of the underprivileged. We hope that the Finnish working people of America will be aroused to work together in a huge organized effort against the might of the cruel moneyed powers. Only the working people themselves can improve their miserable conditions...."

In May 1904, less than a year after its first issue, the *Työmies* moved to Hancock, Michigan, to serve the largest Finnish community in America. It was in Hancock that Leo Laukki, after successfully evading the Russian czar's police and fleeing the Grand Duchy of Finland, first found work as an editor of the *Työmies* in 1907.

THE FINNISH FEDERATION

Author Carl Ross wrote that "Finns were stubborn, non-conformist, often rebellious, and generally clung to their own ethnic community." Many never learned to speak English and, for the most part, tried to remain within their Finnish communities. About 1904, as the Labor Movement began gaining strength and momentum, many workers' clubs were formed in Finnish communities.

In 1906, the Finnish Federation was organized in Hibbing, Minnesota, when about 2,500 members of the Finnish workers' clubs throughout America gathered. After meeting for a week, the newly formed Finnish Federation ended in August with a parade and speeches in both English and Finnish. The longest speech given during the celebration was about the Labor Movement.

The Finnish Federation was divided into three districts with each district having their own newspaper, which included local, national, and international news. Stamps were sold to raise money. The Federation sold stamps for 40 cents, and each individual organization sold them for 50 cents, keeping a dime from each stamp.

With its established factories and skilled building trades, the Eastern District was the most moderate of the Federation's three districts. Their newspaper was the *Raivaaja*, which had begun printing in 1905 in Fitchburg, Massachusetts, with Taavi Tainio as its first editor. Tainio, a Finnish SDP member, had fled the Grand Duchy of Finland to avoid incarceration after the 1905 Russian Revolution.

The Finnish Federation's Western District was more radical than the Eastern District. The Western District did not have a newspaper affiliated with the Federation in 1906, and the Federation's board of directors determined the newspaper would be located in the city that raised the most money for the establishment of a newspaper. In December 1907, the first issue of *Toveri* was printed in Astoria, Oregon. *Toveri*'s first editor was Aku Kissanen,* a prominent Finnish SDP member who, like Taavi Tainio, was a fugitive following the Russian Revolution.

The Finnish Federation's Midwest District was the most radical of the three districts and was a hotbed of unrest in the region surrounding Lake Superior during the early 1900s because of the mining and transporting industries where most of the immigrant Finns worked. The *Työmies* was selected as the District's newspaper, which was then printed in Hancock, Michigan. The editor was Finnish SDP member Kaapo Murros, who was also a Grand Duchy of Finland exile. Soon after the Finnish Federation was formed, Murros was replaced as editor by Finnish fugitive Leo Laukki.

The newspapers provided Finnish immigrants news from the Old Country, economic and historical articles, short stories, poetry, political and cultural events, and even personal ads from people looking for partners. Correspondents from throughout the nation had their articles published in all three papers and linked Finnish immigrants nationally.

Newspapers were also an excellent way to spread propaganda. The Federation's papers were sometimes called "the worker's best friend," and the Finnish Federation's newspaper kept fanning the flames of radicalism and workers' injustices. The Finnish communities provided a powerful network of like-minded readers who could be swayed by the Federation's social, political, and economic beliefs.

The Finnish Federation, led by numerous Finnish SDP fugitives,

---

* In 1911, Aku Kissanen was replaced by Santeri Nuorteva, a prominent Finnish Federation leader and Finnish SDP member who was also a wanted Finnish fugitive. Nuorteva was replaced in 1913 by John Wiita.

Work People's College circa 1910 *IHRCA, Anderson Library, U of MN*

Yrjö Sirola was a very influential figure within the Finnish American community in both the Labor Movement and the Communist Movement. After returning to Finland, he became an instigator of the Finnish Civil War. *Wikimedia Commons*

was determined to fight American capitalism through political action and labor organization. Within a year came the first battle, and defeat, with Minnesota's 1907 Mesabi Strike. In the coming years, any victory against the powerful extracting and transportation corporations would prove elusive.

THE WORK PEOPLE'S COLLEGE

In 1903, an 18-room building was purchased about ten miles south of Duluth in Smithville, Minnesota. The school building was originally a seminary named People's College (*Kansan Opisto*). Almost immediately, a struggle ensued between those who wanted a seminary and those who wanted a more expanded curriculum in the Finnish language. One of the incorporators was Alex Halonen, a radical agitator from Finland, who began selling shares for the school for one dollar each. Halonen traveled as far as California and sold shares to fellow radicals and by 1907, the radicals controlled the Board of Directors.[4]

The school's name was changed to Work People's College (*Tyovaen Opisto*) and probably became the most important institution during the Finnish Labor Movement. Leo Laukki, a recent editor of the *Työmies* newspaper in Hancock, Michigan, became the director and an instructor in 1908. Laukki was described as an electrifying lecturer but quick-tempered and unyielding. His radicalism had a tremendous influence on the regional Labor Movement, and many scholars believe it was greater than that of any other individual.

Also in 1908, The Finnish Federation accepted the Work People's College (WPC) as its educational institution and began partially funding it through an annual fee of one dollar per member. The Finnish Federation needed public speakers and organizers. The Federation's newspapers and Finnish-owned businesses needed business managers, editors, and bookkeepers. The WPC provided the education needed to fill these positions.

Only eight students enrolled in the first year, but that number increased to 100 by the next year. In the third academic year 136 students enrolled, which included 33 women. Most of the students were young working-class Finnish immigrants. For some, the four-month course was their only formal education, even though 90 percent of all Finns were literate. In the early years of operation, the

Finnish Federation paid all expenses.*

Courses offered included history, economics, biology, public speaking, English, civics, citizenship (preparing students to become U.S. citizens), evolution, (Marxist-leaning) economics, and Tactics of the Labor Movement. The Business Department students also learned bookkeeping, commercial arithmetic, commercial law, and correspondence for jobs at the Finnish Federation, its newspapers, or other businesses.

John Wiita, who had moved to Superior in November 1905 when he was 17, had worked as a longshoreman on the Superior docks and as a railroad car repairman before enrolling as a student at the WPC in the fall of 1909. Wiita became interested in leadership and the Labor Movement at that time, serving first on the WPC Board of Directors in 1909 and later as an assistant instructor at WPC while attending classes and serving on Finnish Federation executive committees.

Perhaps the most significant administrator of the WPC was Yrjö Sirola, who became the director in 1910 at the request of Leo Laukki.** Like many of the other Finnish radicals, Sirola was evading imprisonment when he arrived in America. At the WPC, he taught various subjects while serving as director and influenced hundreds of students during his tenure. His favorite subject was history, but he also taught civics, American citizenship prep classes, and methods of organization – specifically labor organizations. He wanted his students to think and not just listen. John Wiita stated, "I well remember how he suddenly stopped his lecture, putting his forefinger over his nose, and began questioning his students. He was asking what lessons we should learn from certain historical phenomena or the actions and the deeds of certain historical leaders and their methods and actions. He taught us to be future leaders and to

---

* Beginning in the fall of 1912, the students paid $20 each month for tuition, food, and lodging. The fee increased to $22 per month the following year.

** Laukki and Sirola had both worked for the *Kansan Lehti* in the Grand Duchy of Finland. Sirola, the son of a Lutheran minister, had studied at a seminary before turning to a newspaper career. He had joined the Finnish SDP in 1903 and became acquainted with Vladimir Lenin when Lenin joined the Second International in 1905. When Sirola was in his mid 30s, he began serving in the Finnish Parliament and was the Deputy Speaker in 1908 and 1909.

be well prepared in advance of meetings."

Sirola became more radical while in America and stated that, at times, demonstrations and strikes were sometimes necessary to advance workers' demands. Sirola moved from a political centrist to believing more in revolutionary tactics, but he did not believe in the IWW's ways of advancing their cause by sabotage or destruction of property.

About the time Sirola arrived at the WPC, radicalism and unionism were becoming stronger in the WPC and Finnish Federation. The radicalism of those years was caused by social, economic, and political factors. Capitalism was strong, with the Labor Movement believing there was no ceiling for corporate wealth and no ceiling for the disregard of their workers.[5]

When Yrjö Sirola began his directorship at WPC, the student body was unusually large and included Finnish miners, loggers, domestic workers, mechanics, carpenters, and factory workers from northern Wisconsin, Minnesota, and Upper Michigan. This coincided with the opening of a second building which included classrooms and a dormitory.

Yrjö Sirola returned to the Grand Duchy of Finland in 1913. During his years in America, he joined the Finnish Federation and became an important, well-known national leader. Sirola built the WPC into an important educational institution with its most successful academic year being the 1913-1914 school year when 160 students enrolled.

Because of his many associations, Yrjö Sirola remained very influential even after leaving his directorship at the WPC in America and played an influential role in the Labor Movement's Finnish radicalization.

The Labor Movement on the Keweenaw Peninsula

The beginning of the twentieth century saw lower profits and less copper in the ore extracted from increasingly deeper mines on the Keweenaw Peninsula. Even the mighty C & H struggled to maintain the stellar dividends paid to its shareholders during the last two decades of the 1800s. In 1900, a ton of ore extracted by the C & H yielded 50 pounds of copper. Ten years later, the yield had dropped to 25.8 pounds. Decreasing productivity, an increasingly unskilled workforce – usually recent immigrants with no training in operating modern equipment – and the competition from more profitable Western mines were constant pressures on mine managers.

Efficiency experts were hired by the mining companies, and the mine bosses knew how much work the miners and trammers were capable of doing. The bosses told the workers what they expected. If productivity goals were not met, the worker was warned, reprimanded, or fired. There was a constant pressure for greater productivity as the chasm between workers and management grew during the early 1900s. As an increasingly higher efficiency was demanded by those working above ground, there was a growing discontent in the shafts and drifts in the ever-deepening mines below.

In July 1906, a Finnish-speaking organizer for the Western Federation of Miners (WFM) riled the audience in a Finn hall in Rockland, Michigan, and soon after, 280 of the 300 local mine workers walked off their jobs on strike. A confrontation developed soon after, and law enforcement fired into the crowd, killing two miners. That night, 110 Finnish men were arrested for disturbing the peace, and 13 of them were charged with the murders. Meetings were held, and headlines in the Finnish Federation newspapers across America helped raise the needed legal fees. The unfair charges were dropped, but the event was a big boost for the Finnish Labor Movement. Many Finns began associating themselves with the WFM, which was considered a militant union by the mine owners.

THE LABOR MOVEMENT ON THE IRON RANGE

There were a lot of strikes in the early 1900s with the mining companies' owners doing everything they could to stop them without acceding to the workers' demands. Miners of different nationalities, most of whom didn't speak English, were deliberately mixed in work teams to keep miners divided and unable to communicate and strategize. Spies were hired and worked alongside with the miners, creating distrust. Wildcat strikes resulted in blacklistings, discrimination, and firings of the migrant workers – mainly Finns, because they were generally more organized and experienced against the unfair labor practices.

Mining labor organizers had a difficult task because of the various nationalities and languages. The WFM's local union in Eveleth, Minnesota, was divided into Finnish, Italian, and Slavic sections with miners of each nationality representing the needs of his ethnic group.

Finns, who were considered to be the most radical and revolutionary, became a driving force for unionism. The Finn halls, which were in nearly every Finnish community, bustled with speakers and union activity. By the early summer of 1907, the WFM had enrolled 2,500 miners who worked on the Mesabi Range.

The 1907 Mesabi Range Strike began on July 16, 1907, when workers at the Twin Ports iron docks struck, causing a spontaneous strike of the miners. On July 17, the WFM asked the Oliver Mining Company for an 8-hour day, $2.50 per day for open-pit miners, and $3 per day for underground miners. The mining company flatly refused to negotiate and instead fired 300 miners.

All mines on the Mesabi Range were shut down, and over 20,000 miners struck. The Oliver Mining Company, representing U.S. Steel, hired hundreds of replacement workers directly from Europe, who didn't know they were working as scabs.* Violent resistance including beatings occurred because of the 1,000 armed guards and law enforcement officers hired directly by U.S. Steel. Using the logic, "If they get hungry enough, they'll be forced to work," owners of the mining companies pressured local businesses to cut off credit to the strikers. The strikers responded by forming consumer cooperatives, and the mining-company owners then pressured the wholesalers to refuse delivery to the cooperatives. The Finnish strikers were labeled as the "fiery followers of the Red flag," and 70 percent of Finnish miners never worked in the mines again.

---

*Scabs are workers who work before a strike ends. Sometimes hired as strikebreakers, they are usually compensated for less than the union workers receive.

MEMORIES FROM THE MINNESOTA IRON ORE MINES

It was April 27, 1908, when I was lowered for the first time into the "bowels of the earth." It was on that day that I started tunneling like a mole in the underground mine to earn my daily bread. It was a bit scary in those dark tunnels until I adjusted to the conditions.

"More, more" were the everyday orders of the working boss. "You have to show better results. If you can't get all those cars full you're fired." I put forth all I had because I was penniless, but many of the weaker, older men were fired because they couldn't keep up with the orders of the boss.

Too many men met their death at an early age. The ten-hour shifts were often worked in such poorly ventilated mines that the candle hardly burned, and the lingering smell of the dynamite after blasting was overpowering. It is no wonder what it did to man. In time the underground miner turned pale; his health was gone. The constant fear of death or injury left a grim mark on their faces. And if a death occurred, he was just another victim who had done more than his share to gather wealth for the capitalist millionaire.

The Finnish miners were "front-line" men. The wet, clammy gopher holes were places where the Finns reigned! The best timbermen were the Finns. Numerous repair jobs also belonged to the Finns. One can say that a Finn was used in the most important, the best, and the worst working places in the mine.

A miner barely gets a livelihood from the riches he digs while the millionaire gathers another million into his bottomless bag. Oh, when will a worker be able to free himself from all this wretchedness?

MATTI PELTO
Personal memoir

The Mesabi Range Strike lasted for two months, and the miners lost. Production in the mines resumed. Many workers returned to their jobs, but the most militant strikers (mainly Finns) were blacklisted, and the blacklists were sent as far as Montana to the West and Pennsylvania in the East. Many miners left the area permanently while others tried to buy land for a small subsistence farm.

All of the Finnish Federation newspapers carried stories of the strikes, and the Finn halls rang with shouting at the injustices, but the strike split the Finnish communities between those advocating for peaceful moderation while others were ready for violence.

The 1907 strikes resulted in U.S. Steel joining the open-shop drive by Citizen's Alliance and expelling all unions from its businesses. This affected haulers, construction workers, and sailors as well as miners and dock workers. U.S. Steel and its subsidiaries also refused to sell to all union contractors.

THE COPPER COUNTRY STRIKE OF 1913

There were several reasons for the Copper Country Strike of 1913 that began on July 23. Typically, miners worked 10 to 12 hours each day with one day off per week. Their salary was about $2.36 per day. Each payday, their wages were reduced by the tools they had purchased for their jobs, or food and other personal supplies they had purchased from the company-owned stores. Miners were expected to behave properly and could be fired for fighting, excessive drinking, or for no reason at all. In 1913, the mining companies had begun to replace two-man drills with one-man drills, which most miners strongly opposed. The miners believed that if a miner using a one-man drill had any problems, it could be several hours before he was found in an isolated area of the mine.

Many miners working on Michigan's Upper Peninsula had joined the WFM earlier in 1913. The WFM had successfully organized several violent strikes at mines in the western U.S., and Michigan's copper miners looked with envy at the higher wages and eight-hour days won by the WFM. In Upper Michigan's Copper Country, the WFM warned the mining companies that they would declare a strike if the companies refused to grant concessions or a conference.

The mining companies ignored the warnings.

The resulting strike was the first strike to affect all Copper Country mines. After just the first day of the strike, nearly all mines in the district were closed down with strikers blocking access to the mines. For several weeks, parades occurred almost daily to boost the strikers' morale. The mine owners asked Michigan's governor for National Guard troops to keep the peace, but this only led to confrontations and violence between the troops, striking miners, and law enforcement officials.

The Hancock People's Finnish Home housed both the *Työmies* newspaper and strike headquarters and looked like an armed camp as armed guards protected both the newspaper and strike leaders from Citizen's Alliance, which constantly threatened to destroy the building. The newspaper, which was printed in Finnish, was translated by people fluent in the various languages of the striking miners. The *Työmies* became the target of the mining companies' wrath because it became the voice of the strikers. Later, the newspaper was denied advertising by many businesses affiliated with Citizen's Alliance.

On August 14, an event known as the Seeberville Affair occurred when strikers John Kalan and John Stimac walked across mine property, were told they were trespassing, and ordered off the property. The men ignored the guard's order and kept walking. The guard and a few others then arrived at Kalan's residence and ordered him to follow them for questioning. Kalan refused to go with them, went back into the boardinghouse, and the group of men began shooting at the house. John Stimac and another man were wounded. Two boarders with no connection to Kalan or Stimac were killed, and their funerals were attended by some 4,500 mourners. Six months later, the guards were convicted of manslaughter.

On Christmas Eve 1913, the Women's Auxiliary of the WFM organized a Christmas party for hundreds of strikers and their families. The party was held in Calumet in an upstairs ballroom. At some point during the evening an unidentified man entered the ballroom and yelled "Fire!" The main exit from the ballroom was a steep stairway and, in the ensuing panic and stampede, 73 people were crushed to death in the stairwell, most of them children. The person who shouted "Fire!" was never found.

The disaster gave additional life to the strike. Shortly afterwards, the president of the WFM was shot and then forcibly placed on a train leaving the Upper Peninsula. However, support for the strike declined as organizers left the Copper Country, the WFM ran out of money, and strikers' families experienced great hardships during the winter. Many miners and their families permanently left the Copper Country. Almost nine months after the strike began, the strikers voted to end the strike on April 13, 1914.

THE ORE DOCK WORKERS STRIKE IN THE TWIN PORTS

Shortly after the Copper Country Strike began, ore dock workers in the Twin Ports struck. On July 31, 1913, an accident at the ore docks in Superior, Wisconsin, killed two men and injured two others when there was a miscommunication of workers transferring ore from a Great Northern Railway car into a waiting ore boat. The workers had previously requested that the signaling system be changed, and the deaths caused an immediate strike by 500 Duluth, Mesabi & Northern dock workers. DM&N was a U.S. Steel subsidiary.

The IWW and Leo Laukki became involved in the strike. Demands for better safety conditions as well as a pay increase were answered by the Great Northern Railway when they brought in strikebreakers and armed guards. Disillusioned, the workers had returned to their jobs by August 5, but the strike had caused a backlog in shipping.

On August 6, over 600 ore dock workers employed by a subsidiary of U.S. Steel in West Duluth struck, refusing to load any boats diverted from Superior. A representative of the IWW was kidnapped, and Leo Laukki was attacked by a private guard hired by the Oliver Mining Company. Spies were hired by employers during this time in an attempt to suppress organized labor.

On October 1, the Duluth dock workers were offered a 10-cent per day raise with an additional 10-cent per day raise on October 15. All workers except Finns were promised their jobs. The Finns were all fired and blacklisted.

A COHESIVE FINNISH FORCE

The early years of the twentieth century brought many changes for Finnish immigrants while some aspects never seemed to change. For those working in the transporting and mining industries, the strikes, walkouts, and boycotts brought push-backs by the company owners with firings, strikebreakers, and blacklistings with little improvements in working conditions or wages. In 1910, two-thirds of workers in the copper and iron mines were foreign born, and their annual wages were approximately two-thirds of the annual wages earned by American mine workers.

The Finnish SDP leaders who had fled to America and whose cause was the Labor Movement and overthrow of capitalism continued their work through newspapers, education, and organizations like the Finnish Federation and the Work People's College. Their mission remained unchanged, and they remained in contact with fellow exiles in America and their associates of the Second International still living in Europe. Their efforts in America had produced younger but no less passionate members of the Finnish Federation who would carry their cause well into the future.

The Finnish fugitives and their younger protégés created a cohesive force within the Finnish communities nationwide. Their training allowed them to work as educators, administrators, speakers, or in any of the Finnish newspapers published by the Federation. They were well-respected and trusted within the Finnish communities. By 1913, the Finnish Federation membership exceeded 13,000 in 260 branches nationwide.

The Finnish immigrants who had chosen a life in rural communities seemed far removed from the struggles and unrest of wage earners in the mining and transportation industries. Many farmers worked in logging camps during the winter to generate much needed income and returned to their farms every spring.

Predominantly Finnish communities in northwestern Wisconsin, like Waino and Oulu, only grew because the settlers worked together without outside help. There was community pride every time a new barn was built or a new school opened, and no boss or company profited from their hard work.

3 EVOLVING TOWNS & ORGANIZATIONS

"If the sauna doesn't cure you, death is close at hand."

FINNISH PROVERB

THE OULU FINN HALL* opened in July 1910. It stood on an acre of land that had been donated by Nestor Johnson and was about one-half mile east of the junction of highways B and FF. The early settlers joined together and built the hall with most of the material being donated.

Three years later, in 1913, the Waino Finn hall opened. The two halls were less than five miles apart in the adjacent townships and in different counties, but transportation in the rural communities during the early 1900s was over rough unpaved roads. Cars were a new invention and a luxury most families could not afford.** Walking or riding in a horse-drawn buggy was typical.

Finnish people are known for joining together to strengthen ties of ethnicity, kinship, and community, and the halls in both Oulu and Waino met that need. The hall in Waino, about six miles north of the village of Brule, was built near the Beck School. The original building was rectangular with a small dance hall, stage, and kitchen. Soon, the hall needed to be enlarged, and the Waino Round Hall became known for the beautiful hardwood floors by everyone who loved to dance. It became the local gathering place for

---

* The Finn hall, or *haali*, was the vital center of the Finnish community's activities. Finn halls were built in almost every Finnish community and were used for plays, meetings, dances, classes, sporting events like basketball games or wrestling matches, speakers, and almost every community event. It was the focal point of the Finnish culture with activities for all ages, and everyone was welcome.

** With a price of $850, the first Model T was available on August 12, 1908.

THE OULU FINN HALL

After the Hall's grand opening, "many groups and clubs were organized. The first was the Workers' Society, which had a large membership. There was a dramatics club, mixed choir, a women's organization, and a youth league. Meetings and community programs and entertainments were held and basketball games played. It was a busy place.

"In the early years there were no cars and, if there had been, they could not have been used in the wintertime because of the drifted roads. The town did not own a snow plow to open the roads. Horses were used; they were tethered and blanketed near the sheltered side of the building, waiting patiently for their masters. People used to walk for miles to see the entertainments offered at the hall, despite the zero weather.

"Many romances...had their beginnings in this hall. The children usually accompanied their parents, as babysitters were not invented yet. Many a sleeping child was laid on the stage, wrapped in its mother's coat, some even peacefully slumbering in the cupboard drawers in the kitchen, oblivious to the music and dancing around them."

FROM *HISTORICAL SKETCHES OF THE TOWN OF OULU*

all wedding dances, plays, speeches, festivals, and programs.

In 1910, the first cooperative organization in Oulu was built at the intersections of the future highways B and FF. The Oulu Co-op Creamery, which was less than one mile east of Waino's town line, enabled the farmers in both townships to market their dairy products. The creamery experienced a very shaky start when a severe drought caused a poor hay crop, forcing many farmers to reduce their herds. A few years later, though, conditions had improved, dairy herds were back to their normal size, and the creamery was thriving.

The two townships also worked together and organized the Waino-Oulu Telephone Association in 1913 when they purchased the Loveland Line for $100. The Loveland Line began in the village of Brule, ran north through Waino, and ended at the mouth of the Brule River. The two-mile N.P. Johnson Line in Waino was purchased for $25 and connected to the Loveland Line.

On March 22, 1914, at the Warren School in Oulu, a meeting was held to establish a cooperative store in Iron River, Wisconsin. Board members were elected, and a decision was made to pay the board members $1.50 each for every meeting they attended.

When the competing merchants learned of the organization, they immediately cut off all credit to the new cooperative's members. They quit trading eggs and butter for groceries. And they did everything they could to stop the Finnish cooperative from ever beginning their new enterprise.

The cooperative members persisted, though. An abandoned hotel building was rented for $10 per month and became their new store. A manager was hired for a wage of $65 per month, and a clerk received $32 per month. Both employees received free living quarters. A horse was purchased for delivering groceries and hauling supplies from the nearby Northern Pacific depot.

Matt Jaakkola, one of the board members, loaned the cooperative a stove, a few electric lights, a safe, and a clock with an option to buy them if desired after six months. On November 11, 1914, the Farmers' Co-operative Store held its grand opening. Three years later, the cooperative bought a second hotel building for $2,000.

Oulu saw its first cooperative store – called the Oulu Branch – in 1916 when Henry Kortesmaa sold a building for $15 and the half-acre of land surrounding it for $5 to the Iron River Cooperative. The building stood next to the Oulu Co-op Creamery in the heart of Oulu and near the east border of Waino.

The Waino and Oulu communities had several one-room schools with classes for grades one through eight. There were no school buses, but one large family in Waino had the luxury of a horse-drawn covered wagon for transporting their children. Most children walked to school, and many boys carried guns so they could hunt on the long walk home.

After graduating from the eighth grade, additional education was available in larger towns like Ashland to the east or Superior and Duluth to the west. The Superior Normal School was established in 1893 for training teachers, and many new teachers found their way to Waino and Oulu.

In less than 30 years, Waino and Oulu grew from cutover and heavily forested land to an area dotted with small farms and thriving communities. Every building had been constructed with the materials available from the land with hand tools and the help of neighbors. Every community member had a sense of pride and accomplishment as they sent their children to the school they had helped build, or walked into church, or prepared for a night of dancing in the Finn hall. Strong ties bound the relatives, neighbors, and friends together.

The leaders, educators, editors, and speakers of the Finnish Federation, its newspapers, and the WPC had worked together and built a membership of over 13,000 in the six years after its organization in Hibbing, Minnesota, in 1906. The Finnish Federation was a powerful organization whose newspapers had thousands of faithful readers. Hundreds of students had graduated from the WPC with the training needed for American citizenship or a better paying job.

After serving as the WPC director and educator since 1908, Leo Laukki moved to Hancock, Michigan, in 1911 and rejoined the staff at the *Työmies*. He returned to the Twin Ports during the summer of 1913, supporting the more radical wing of the IWW and helping the IWW leaders during the dock workers strike. He rejoined the WPC as the school's director after Yrjö Sirola* left the school late in 1913.

While Yrjö Sirola was still director at the WPC, he asked John Wiita to join the staff as an assistant instructor. Wiita had to resign from the position as well as his position on the Finnish Federation's Midwest District's Executive Committee in the spring of 1913 when Santeri Nuorteva asked him to join the *Toveri* editorial staff in Astoria, Oregon. After less than one year, though, Wiita returned to the Twin Ports due to a conflict with Nuorteva. In February 1914, Wiita was elected secretary of the Finnish Federation's Middle District just as the moderates and radical members were increasingly at odds. (After the Copper Strike of 1913, many of the more radical members of the Finnish Federation who favored strikes and sabotage had joined the IWW.)

Leo Laukki, after working at the *Työmies* in Hancock during the copper strike, shared the views of the Finnish Federation's more radical members and tried to incorporate those views into the curriculum at the WPC. He was admonished for his efforts by the Finnish Federation, which didn't have much of an effect. The Finnish Federation's Executive Committee then nominated Santeri Nuorteva** to head an investigation of the WPC and its increasingly revolutionary leanings. An enraged Leo Laukki called the investigative committee a *"noitakomitea"* (witch hunt committee) and prevented the investigation.

---

* Yrjö Sirola resigned from the WPC, returned to the Grand Duchy of Finland, and was re-elected to the Parliament as a member of the SDP. His influence in both America and Europe as a gifted speaker, director, educator, and organizer within the Finnish Federation and SDP had a lasting effect for many years.

** Santeri Nuorteva was known as a brilliant scholar and writer fluent in ten languages. He was a member of the SDP and served in the Finnish Parliament from 1907 to 1910 while working as a magazine journalist. Nuorteva was considered a radical revolutionary and was imprisoned by Czar Nicholas II. He escaped after six months and, in 1911, he fled to America with his family and avoided further imprisonment for treason. While living in Astoria, Oregon, he became a prominent leader and spokesman for the Finnish Federation and an editor of the *Toveri*. The Nuorteva family then moved to the East Coast where Santeri became an editor for the Finnish Federation's Eastern District's newspaper *Raivaaja*.

During this time, the IWW attempted to take control of the WPC, but the Finnish Federation's moderate members held the majority in the organization and forced the radical, IWW-leaning members to retreat. The IWW, though, continued in their pressure to control the school.

In 1914, the Copper Strike of 1913 had forced the *Työmies*, which had sided with the striking copper miners, to shut down the newspaper's publication on the Keweenah Peninsula due to a loss of business advertising. Deeply in debt, the newspaper moved from Hancock, Michigan, to 601 Tower Avenue in Superior, Wisconsin. With the *Työmies* now in America's hotbed of unrest, a meeting at the *työmies* Publishing Company in the summer of 1914 founded a second, more radical leaning newspaper and named it the *Industrialisti*.

Before long, the radical members of the Finnish Federation who were pro-IWW made the *Industialisti* their newspaper while the moderate members of the Finnish Federation kept the *Työmies*. An attempt was made by Leo Laukki and the IWW to take control of the entire *Työmies* Publishing Company.* Again, the moderates pushed back and retained control, forcing the IWW to independently publish the *Industialisti* with Leo Laukki as the editor-in-chief.

John Wiita again became the director at WPC, replacing Leo Laukki, who was fired in early 1915 after the school's struggle with the IWW. After less than two years, though, John Wiita resigned from the WPC, moved to Detroit, Michigan, and worked there as a mechanic and machinist. After Wiita moved to Detroit, Leo Laukki replaced him as the director of the WPC and changed it into an IWW-oriented school.

On June 28, 1914, Archduke Franz Ferdinand of Austria and his wife Sophie were assassinated, leading to the beginning of World War I, or the Great War. The Great War was largely fought in Europe, which allowed America to keep its non-intervention policy

---

* At the time of the attempted takeover, the IWW hall in Superior was located at 328 Tower Avenue – three blocks from the Työmies building.

during the first years of the conflict. The war, however, generated an American Red Scare, causing intense scrutiny of the IWW's extremist tactics. For the business leaders in Duluth, the IWW became Public Enemy Number One.

The largely futile strikes during the early 1900s led to a deep division within the Finnish Federation between the moderate members who believed in gradual reforms and the more radical members – most of whom belonged to the IWW – who wanted immediate, confrontational resolutions. In 1915, the Finnish Federation successfully voted to expel the IWW-leaning Finns.

CONTINUING INFLUENTIAL ACTIVISTS

In the year 1916, Otto Kuusinen, Edvard Gylling, and Yrjö Sirola were living in the Grand Duchy of Finland. Oscar Corgan, Leo Laukki, Santeri Nuorteva, Matti Tenhunen, and John Wiita were all living in America. Whether members of Finland's SDP or America's Finnish Federation and IWW, the struggle against capitalism and in support of the Labor Movement remained a vital part of their lives.

Within the next few years, five of the eight Red Finn activists would be forced to flee from their current resident country to a country that, in 1916, was ruled by Czar Nicholas II – a ruler who was very hostile to them. But in this year, no one could have foreseen the life-altering events hurtling toward them.

4 WHERE WERE THE ACTIVISTS IN 1916?

CHOOSING THE RIGHT RING

"Imagine an apparatus consisting of a moving belt, from which hung rings that could be grasped by the people waiting underneath. In this life, every human being has the chance to grasp such a ring and hang onto it, without knowing where the moving belt will take him. A happy life depends on grasping the right ring, which will carry one over the abysses of life, so that when one lets go of it, one will be sure of landing in a safe place. But it is the lot of many men to take hold of the wrong ring, and to land in a dangerous place far removed from where they had hoped to be. Others seize the right ring but let go of it too soon or in the wrong place."

OTTO KUUSINEN
Printed in *Pravda*

OTTO KUUSINEN AND EDVARD Gylling were both serving in the Finnish Parliament as SDP members in 1916. Kuusinen also continued working for the SDP newspaper *Työmies* in Helsinki, which kept him in contact with his associates in America's Finnish Federation. Edvard Gylling, who had a PhD, was a professor of statistics at Helsinki University.

Yrjö Sirola had joined his friends and associates again when he was re-elected to the Finnish Parliament as a member of the SDP in 1916, the same year the Finnish SDP won 46 percent of the seats in Parliament and became the majority party. Sirola was also elected to the SDP's Executive Committee in 1916.

THE 1916 MESABI RANGE STRIKE

"By 1916, U.S. Steel projected record profits. These profits didn't trickle down to workers. On June 2, 1916, Joe Green threw down his tools at the St. James Mine near Aurora... 'To hell with such wages. We've been robbed long enough. It's time to strike.' Others joined him. By the next day, 5,000 miners had walked out of the mines. The strike was on. The only union willing to assist the strikers was the IWW. The IWW aimed to overthrow capitalism. When their organizers arrived on the Range, the tensions rose."

ELIZABETH GURLEY FLYNN,
IWW Organizer, 1916

Leo Laukki had become increasingly aligned with the IWW, and the IWW was in control of the Labor Movement in 1916 when the Mesabi Range strike began on June 2 in Aurora, Minnesota. By June 14, over 16,000 miners were on strike. The miners wanted an 8-hour workday, not the 10- to 12-hour day they currently worked. They also wanted to be on company time for commuting to their work site – often thousands of feet underground – and a pay increase. The miners also complained about an unfair contract system that allowed the mining captains to collect bribes before giving out the more favored work assignments.

U.S. Steel hired 1,000 armed guards, who attacked the strikers even during peaceful rallies and parades in neighboring towns. Any business who sided with the strikers saw their credit discontinued because, by then, U.S. Steel controlled virtually all of the Iron Range, Duluth, and Superior.[1] The strike ended on Sept 16 after the company bosses said they "might" improve working conditions if they didn't need to deal with the IWW. They also promised a 10-percent raise and an 8-hour day beginning May 1, 1917.

WESTERN UNION TELEGRAM

VIRGINIA MINN   JUNE 14 1916
    M A HANNA AND CO
    CLEVELAND O

ABOUT TWO HUNDRED FIFTY MINERS MARCHED INTO TOWN THIS AFTERNOON HELD A MEETING IN SOCIALIST HALL REPORTED HAYWARD IS IN TOWN ALL QUIET
C E HENDRICK

WESTERN UNION TELEGRAM

DULUTH MINN   JULY 1 1916
    M A HANNA AND CO
    CLEVELAND O

GOVERNOR ISSUED PROCLAMATION ORDERING SHERIFF ARREST ALL PERSONS WHO HAVE OR ARE PARTICIPATING IN RIOTS OR UNLAWFUL ASSEMBLIES AND CHIEF OF POLICE DULUTH SAYS WON'T ALLOW AGITATING IN DULUTH COUNTY ATTORNEY SAYS WILL BACK SHERIFF UP AND MAXIMUM PENALTY FIVE YEARS STILLWATER THIS WILL KILL STRIKE AND DON'T BELIEVE ANY DANGER OF STRIKE ON LOCKS MESABA CONDITIONS SAME AS YESTERDAY OUR PROPERTIES WORKING HART SAYS COULD NOT INCREASE WAKEFIELD DAILY PRODUCTION BEYOND SCHEDULE PRESENT TIME
J D IRELAND

(Source: *Minnesota Discovery Center, Chisholm, Minnesota*)

In 1916, **Santeri Nuorteva** and his family were living on America's East Coast. Nuorteva continued working within the Finnish Federation and as an editor of the Federation's Eastern District's newspaper, *Raivaaja*.

John Wiita was living in Detroit and working as a mechanic in 1916 while remaining in contact with members of the Finnish Federation.

Matti Tenhunen, as the publishing director of the Finnish Federation's *Työmies* newspaper, had moved with it in 1914 from Hancock, Michigan to Superior, Wisconsin. Now in the hotbed of the Labor Movement, the newspaper began to thrive and shed its massive debt.

Like John Wiita and Matti Tenhunen, **Oscar Corgan** was in his late 20s in 1916 and was an activist for the Labor Movement. Four years earlier, he had filed the first papers toward American citizenship. While living and working in a copper mine in Hancock, Michigan, he had taken classes and learned to speak English. In 1916, Corgan was living in Superior, Wisconsin, and was the chairman of the Longshoremen's Union.

> **TUESDAY, AUGUST 15, 1916, DULUTH MINNESOTA**
>
> *W.B. Jones, vice president, and organizer of the Longshoremen's union, Charles Swanson, local organizer; Joseph Moratzki, secretary of the coal strikers' union, and Oscar Corgan, chairman of the strikers' union, were last night appointed at a meeting of the strikers' union, held in the Finnish hall, to meet dock superintendents at their offices this morning to come to an agreement on the strike situation. Nearly 600 men and women attended last night's meeting.*

In 1916, the eight radical Finnish activists were unaware that their lives would soon change because of a member of the Second International who was currently living in exile from his homeland, the Russian Empire. That man was Vladimir Lenin.

The Communist Chasm: How the Dreams of a Better Life Became a Terrible Nightmare

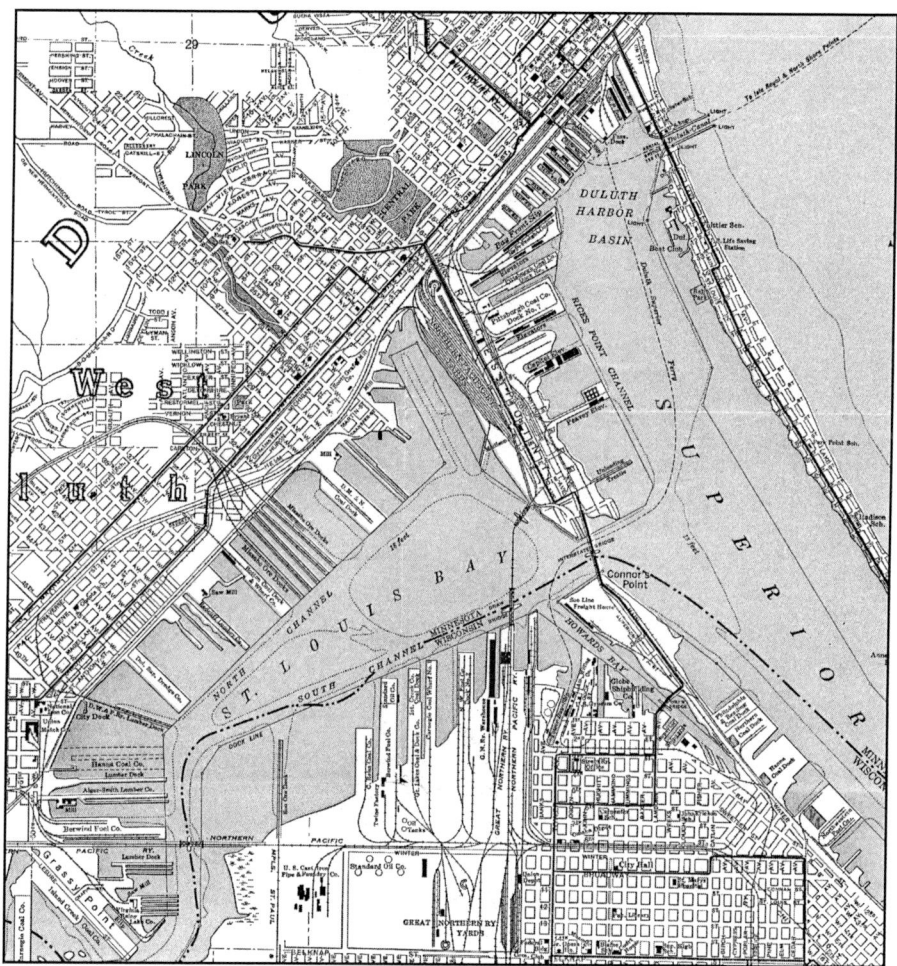

THE TWIN PORTS HARBOR CIRCA 1916

The Twin Ports cities of Superior, Wisconsin, and Duluth, Minnesota, teemed with activity in the early 1900s with ships from the east and multiple rail lines radiating from the harbor areas. The Twin Ports are 2,300 miles from the Atlantic Ocean, making them the farthest inland harbors in the U.S. that are open to sea-going vessels.

Elevators were built to hold grain from the far western states. Ore docks were built for iron ore from the Iron Range. At one time, the Twin Ports' tonnage exceeded that of New York City's harbor. In 1916, a shipyard was built on the St. Louis River. Submarine chasers and tankers were built in the shipyard.

Many ethnic groups were represented in the Twin Ports, but Finnish immigrants were the majority group. At one time, the Twin Ports had the largest Finnish community in the world outside Finland. Finn Town was located close to the Aerial Lift Bridge. *IHRCA, Anderson Library, U of MN*

THE KALIEDOSCOPE TWISTS

The year 1917 seemed to be a fairly innocuous year. It wasn't the beginning of a century or even a decade. No world wars began in 1917, although World War I, the Great War, continued before ending late the following year. There were some civil wars in 1917, though. A monarchy ended, and there were some very radical changes in some governments.

In 1917, a secret telegram was confiscated and decoded, and that telegram played a major part in America's involvement in World War I. People around the world were stunned by the collapse of the mighty Russian Empire, but no one could have foreseen that the collapse would send thousands of Finnish Americans and their families over a decade later across the Atlantic Ocean to Karelia, then a province of the mighty Russian Empire.

5 THE YEAR 1917: A TIME OF CHANGE

"Some of us let dreams die, but others nourish and protect them; nurse them through bad days till they bring them to the sunshine and light which comes always to those who sincerely hope that their dreams will come true."

PRESIDENT WOODROW WILSON

THE DRAFT BEGINS IN AMERICA

In 1917, Woodrow Wilson, the 28th American President, was serving in his second term. Wilson, who had narrowly defeated Charles Hughes in 1916, had run on the slogan, "He kept us out of the war." After the *Lusitania* was torpedoed in 1915, President Wilson cautioned Germany that America would not remain neutral if Germany instigated acts of aggression or continued submarine warfare, which violated international law. Germany had complied until early in 1917.

On January 19, 1917, a coded telegram was sent by Arthur Zimmermann, a *Staatssekretär* (high-level civil servant) in the German Foreign Ministry. The telegram was sent to Heinrich von Eckardt, Germany's ambassador to Mexico. Zimmermann sent the telegram in anticipation of the resumption of unrestricted submarine warfare by Germany on February 1, an act the German government presumed would almost certainly lead to war with America. The telegram instructed Ambassador Eckardt that if the United States appeared certain to enter the war, he was to approach the Mexican government with a proposal for military alliance.

The telegram, however, was intercepted by the British military, which cracked the code of the telegram. The telegram, known as the Zimmermann Telegram, was released to the American public in March 1917. In part because of an enraged public over the telegram, America declared war on Nazi Germany on April 6.

THE ZIMMERMANN TELEGRAM

The decoded telegram was translated as follows:

We intend to begin on the first of February unrestricted submarine warfare. We shall endeavor in spite of this to keep the United States of America neutral. In the event of this not succeeding, we make Mexico a proposal of alliance on the following basis: make war together, make peace together, generous financial support and an understanding on our part that Mexico is to re-conquer the lost territory in Texas, New Mexico, and Arizona. The settlement in detail is left to you. You will inform the [Mexican] President of the above most secretly as soon as the outbreak of war with the United States of America is certain and add the suggestion that he should, on his own initiative, invite Japan to immediate adherence and at the same time mediate between Japan and ourselves. Please call the President's attention to the fact that the ruthless employment of our submarines now offers the prospect of compelling England in a few months to make peace.

Signed, ZIMMERMANN

(Source: *En.wikipedia.org/wiki/Zimmermann_Telegram*)

On May 18, 1917, President Woodrow Wilson proclaimed the beginning of the national mandatory conscription, or draft, and gave it a patriotic tone, making service in the military sound like a grand overseas adventure. On June 5, conscription registration began. Wisconsin became the first state to meet its draft quotas.

Many immigrants – particularly immigrants who couldn't speak, read, or write English – did not understand that registering for the draft was mandatory. This became an excuse for raids and intimidation on groups, particularly Finns, who were seen as radical agitators in the Labor Movement.

Congress passed the Espionage and Sedition Acts of 1917, making it illegal to criticize the government's war policies. In September, federal officials armed with search warrants raided IWW halls nationwide and seized files, books, and pamphlets – anything that could potentially be used for propaganda against the government.

Two days later, federal and local officials stormed several homes and boardinghouses in the Finn Town area of Duluth, Minnesota, arresting 69 "slackers" who did not or could not show their draft cards. IWW literature, song books, and dues books were also seized. The next day, 28 of the 69 Finns who had been arrested were released from jail because they were too old to be drafted. The 41 Finns remaining in jail were forbidden from discussing the draft with any visitors and were required to speak only English so their captors could understand what they were saying.[1]

Leo Laukki had been investigated during the early summer of 1917. Then, in July 1917, Laukki was arrested along with other IWW members for violation of the vagrancy ordinance. Their release from jail came fairly quickly but didn't last long. The following month, Leo Laukki and 165 other IWW members were arrested once again.

On October 21, Leo Laukki and numerous other IWW leaders were indicted for conspiring to "prevent, hinder, or delay the United States from carrying on the war with the German government." Laukki and the other leaders were jailed and awaited sentencing for what the government viewed as anti-war subversion tactics.

After the draft began, the Finnish Federation and their newspapers also faced increased scrutiny. During World War I, articles about national and international subjects in the *Työmies*, *Raivaaja*, and *Toveri* had to regularly be translated into English and given to government censors for inspection. During this time, the *Toveri* editor, William Reivo, was imprisoned for publishing some anti-war material.

John Wiita left Michigan and returned to Superior in the fall of 1917. His job as the front-page editor of the *Työmies* newspaper didn't last long, though. To avoid being drafted, Wiita changed his name to Henry Puro and fled into Canada where he lived for several years.

The Cooperative Central Exchange

Daily train service through northwestern Wisconsin on the Northern Pacific or DSS & A rail lines in 1917 still provided the primary transportation for moving people and goods over longer distances, but there was a network of roads within the communities that were for the most part primitive and impassible during inclement weather. Oxen- or horse-drawn wagons and buggies were still a very common sight, although seeing a motorized vehicle was no longer rare.

Trains brought food and supplies to the small-town depots along the rail lines for the stores that were owned by individuals or groups who had placed orders at the wholesale companies in the larger towns like Superior and Ashland in Wisconsin or Duluth, Minnesota. In the northern Wisconsin communities like Waino and Oulu, store owners negotiated several miles of primitive roads to the nearest depot. Farmers brought their produce, eggs, and cream to the local stores and creameries where it was then brought to the closest depots and shipped by train to the wholesale companies.

The Co-op Central Exchange (CCE) was organized on July 30, 1917, during a meeting in the Työmies building in Superior, Wisconsin. Matti Tenhunen, then the manager of the Työmies Publishing Company, was a key participant as well as members from 15 area Finnish-owned cooperative stores. The members met to discuss ways to overcome the discriminatory credit and supply practices of the regional wholesalers against the small member-owned cooperatives (mostly Finnish owned) who were competing against privately owned stores in the region surrounding Lake Superior.

An article titled "Co-operative Buying May Broaden Scope" on August 26, 1917, in the *Duluth News Tribune* stated: *"During the years that the several cooperative stores have been in business, they have had to combat obstacles which have made their existence rather precarious... This brought the Finnish cooperative stores together, and a union was formed here a short time ago. The committee, which is in charge of the preliminary work of organizing the purchasing headquarters, has commenced to realize that other cooperative stores have the same difficulties to overcome, and Matti Tenhunen has commenced correspondence with them with a view of bringing them into the union."*

The CCE began with 15 stores pooling their small orders, thereby qualifying for a larger discount on their purchases from the wholesale companies. The stores started the CCE with a working capital of $15.50 and realized a profit of only $268 in 1917.* The CCE was strongly affiliated with the Finnish Federation and grew to a network of over 200 cooperative stores in Upper Michigan, northern Wisconsin, and northern Minnesota.

In the beginning, the *Työmies* newspaper was chosen as the official organ of CCE, and the two organizations had very close ties. The Finnish Federation and the Työmies Publishing Company helped the fledgling CCE with publicity, education, and business. The first manager of the CCE was John Nummevuori whose sparse office – consisting of a table, two chairs, and a typewriter – was in a small room in the Työmies building. At the time, Nummevuori was a veteran manager of the Työmies Publishing Company.

Bookkeeping and management skills were taught in Finnish by the CCE at the annual Exchange Finnish Cooperative Training School, which was a six- to eight-week course. Matti Tenhunen was an instructor as was the Education Director, George Halonen. The basic bookkeeping course and a training course for store managers began in 1918, and the majority of the cooperative store managers were graduates of these courses.**[2]

The CCE's Board of Directors quickly realized that becoming a wholesale company would effectively streamline the CCE supply chain. At first, horse-drawn wagons delivered orders from the CCE wholesale building to the cooperative stores in Superior and Duluth. Trains delivered food and supplies from the CCE wholesale to the depots nearest the community cooperatives in Michigan, Wisconsin, and Minnesota. Farmers who were members of the cooperative stores bought most of what they needed from the stores and brought their farm products to their local stores. Trains then transported the products to and from the CCE, effectively cutting out the competing

---

* Beginning in 1928, the CCE's profit exceeded $1 million annually.

** In 1920, Oscar Corgan was still a rail car repairman, but the classes he took at the Exchange Finnish Cooperative Training School dramatically changed his life. When his first daughter Mayme was born in 1923, Oscar was the manager of the Co-op Store in Brule, Wisconsin.

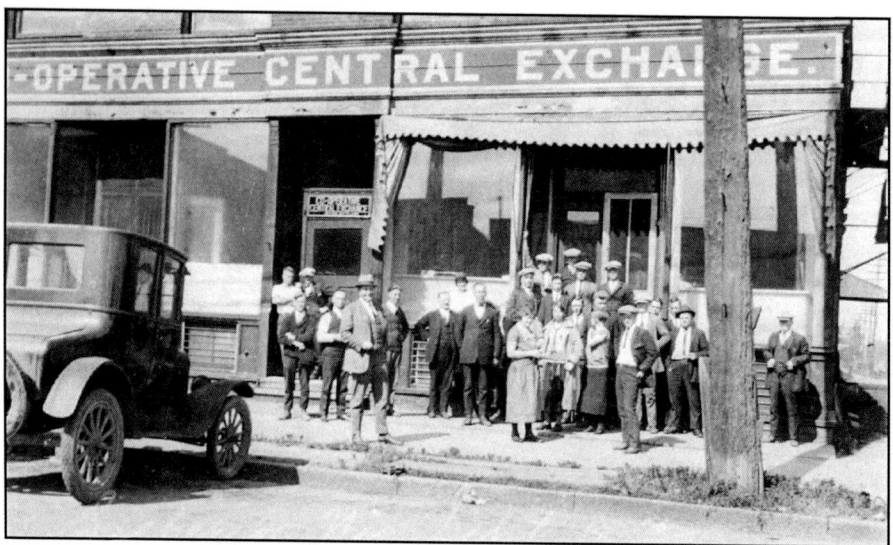

Students of the courses sponsored by the Co-operative Central Exchange gather outside the building in 1924. Superior, Wisconsin. *IHRCA, Anderson Library, U of MN*

One of the most popular items sold by the CCE in every cooperative store was Red Star Coffee. (Note the hammer and sickle on the can.) Until the attempt at a hostile takeover by the communists, the CCE remained politically neutral and worked harmoniously with them. *IHRCA, Anderson Library, U of MN*

wholesale companies and enabling the member-owned cooperative stores to thrive.

Because of the CCE's close affiliation with the Finnish Federation, they initially chose the Federation's bank as their own. But on October 16, 1917, in an article entitled, "Workmen will have Own Bank; is Incorporated," Workers Mutual Savings was chosen as the name of a new bank in Superior, Wisconsin. Matti Tenhunen, manager of the Työmies Publishing Company and one of the bank's incorporators, stated, *"Our people* already have one bank on the same plan* [as a cooperative bank] *located in Fitchburg, Massachusetts. That bank has had great patronage from here, but the distance from the headquarters made it almost impossible to obtain loans from the bank... All* [cooperative banks] *work under the cooperative principle, which is designed to give depositors the best service at the lowest cost and with absolute safety."*

THE BOLSHEVIK REVOLUTION

In 1914, Vladimir Lenin had decided that the time was perfect to overthrow Russian Czar Nicholas II, but before Lenin and his fellow Bolsheviks could move forward with their plans for a revolution, World War I began. By 1917, it seemed to Lenin that the war would never end and that the perfect time for his revolution was rapidly disappearing. But on March 15, 1917, the long reign of the House of Romanov, which had ruled the Russian Empire since 1613, ended when war-weary soldiers summoned enough fighting spirit and forced Czar Nicholas II to abdicate his reign or face a violent overthrow. Shortly after his abdication, 18 of the 65 Romanov family members were murdered with the remaining 47 family members fleeing for their lives into exile.

At the time of the revolution, Lenin was living in Germany but quickly relocated to Petrograd. By the time he arrived in Petrograd in April 1917, the Provisional Government had full power. Lenin rallied his comrade Bolsheviks by declaring the Provisional

---

*Tenhunen was referring to the Finnish Federation and their bank in the Eastern District.

Joseph Stalin: Vladimir Lenin's Protégé

Joseph Stalin was born on December 18, 1878. He was almost ten before he started school but excelled academically. In August 1894, Stalin enrolled in a seminary. As he grew older, he gradually lost interest in his studies and was often confined to his cell for rebellious behavior – talking in class, fighting, and refusing to doff his hat to the monks.

Stalin was 20 years old when he left the seminary in April 1899. Before leaving, he had declared himself an atheist, joined a forbidden book club, and began studying the philosophy of Karl Marx while attending secret workers' meetings at night.

In May 1900, Stalin organized a clandestine workers' meeting at which he encouraged many attendees to strike. This brought him to the attention of the Czar Nicholas II's secret police. He avoided arrest for over a year by using aliases and moving constantly. In November 1901, he was voted into the executive committee of the Marxist party, the Russian SDP.

His activist activities led to his arrest in April 1902, and he was sentenced to three years of exile in Siberia. Before he escaped from his exile, the Russian SDP had split into the Bolsheviks and Mensheviks. Stalin joined the Bolsheviks and began working with Vladimir Lenin, whom he regarded as his mentor. They had first been introduced at a conference for the Second International in the Grand Duchy of Finland in 1905, where they also met with the leaders of the Finnish SDP, including Yrjö Sirola.

Vladimir Lenin and Joseph Stalin agreed to raise money for the Bolsheviks by committing armed robberies, kidnappings, counterfeiting, and running extortion rackets. Stalin's gang ambushed an armed bank convoy in June 1907, using homemade bombs and guns. Over three dozen people were killed, but Stalin's entire gang escaped. Stalin was imprisoned in 1908 and became the leader of the Bolshevik inmates. He organized discussion groups and ordered the executions of any suspected informants.

From February 1909, he was exiled and escaped numerous times, escaping for the final time in February 1912 when he fled to St. Petersburg and began editing the daily newspaper, *Pravda*. By 1917, Stalin was considered one of the top Bolshevik leaders, and his newspaper *Pravda* was the Bolshevik mouthpiece.

Government to be complete imperialists and undeserving of their Bolshevik support. Lenin said that only a government ruled by peasants, workers, and soldiers (all collectively known as Soviets) could properly rule, raising the battle cry of "All power to the Soviets!" The Bolsheviks at that time constituted a minority within the Soviets, but Lenin believed that they must somehow topple the Provisional Government.

From March to September 1917, the Bolsheviks remained a minority but, in July, the Bolsheviks bravely staged an armed demonstration in Petrograd, which was stopped by armed members of the Provisional Government. Joseph Stalin kept Lenin, who had been labeled as a "German agent," from being arrested by hiding him in various safe houses in Petrograd and then helping Lenin escape to the Grand Duchy of Finland, which was still part of the Russian Empire. During the weeks Lenin was in hiding, Stalin commanded the Bolsheviks.

By autumn, the Provisional Government had lost the majority's support, and the Soviets – the people – demanded an immediate change. The still-exiled Lenin and his Bolsheviks became the majority of the Soviets by the end of September.

Beginning in late September, Lenin began sending an avalanche of letters and articles from his hidden location in Finland. His correspondence urged the Soviets – the peasants, soldiers, and workers – to make their choice immediately: Continue their miserable existence or become the ruling majority. Lenin ruthlessly expounded that the Provisional Government was a dictatorship of the bourgeoisie, the propertied minority, and must be overthrown. The Bolsheviks would soon stage the second Russian Revolution of 1917.

In the latter half of October, a well-disguised Vladimir Lenin left Finland for Petrograd, arriving there in time for a Bolshevik Central Committee (BCC) meeting on October 23. After a very contentious 10-hour debate, Lenin won over a majority of those attending to favor an armed takeover of the Provisional Government. Secret training of the sailors and soldiers, called the Red Guard, began under the direction of Leon Trotsky while Lenin remained hidden in Petrograd. In the evening of November 6, Lenin sent a letter to the BCC, stating the time was right to arrest the leaders of the Provisional Government.

On November 7 and 8, the Bolshevik-led Red Guards overthrew the Provisional Government and proclaimed that state power had passed into the hands of the Soviets. By this time the Bolsheviks constituted an absolute majority of the Soviets and voted overwhelmingly to accept full power with Lenin elected as chairman of the Council of People's Commissars.

Overnight, Lenin emerged from his hideout and evolved from a sought-after fugitive to the leader of the largest country in the world. Since his youth he had spent his life dreaming of building a party that would win such a victory and now, at the age of 47, he and his Bolsheviks had triumphed. "It makes one's head spin," he confessed. But power neither intoxicated nor frightened Lenin. Instead, he became even more focused than before. With a clear vision, he began steering the government toward consolidation.

THE GRAND DUCHY OF FINLAND BECOMES THE REPUBLIC OF FINLAND

With Vladimir Lenin now in charge, the Russian-controlled Grand Duchy of Finland declared and peacefully received its independence on December 6, 1917, eventually becoming the Republic of Finland. At the time of its independence, however, Finland found itself bitterly divided internally between the White Finns and the Red Finns on most political, social, and economic issues.

The White Finns were comprised mainly of the Swedish-speaking middle and upper classes plus the peasants and wealthy farmers living in the northern two-thirds of the country. The White Finns strongly rejected the ideology of communism and generally embraced capitalism.

Landless rural cottage dwellers and many urban workers generally made up the communist-leaning Red Finns, who vehemently rejected capitalism. Many Red Finns had left a life of farming for work in factories where they endured long, hard hours for very little pay and believed they were being exploited by the money-hungry capitalist factory owners.

The SDP was the majority party in Finland's Parliament and was composed of a Red Finn majority within the SDP. At the end of

1917, the SDP leaders of Finland's Parliament, including Yrjö Sirola, Edvard Gylling, and Otto Kuusinen, were secretly conspiring for a Bolshevik-style takeover of the Finnish government like their Russian associates had successfully accomplished. In November 1917, after Vladimir Lenin successfully became Soviet Russia's leader and shortly before the Grand Duchy of Finland gained its independence, Joseph Stalin – as one of the Bolshevik leaders – met with Yrjö Sirola in Petrograd.[3]

Members of Finland's exiled Central Committee. Kullervo Manner, center in a suit, was chosen to be the President of Red Finland. Yrjö Sirola, far right, was a top influential Red Finn leader in Finland's Civil War. Standing behind Sirola is his wife, Mandi. *Wikimedia Commons*

SOME PUSHBACK AGAINST COMMUNISM

The stunning success of Vladimir Lenin and his Bolsheviks reverberated not only throughout the Russian Empire and Europe but across the Atlantic Ocean to America and Canada and around the world. The Bolshevik Revolution created a safe haven in Soviet Russia for radical refugees and soon welcomed the thousands of Red Finns fleeing from Finland following the Civil War.

Vladimir Lenin formed the Communist Party of Russia. When he began organizing the Communist International, Yrjö Sirola and Otto Kuusinen were also involved in its formation. Communist parties were established in numerous countries throughout the world, but not without some significant pushback from those vehemently opposed to communist principles.

6

THE 1917 AFTERMATH

"When you flee from a wolf, you run into a bear."

Finnish proverb

The Finnish Civil War

The newly independent Republic of Finland began 1918 as a deeply divided country. After the collapse of the Russian Empire, the power struggle between the Red Finns and White Finns intensified until January 27 when the Red Finns declared Finland to be the Finnish Socialist Workers' Republic (FSWR), launching Finland into a short but brutal Civil War.

Among the Red Finn leaders who had plotted to create the FSWR were Edvard Gylling, Otto Kuusinen, and Yrjö Sirola. On March 1, 1918, while the leaders of the FSWR still felt victory was assured, Edvard Gylling and Oskari Tokoi, as representatives of the FSWR, signed a peace treaty with Russia in St. Petersburg. Vladimir Lenin and Joseph Stalin represented Russia in the signing. But in what the Red Finn leaders felt was their new country, unrest continued.

When the Finnish Civil War began, Santeri Nuorteva was living in Fitchberg, Massachusetts, and working for the Finnish Federation's *Raivaaja*. Nuorteva had enthusiastically sided with the Russian Bolsheviks and strongly supported the FSWR, so it came as no surprise when Yrjö Sirola asked him to be America's official FSWR representative. Nuorteva immediately resigned from *Raivaaja* and moved to New York City where he set up an aid office for the FSWR. He then relocated to Washington, D.C., where he opened his Finnish Information Bureau on March 30, 1918. At that time Nuorteva was considered to be an accredited agent of the FSWR.[1] At the same time, though, the Red Finn leaders were beginning to feel less optimistic about the Civil War's outcome.

From the beginning of the Finnish Civil War, the Red Guard was at a disadvantage because of food shortages, a poorly trained military force, and a lack of equipment. Just over a week after Santeri Nuorteva opened the FSWR's Finnish Information Bureau in Washington, D.C., Yrjö Sirola was in Petrograd discussing with Russia's leaders a potential need for a safe haven for the Red Finns. Sirola set up an office in Moscow to aid Red Finn evacuees on April 14, 1918.

Edvard Gylling, a prominent Red Finn leader
Wikimedia Commons

Edvard Gylling commanded the final battle of the Finnish Civil War but, on May 15, 1918, the White Finns declared victory. Over 38,000 Finnish citizens and soldiers on both sides had perished in less than four months, and the victorious White Finns drove most of the Red Finns from the country. As many as 13,000 Red Finns escaped to Soviet Russia while thousands of others fled to other European countries or North America.

Otto Kuusinen was well-known to be one of the Red Finn leaders responsible for Finland's Civil War. He had been involved in creating the FSWR and was named its Minister of Education. As one of the leaders, Kuusinen was aware that he would be executed if he was captured by the White Finns. Leaving his family behind, he fled to Russia.

Yrjö Sirola was in charge of coordinating the evacuation of the fleeing Red Finns and their leaders to Vladimir Lenin's Soviet Russia. On August 29, 1918, Sirola and Kuusinen, along with Kullervo Manner, were the organizers of the Finnish Communist Party while living in Moscow. Sirola became its first chairman.

Later, historian Anthony Upton wrote of the Finnish Civil War:

"The choices before the leaders were unconditional surrender, a glorious fight to the finish in Finland ending in almost certain martyrdom, or a prudent withdrawal with a view to a future return. It was not a difficult choice to make, and did not mean, as their detractors had always claimed, that they were weak and cowardly men who betrayed their faithful but deluded followers. They were Marxists and could see their defeat as only an episode in the class war, which always continued, and their duty was not to indulge in glorious gestures of defiance, but to persevere in the struggle."

SOME OF THE INFLUENTIAL RED FINN ACTIVISTS REUNITE IN RUSSIA

While Finland was struggling with its Civil War, and World War I was tearing Europe apart, Leo Laukki and his fellow IWW members were brought to trial in America. Known as the "Case of the 166," the trial began on April 2, 1918. All were found guilty of attempting to overthrow the government, opposing the war, advocating for the destruction of property, and violence. Laukki was given a 20-year prison sentence and fined $20,000 (about $250,000 in today's dollars). Bail was posted by the IWW Defense Fund for Laukki and, while released on bail and supposedly waiting to appeal his case, Laukki jumped bail – much to the consternation of the IWW – and fled to Russia, where he joined Yrjö Sirola and Otto Kuusinen.

As a leader of the FSWR, an arrest warrant was issued for Edvard Gylling by the victorious White Finns, and he was the only Red Finn leader who escaped to Sweden. While living in Stockholm for two years, Gylling joined the Finnish Communist Party. He also wrote to Vladimir Lenin, expressing his desire to make Russia's Karelian province the permanent home of the Red Finns who had fled Finland. Lenin had no interest in his plan, but he did request that Gylling move to Karelia and lead the province.

After the Bolshevik Revolution and shortly before World War I ended, Vladimir Lenin wrote a letter appealing to all American workers to join the Communist Revolution that he began – a revolution that he wholeheartedly believed would end capitalism. (Santeri Nuorteva collaborated in translating the letter into English.) The letter was dated August 20, 1918, at a time when many non-communist Americans were beginning to fear that a Bolshevik-style Revolution might also be attempted within the United States. Their fears were no doubt heightened when the Communist Party of the U.S.A. (CPUSA) was organized the following year on May 1, 1919, but it was not recognized as a legal organization in America.

LENIN'S LETTER TO AMERICA'S WORKERS

"Four years of the imperialist slaughter have not passed in vain... Four years of war have shown in their results the general law of capitalism as applied to war between the murderers for the division of spoils: That he, who was the richest and mightiest profited and robbed the most; that he who was the weakest was robbed, decimated, crushed, and strangled to the utmost.

"The American billionaires were the richest of all and geographically the most secure. They have made all, even the richest countries, their vassals. They have plundered hundreds of billions of dollars... Every dollar is stained with the filth of 'profitable' military deliveries enriching the rich and despoiling the poor in every country. And every dollar is stained with blood – of that sea of blood which was shed by the ten millions killed and twenty millions maimed in the great, noble, liberating and holy war...."

Lenin then went on to quote Eugene Debs, a prominent American in the Labor Movement, who stated in 1915 that he would *"rather be shot than vote for loans for the present criminal and imperialist war. I [Debs] know of only one holy and legal war: The war against the capitalists, the war for the liberation of mankind from wage slavery!"*

Continuing, Lenin wrote: *"I am not at all surprised that [President Woodrow] Wilson, the head of the American billionaires and servant of the capitalist sharks, has thrown Debs into prison. Let the bourgeoisie be brutal to the true internationalists... The more obduracy and bestiality it displays, the nearer comes the day of the victorious proletarian revolution...*

"The first country which demolished the galley chains of imperialist war was our country [Russia]. We [the Bolshevists] made the greatest of sacrifices in the struggle for the demolition of this chain, but we broke it. We are beyond imperialist dependence, we raised before the whole world the banner of struggle for the complete overthrow of imperialism...

"In a word, we [the Bolshevists] are invincible, because the world proletarian revolutionists are invincible."*

---

* Translated by Einde O'Callaghan with excerpts printed in *Labor Action*, January 29, 1945.

Gylling met an American foreign correspondent while living in Stockholm and told the correspondent, Carl Sandburg,* of his harrowing escape from his homeland. The following article appeared in *The Evening News* in Harrisburg, Pennsylvania, on March 4, 1919.

FINN REBEL HID WEEKS AND THEN MAKES ESCAPE

Two years ago, Edvard Gylling, PhD, was professor of statistics at the University of Helsinki, Finland… He belonged to the aristocracy, the ruling class. Today he ought to be sitting in the seats of the respectable people who govern Finland.

Edvard Gylling, however, didn't want to be respectable. He is today in the eyes of the government of Finland an outlaw, a traitor, under sentence of death for treason.

Once, twice, three times, the Finnish junker government has reached out with writs of extradition calling for Edvard Gylling to be taken from Stockholm, where he now lives, and brought back to Finland to be shot as a traitor. And once, twice, three times the Socialist-Liberal government equalities of Sweden have said in effect to Finland: "Hands off this man! Whoever takes him must come with clean hands."

Held Finance Ministry

Gylling was Finance Minister of the Peoples Republic of Finland, set up by Red Guards in 1918 and overthrown in April and May by Finnish White Guards reinforced by Prussian battalions taken from the Western Front in France.

"I was against the revolution and advised another course," Dr. Gylling said to me, "but the workingmen were for it. It was a mass drive. They could not be stopped. I had to be for them or against them, so I joined them and went the limit. We took the railroads, the banks, the big landed estates, the factories, all the industrial property in Finland, except that of the cooperatives… The aim was to achieve a social revolution…."

---

*Carl Sandburg was born in Galesburg, Illinois, to Swedish immigrants and became a famous, three-time Pulitzer Prize-winning author and poet. During late 1918 and early 1919, he was a foreign correspondent for the Newspaper Enterprise Association based in Stockholm, Sweden.

REPORT ON IWW OR BOLSHEVIK ACTIVITIES BY INFORMANT J.S. PETERSON ON FEBRUARY 13, 1919

To William E. Allen, Bureau of Investigation

Among those who have been most conspicuous as troublemakers in and around Boston are:

Louis C. Frain: (Italian), now just through serving a month in New York for violation of the Espionage Act.

N.I. Hourwich: (Jew), radical speaker in Russian.

Santeri Nuorteva: (Finn), sponsor of the social revolution. In all of the radical meetings held in Boston for the past three months, where the audience has been predominantly foreign born, the speakers appear to extol internationalism and to deride the actions of the U.S. government. These forceful speakers time and again have aroused audiences of 2,000 or more to fever heat. When not on the platform, these speakers are writing for many revolutionary publications...

These agitators are carrying on IWW propaganda in foreign languages, and each has a command of six languages other than English. Hence patriotism means nothing – law and order, less than nothing...

The sanest way to deal with these professional troublemakers would be to outlaw them from the country for which they hold no respect. They surely cannot further the future good of America by influencing the immigrant population...

Corresponding foreign language newspapers include Finnish newspaper *Raivaaja*, Editor **Wilho Boman**, 47. Certain issues that were barred from the mails serves only to bring out more rabid issues which are freely sold at the meetings....

Respectfully submitted,
J.S. Peterson, Informant

(Entire document is in DoJ/Bol Investigative Files, NARA collection M-1085, reel 923, file 167630)

Executions of Revolutionists

"I was in Vyborg April 29, German cavalry and Finnish White Guards had captured the city after a week of fighting. I was told by eyewitnesses of the execution of revolutionists by [the] hundreds...

"I hid in a cellar of a workingman's house. A comrade was with me. The first two days we had nothing to eat. We heard the boots of soldiers searching the kitchen over our heads. We heard them come down and knock the butts of their guns against the false wall we were hiding behind. We were cramped so close we couldn't stand up or move around. Believe me, we were a sight when we came up, dirty, and eleven days of whiskers on our faces.

"I went at night to another house. There I stayed three weeks in a garret, reading the newspapers and hearing from day to day how the White Terror was driving everything before it, and how the Labor Movement of Finland was gone to hell in a grand smash.

Escape in Disguise

"I shaved my face and smeared it with coal dust. I put on a suit of overalls. Using a passport friends had bought for me, I went to the railroad station and bought a ticket for Helsinki, the capital of Finland, the last place I would be expected. On the train I read newspapers telling how if I was captured I would be shot on the day they got me.

"In Helsinki I stayed at eight different workingmen's homes. They were under suspicion and their homes were searched nearly every day by squads of White Guards. I grew a beard all over my face. I put on goggles. Then with six comrades I started on a trip to Abo. They got a passport and railroad ticket. They sat in seats behind, in front, and across the aisle from me. And so I got to Abo and there saw my wife and three children.* There I hid three weeks. Stowed away in a coal box by a seaman on a steamboat running to Stockholm. I came here."

---

* Gylling was later reunited with his family when they joined him in Karelia.

Toveri editor Santeri Nuorteva, center. Photo taken in Astoria, Oregon.
IHRCA, Anderson Library, U of MN

Santeri Nuorteva's Finnish Information Bureau in Washington, D.C., was very short-lived with no reason for continuing after the Finnish Civil War ended just six weeks after the office opened. But Nuorteva soon found employment as the secretary to Lenin's American representative named Ludwig Martens and became very influential in the official affairs of Russia, which brought him to the attention of the American Military Intelligence Division. The Military Intelligence Division began monitoring his activities and, by August 1918, Santeri Nuorteva was labeled as a dangerous international radical, and "an agitator of the extreme type."

The heightened scrutiny of Nuorteva cost the Russians dearly later that year. When Carl Sandberg prepared to leave Sweden for America at the end of 1918, he was given a $10,000 check for Nuorteva. The check was confiscated when he was searched at the port of New York. Nuorteva tried in vain to recover the check.

Nuorteva was believed to be one of the most important figures in America's Communist Movement, and his continued activities resulted in him being called before a U.S. Senate committee investigating Bolshevik propaganda in 1919. Facing arrest, he fled to Canada under a false name. Canadian authorities were soon pursuing him, and he fled to England, arriving in June 1920. He was put under scrutiny immediately by Scotland Yard as he attempted to establish commercial ties between England and Soviet Russia. He was again regarded as extremely dangerous, and England arrested him for domestic subversion. Nuorteva was deported by British warship to Russia, arriving there in late July 1920. With his fluency in many languages, Santeri Nuorteva became a valued member of the Comintern.[2]

AMERICA AFTER WORLD WAR I

On November 11, 1918, Germany accepted an armistice, and World War I came to an end. Over 14 million soldiers and civilians perished during the war including 112,000 American soldiers.

Unions had enjoyed an increase in membership during the war, but now the labor force was flooded with war veterans seeking work. Women, who had been employed to replace men during the war, suddenly found themselves unemployed. An antagonism toward immigrants and African Americans grew. The glut of workers wiped out most of the gains made by the unions during the war, and their memberships fell. Inflation increased as business owners cut the wages and benefits gained by the workers during the war.

The first Red Scare began immediately after the successful Bolshevik Revolution and was the perceived threat that a similar event would occur on American soil. Political scientist Murray B. Levin wrote that the Red Scare was a "nationwide anti-radical hysteria provoked by a mounting fear and anxiety that a Bolshevik Revolution in America was imminent – a revolution that would change church, home, marriage, civility, and the American way of life." Newspaper sensationalism increased Americans' anxieties and anti-foreign sentiment by claiming that all immigrants believed a radical overthrow of capitalism was their path out of poverty.

In 1919, there were over 3,600 strikes in America with over 4 million workers involved at various times. The strikes impacted the steel industry, railroads, shipping, and even police departments. The newspapers portrayed the strikes as "radical threats to American society" that were inspired by "left-wing, foreign *agents provocateurs*."

The Great Steel Strike of 1919 affected over 350,000 workers, and U.S. Steel depicted the strikers as "undesirable foreigners" – despite the fact that they had employed the agents who had initially encouraged the "undesirable foreigners" to leave their homelands and come to America. The workers wanted better conditions than what they had and demanded one day off each week with 11-hour day shifts and 13-hour night shifts.[3] U.S. Steel's answer was to employ returning World War I veterans as strikebreakers.

No meetings were allowed during the Great Steel Strike, but Santeri Nuorteva – before he fled to Canada – and his longtime friend Wilho Boman* were scheduled to speak in Woodlawn, Pennsylvania, in the spring of 1919. The Finnish hall was filled, but everyone was arrested and jailed before the meeting began. During this time, the federal government consistently targeted radical immigrants, contending that speaking in a foreign language was a display of disloyalty to America.

In April 1919, government agents uncovered a plot to mail three dozen bombs to prominent political and business leaders. Among those targeted were John D. Rockefeller, J.P. Morgan, Supreme Court Justice Oliver Wendell Holmes, and U.S. Attorney General Alexander Palmer. Two months later, on June 2, 1919, Alexander Palmer was again a target when eight bombs exploded simultaneously in eight cities. No one was killed except the bomber, an Italian-American radical, who died outside Alexander Palmer's house in Washington, D.C.

Attorney General Palmer used his Department of Justice to launch the Palmer Raids, which allowed federal agents to enter and search homes without regard to constitutional rights. Lawyers accused Palmer of illegal acts and wanton violence, but newspaper editors applauded the raids. *The Washington Post* declared, "There is no time to waste on hairsplitting over the infringement of liberty."

---

*Nuorteva and Boman were friends since they had first met in Finland as members of Finland's SDP.

The New York Times gave the raids an even more positive approval when it stated the injuries of those arrested were merely "souvenirs of the new attitude of aggressiveness which had been assumed by the federal agents against Reds and suspected Reds."

The culmination of the unprecedented number of strikes in 1919, the Palmer Raids, and the Red Scare was the "Russian Ark," which departed New York City on December 21, 1919. On board the USAT *Buford* were 249 radical immigrants who were suddenly and unexpectedly being deported as "America's Christmas present to Lenin."

The families of the deportees were informed of their relatives' departure only after the *Buford* was at sea, and the *Saturday Evening Post*'s comment echoed those of many Americans during the Red Scare years: "The *Mayflower* brought the first builders to this country; the *Buford* has taken away the first destroyers." Once in Russia, the deportees were left to choose between making a new life in Russia or finding a way to reunite with their families and friends in America.[4]

THE COMINTERN AND KARELIA

After the Bolshevik Revolution, the Bolsheviks soon became known as the Russian Communist Party, and Vladimir Lenin believed that any communist parties formed in other countries must adhere to the rules established by the Russian Communist Party in order to have the best chance of overthrowing their capitalist leaders.

In January 1919, Yrjö Sirola represented the Finnish Communist Party at the first meeting to organize the Communist International, or Comintern.* The Comintern was formally organized in March 1919 after Vladimir Lenin requested that Otto Kuusinen write the organizational papers. Kuusinen, who became the Comintern's Secretery General, was also a member of the three-person Comintern's Inner Commission.

The first voting delegates included Yrjö Sirola, Otto Kuusinen, Vladimir Lenin, and Joseph Stalin. Other voting delegates were communist-party members from Great Britain, Germany, and France.

---

* The Comintern was also known as the Third International.

America, which had no communist party until May 1919, was not represented. At the first official meeting, Lenin expanded membership in the Comintern but accepted affiliations only if the other interested international organizations imposed strict discipline and adhered to all Comintern rules.

In the fall of 1919, Lenin asked Otto Kuusinen to investigate a situation in Finland. Shortly after secretly arriving in the country, the Finnish police were looking for him, forcing him to hide in homes of various sympathizers. Kuusinen spent a few nights near Helsinki in the home of Leo and Aino Sarola and, during that time, a romance began between Otto and Aino.

In 1920, Otto left Finland and lived for a time in Stockholm, Sweden. While living in Stockholm, he began writing poems for Aino, who always received them by private courier. One time, Aino received a letter from Otto that was addressed to Finnish Prime Minister Rafael Erich.

Rafael Erich and Otto Kuusinen had attended school together beginning at a young age and extending to their time at Helsinki University. As a young man, Kuusinen was more moderate and originally believed that every country had a different path to achieving their anti-capitalistic goals. The beliefs of both men had diverged as Kuusinen became more radical. In the letter that Aino delivered to the Finnish Prime Minister, Otto begged his old friend to reconsider and end the persecution of Red Finns. After reading the letter, Rafael Erich's short answer was: "Tell the sender that I shall not reply."[5]

While still living in Sweden, Edvard Gylling wrote to Vladimir Lenin on March 20, 1920, and again expressed his desire to make Karelia – a remote, underdeveloped region in northwestern Russia – the permanent home of the exiled Red Finns. Like Gylling, Lenin had plans for Karelia, too, but he wanted the province to act as a "neutral territory" between Finland and Russia. In Lenin's mind, choosing a Red Finn, such as Gylling, to lead Karelia would maintain stability within the province.

Gylling moved to Karelia in May 1920 and met with Lenin shortly after arriving, proposing that Karelia should be an experimental economic area. On June 8, 1920, the Karelian Workers' Commune* was established with Edvard Gylling as the chairman. At the time, Karelia had very few agriculture or industrial enterprises with little or no opportunities for education. Gylling envisioned Karelia as a land where exiled Red Finns could live harmoniously as the majority population, and he dreamed of transforming Karelia into a model economy. From the beginning, he thought of Karelia as the "Greater Red Finland" and wanted Red Finns to take pride in developing their own country. Soon after becoming Karelia's leader, Edvard Gylling had developed an immigration plan focused on bringing communist-leaning Red Finns to Karelia.

A commonly known shortage of skilled workers plus the need for modern equipment and technology throughout the Soviet Union seemed to perfectly fit in with Gylling's plans, but Gylling knew that Lenin had to make the first move.

Author Carl Ross wrote: "The Finnish Federation's claim to prominence was launching Finnish American radicals into a communist orbit."[6] The Federation slowly began shifting its focus from the Labor Movement to the Communist Movement in October 1919 during its Fifth National Convention in Chicago, Illinois. Prior to the convention, some radical factions within the Federation's three districts wanted the Federation to join the Communist Party (even though the CPUSA was an illegal organization operating underground in America) while others wished to lean toward the Socialist Party of America. The Federation's convention began as a deeply divided organization, and Adolph Salmi of the *New York Call* wrote on October 25, 1919, "It is certain that the convention will see a breach in its ranks... A few Finnish locals have already demanded that the Finnish Federation should join the Communist Party, but

---

* In 1923, the province became known as the Karelian Autonomous Soviet Socialist Republic, also known as Karelian ASSR.

Pictured are two of the cooperative stores within the CCE region. Above is the Brule Co-op, built one block from the Northern Pacific depot in Brule, Wisconsin. Oscar Corgan was one of the early managers. *Author's collection*

Below is the Cherry Co-op, a store that served the Iron Range in Cherry, Minnesota. *IHRCA, Anderson Library, U of MN*

this is not likely to happen, although it is possible that some of the Finnish locals will secede and go to the Communists."

In a supposed attempt to preserve unity, the Federation's leaders proposed disbanding the three districts and combining them into one with a Central Committee distributing the material for all three newspapers. Then, the news for the nearly 17,000 members would be centralized with the communist-leaning and highly experienced propagandist, Wilho Boman, who had already been designated to head the Central Committee. Many believed, though, that the proposal was merely an attempt to bring the moderate "renegade" Eastern District under tighter control of the radical Midwest District.

The proposal to combine the three districts into one, which most believed was Wilho Boman's idea, caused even more discord and outrage than before, and thousands of non-Communist Finns ended their memberships with the powerful organization. The Eastern District, being the most moderate of the three districts, flatly refused to follow the other two districts into a more communist-leaning future. By Christmas 1920, the Eastern District of the Finnish Federation and its newspaper, *Raivaaja*, had split completely from the remaining two radical districts and formed its own Finnish organization.

After losing the *Raivaaja* newspaper in the Eastern District, the Finnish Federation established the *Eteenpäin* (Forward) newspaper in May 1921. The newspaper, as well as the *Työmies* and *Toveri* newspapers, soon came under the control of pro-communist factions. By that time, about half (or 6,000) of the remaining Finnish Federation members were members of or leaned toward the CPUSA. The bitter split within the Finnish Federation marked the end of the harmonious cooperation in the close-knit Finnish-American communities and the beginning of the fighting for control of the Finn halls.[7] Within the next few years, the Finnish Federation membership was almost exclusively pro-communist.

THE GOOD TIMES ARE NOT FOR EVERYONE

The 1920s in America were years of growth, prosperity, and cultural change. Sales of automobiles exploded, and people had more money to spend on sporting events in giant new stadiums and on movies in brand-new theaters. Increasingly, people had radios in their homes where the whole family gathered around in the evenings and listened to stories and news. Occasionally, an airplane sent everyone within hearing racing outside to witness the still-unusual overhead spectacle. Telephones and electrical appliances became necessities in everyone's lives.

European factories, rail lines, roads, and even entire cities had to be rebuilt after the end of World War I, and the well-developed, industrialized America was ready to help. By the middle of the decade, Western Europe was well on the way to joining America in unprecedented economic growth and new lifestyles. For many Americans, this decade was The Roaring Twenties when anything was possible and the good times would never end (the French knew the 1920s as the "Années Folles" – crazy years). But for many American immigrants and their families, the earlier strikes and blacklistings had had a negative effect that seemed impossible to overcome. During The Roaring Twenties, "Karelia" began looking like a beam of hope at the end of a long dark tunnel for many Communist Finns.

After Vladimir Lenin's death and Joseph Stalin's ascension to power, there was a noticeable shift in the priorities of the Communist Party of Russia. Stalin believed that the well being of the Communist Party of Russia – and Stalin himself – were of greater importance than any other communist group, and every true communist, regardless of nationality, should work toward Russia's greater good.

Joseph Stalin's new priorities caused a shift in focus from the Labor Movement to the Communist Movement. Communist Party members became more radical, and the American Finnish communities in northern Wisconsin and elsewhere experienced a widening political divide as the Communist Finns began a hostile takeover of their community halls.

7

THE ROARING '20s

"The radical element of the Labor Movement became enamored with communism."

THE *TYÖMIES*
"For the Common Good"

When Karelia was established under the leadership of Edvard Gylling in 1920, Matti Tenhunen was the publishing director of the *Työmies* and was soon printing articles about the exciting achievements happening in Karelia. In 1921, the Soviet Karelia Relief Committee was established in New York City. It was coordinated by CPUSA member George Halonen, who had also been named as America's representative to Karelia. Halonen originally oversaw the Finnish-American donations to Karelia through the Relief Committee. He also coordinated the fundraising efforts for the new republic with articles in periodicals such as the *Työmies*. As Halonen became increasingly busy, Matti Tenhunen was enlisted to help him.

Before long, Tenhunen was in charge of the Soviet Karelia Relief Committee in America and supervised its finances. Some, but not all, of the money raised went directly to Karelia. Needed supplies and equipment were also purchased with the funds and sent to Karelia. From the beginning, there was an effort to coordinate the needs of Karelia with funding by the Communist Finns in North America through the Soviet Karelia Relief Committee, and that effort was very successful.[1]

By 1921, the communist government led by Vladimir Lenin had crushed all opposition parties within the Russian Empire on the grounds that they had opposed or failed to totally support the communist cause. But instead of relaxing as the new ruler of the Soviets (the People), Lenin now believed that there was more opposition and danger to his new regime than ever, since the peasantry and many of the working class had already become dissatisfied with the new regime. To repress the dissidents of communism, Lenin ruthlessly demanded increasingly tighter controls and "show trials" that frequently resulted in executions. This violent time in the Soviet Union was known as the Red Terror and led to tens of thousands being executed or sent to concentration camps. Lenin frequently stated his opposition to the one-man rule, but his orders for merciless destruction of all opposition seemed to be otherwise.

Lenin also knew that unskilled workers and farmers in the vast Russian Empire posed another problem. To alleviate the problem, Lenin and other communist leaders began discussing the recruitment of skilled workers and farmers from other countries. Soon, there was a series of new laws that set conditions for immigrant farmers and workers.

Initially, Lenin desired skilled farmers and workers who would immigrate in small organized groups and work together in factories or on communal farms. Lenin believed that Karelia in particular could be developed into a showcase for displaying to the world the potential of communism. The immigrants were to be exempt from military service if they obeyed all laws and would be exempt from taxation for five years.

Lenin argued that, "A dozen... a hundred highly-qualified foreign workers could teach a hundred or a thousand Russian workers by working with them."[2] However, he feared that immigrants unprepared for the harsh conditions they would encounter would return home and damage the Soviet Union's image. The government's solution to the problem was a required signed declaration by the immigrants, stating that they were aware of the harsh conditions. Laws were passed that turned away unskilled immigrants who would not be able to sustain themselves.

An early major source for the Soviet Union's needed work force were the recent Finnish and Russian immigrants to the United States and Canada. Many of these immigrants had not adapted well to their new lives, having arrived after much of the available land had been purchased, which forced them to work in the mining, lumber, or transportation industries with long hours and low pay – if the jobs were even available. Many Finns active in strikes had been permanently blacklisted from ever working again, and many others had a difficult time leaving their Finnish communities to seek employment, because they were only fluent in Finnish.

In the early 1920s, emigrants from the United States and Canada to the Soviet Union were told that their help was needed to restore the economy. Many leaving North America brought their tools and equipment as well as the supplies needed for two years. Farming equipment was especially needed in the relatively primitive regions (most peasant farmers in the early and mid 1920s still harvested their crops using reaping hooks and scythes). But despite Lenin's best efforts to infuse his country with an increased workforce with their modernized ideas and equipment, his country failed to thrive as he had hoped.

By 1922, Lenin believed that the continued weakening of his new government was caused by too much red tape and incompetence. He also believed that Joseph Stalin was a big part of the problem as Stalin was seemingly trying to concentrate large amounts of power into the government's center, which Lenin firmly believed was not part of the communist doctrine. Yet despite Lenin's misgivings, Stalin was elected to be the General Secretary of the Communist Party in April 1922, thereby concentrating even greater power. He also oversaw the establishment of the Soviet Union* in 1922 and forged close ties with Cheka.** Leading to even more fragility and discord, most of the communist leaders showed little-disguised disdain for non-Russians residing in any province but Russia.

Lenin's first stroke occurred in May 1922, leaving him partially paralyzed and unable to speak. The following month, however, he had recovered enough to devote himself completely to the formation of the Union of Soviet Socialist Republics (USSR), of which he was named Chairman. During this time though, with his previous

---

* Russia, or Soviet Russia, was the largest province of the Soviet Union. Russia's capital is Moscow.

** Cheka, the secret police, became known as the NKVD. It is currently known as the KGB.

robust health failing, Lenin felt increasingly helpless as he watched Stalin gain ever-increasing power as he worked toward the concentrated type of government that Stalin, not Lenin, envisioned.

In the summer of 1922, Aino Sarola was stranded in Berlin, Germany. Her trip to Berlin from Helsinki on a business trip went smoothly, but then a German railway strike had ground all train services to a halt. While waiting for the strike to end, she had met Otto Kuusinen's friend, Yrjö Sirola. Sirola was working for the Comintern in 1922 and had been ordered by Lenin and Kuusinen to Berlin on business. (As was common for Russian Comintern members, Sirola was traveling anonymously with a forged Norwegian passport.) He invited her to Moscow, where she and Otto were reunited, and she never returned to her husband in Finland. She and Otto Kuusinen were married later in 1922.

In her memoir *Rings of Destiny*, Aino recalled: "I had not been in Moscow long before I began to realize how hard and joyless life had become for the majority of the population since the Bolshevik Revolution. I particularly doubted the concept of a 'classless society,' since I could see there was a large difference between the life led by the workers and that of the 'soviet artistocrats.' Our own example was as good as any.

"Each year we received a new car, which we did not pay for and, thanks to the generosity of the 'classless society,' we had the free use of our apartment, our *dacha* [vacation cottage], a chauffeur and a housekeeper... Our housekeeper, who could neither read or write... when she went shopping for us she did not need any money, only three small books that she presented in the different shops. One was for the State dairy, where she got milk, butter, eggs and cheese; another for the State butcher's, where she obtained meat and poultry; and the third for the State fish shop, where she 'bought' fish and caviar.

"All food was rationed, and only small quantities were available... But the high-ranking officials, who had an unlimited number of ration books, could order as much of the foodstuffs as they wished. Queues formed from early in the morning, and a policeman was on hand to keep order. As each customer came out of the shop with a couple of small packets, another was allowed in. Our cook didn't have to queue, however. As soon as she showed the policeman the book, he called out: 'Make way, make way!' As she came out of the shop laden with parcels, the women outside would shout at her angrily, not only because she had been let in the shop before them, but also because she had been allowed to buy so much... We never paid a kopeck... [Our purchases] were paid for by the 'classless' society."

After they married, Aino immediately began helping Otto with Comintern tasks, even though she wasn't officially hired until 1924. The Comintern's headquarters in Moscow was known as the "Headquarters of the World Revolution," and the large budget needed to operate the organization came from every Communist Party member, in every country, who paid annual dues of one-half of one percent of their wages. The Comintern released propaganda for foreign Communist Parties and used phrases like the "Founding Congress of the Communist International" to make Communist Parties in foreign countries eager to participate. What the Comintern expected was that every Communist Party in every country work toward revolution and the overthrow of capitalist governments.[3]

No matter which country had a problem or concern, all important decisions concerning Comintern affairs were made by the Russian Comintern leaders, and no decision was made without asking for Otto Kuusinen's opinion. He was the most powerful Finnish exile in Russia, and he reported directly to Lenin and Stalin.[4]

Vladimir Lenin's political activities came to an end on March 10, 1923, when another stroke again robbed him of speech. Ten months later, on January 21, 1924, Lenin suffered a final massive stroke and died that evening at the age of 53. Joseph Stalin took control of his funeral arrangements and, to keep a high profile, was one of Lenin's pallbearers.

Against the wishes of Lenin's widow, Lenin's body was embalmed and laid to rest in a mausoleum in Moscow's Red Square. Lenin was succeeded as the chairman of the Soviet Union by Joseph Stalin.

The Finnish Federation's three newspapers actively promoted Karelia in every way they could in the early 1920s. Optimistic articles about Karelia's many supposed achievements appeared regularly along with requests for much-needed aid, which was sent through the Soviet Karelia Relief Committee in New York City. In the Finn halls, impassioned speakers described Karelia as a country in need of hard workers. Edvard Gylling, who saw the recruitment of North American Communist Finns as a way to increase Karelia's Finnish ethnicity, began working with trade unions and promoters in both the United States and Canada during this time.

Interest in Karelian immigration began in the early 1920s and, in 1922, the first American Communist Finns established a fishing commune in northern Karelia. In October 1925, Communist Finns from Cobalt, Canada, arrived in Karelia with hopes of establishing a farming commune. Slowly, Edvard Gylling's dream of a Red Finland seemed to be turning into a reality.

Immigration From Cobalt, Ontario, Canada

Approximately 325 miles northeast of Sault Ste. Marie, Michigan, lay the mining town of Cobalt, Ontario. In 1917, over thirty mines in the area provided work for hundreds of immigrants from Finland, Russia, Italy, and Poland as well as French and English Canadians. Many of the Finnish immigrants had left a farming life in the Old Country, lured by mining-company agents who promised steady work and a good life.

In 1917, as World War I raged throughout Europe, the Ahokas family arrived in Cobalt. Elis and Emma, both in their mid 30s at the time, immigrated to Canada with their only child Vieno. In Finland they had farmed on rented land but, in Cobalt, Elis joined many other Finnish immigrants and found work in one of the area's numerous mines.

During the 1920s, Finnish residents in Cobalt started reading increasingly glorified stories in their Finnish newspapers about Russia's "Workers' Paradise" in Karelia where people were treated with respect, where there was work for everyone, and where everyone was equal. Impassioned speakers in the Cobalt Finn hall encouraged people to leave their homes for Karelia if they desired a better life, and many of Cobalt's Communist Finns were interested.

In addition to Elis and Emma Ahokas, most of the Communist Finns interested in Karelia had been farmers in Finland and still longed for that life. One resident declared, "Haven't we worked too long below ground inhaling coal dust? Maybe we should think about jobs above the ground." They still yearned to till the land, to have dirty hands and clothes from the dirt found above the ground and not below. Many decided to move to Karelia, create an agricultural commune, and realize their dreams of working on the land together for the good of the entire society.

On August 8, 1922, the first meeting of the residents interested in a Karelian commune took place in Cobalt's Finn hall. The future agricultural commune was named Säde, meaning "The Ray of Light." The membership fee was set at $105, which would go to their machinery fund. After arriving in Karelia, every member would be required to work for two years without compensation, but they would receive free meals and housing.

Families of the future commune had to pay for their own travel expenses and buy the supplies and clothing needed for the first two years. Donations arrived from Communist Finns who had no plans for moving to Karelia but supported the cause, fundraising events brought in more money, and the future commune's management committee began searching for the needed farm equipment and supplies.

As time went on, Emma Ahokas voiced increasing concerns about moving to Karelia, worried that her family's new life would be harder than their life in Cobalt. Elis, however, was steadfast and stated, "Consider what a great future we are going to have in a land of working people where all men are equal and free. Sad days behind, brighter days ahead."

It took three years to generate the necessary funds, but eventually $14,000 was raised. The equipment and supplies they would need were purchased. The group who would do the preliminary work and locate the land for their commune was selected and left for Karelia with high hopes for a better life in the fall of 1925.

JOSEPH STALIN'S QUEST FOR POWER

After the death of Vladimir Lenin, Joseph Stalin became the most powerful person in the Soviet Union, and he yearned to consolidate his power even more. Stalin envisioned a Soviet Union, and Russia in particular, equipped with modernized tools and technology equal to that of the Western nations. As The Roaring Twenties continued before slowly trembling to a stop and tumbling into the Great Depression, Stalin remained laser-focused on his goal.

Stalin demanded the dismantling of the various ethnic groups within the CPUSA, mandating that their loyalty must not stay within their groups but must be totally focused on the Communist Party of Russia. The harmonious cooperation and kinship within the American Finnish communities ended as the Communist Finns became increasingly more radical and aligned with the Communist Party, driving a wedge between the two Finnish groups. The Communist Party's attempt to seize control of the CCE and its finances was met with a surprisingly forceful resistance and permanently polarized the Finns and the Communist Finns. Yet Stalin's dream in the late 1920s, known as the First Five-Year Plan, continued to move forward.

8 JOSEPH STALIN'S DICTATES

"We are fifty or one hundred years behind the advanced countries. We must make up this distance in ten years or they will crush us."

JOSEPH STALIN

THE DISSOLUTION OF THE POWERFUL FINNISH FEDERATION
With Vladimir Lenin deceased, Joseph Stalin slowly seized complete control of the Soviet Union, the Communist Party of Russia, and the Comintern. In 1925, Stalin shifted his primary goal from a communist world revolution to the requirement that all communist parties defend the Soviet Union above all else. Stalin's proclamation was that "an Internationalist is one who is ready to defend the Soviet Union without reservation, without wavering, unconditionally; for the Soviet Union is the base of the world revolutionary movement, and this revolutionary movement cannot be defended and promoted without defending the Soviet Union."[1]

Next, the Moscow-based Comintern ordered all communist parties, including the CPUSA, to immediately reorganize by dissolving the different language branches and combining them instead by town or area. Otto Kuusinen, then the chairman of the Comintern's American Commission in Moscow, was in charge of guiding the dissolution of the American language groups. Otto Kuusinen, Joseph Stalin, and other leaders in Soviet Russia believed that by blending the different communist-American ethnic groups, they would combine the various radicals into an ideological and political subservience to Russian Communism.[2]

America's Finnish Federation, whose executive board was made up of all Communist Finns, was against Moscow's Bolshevization with the greatest opposition coming from the Midwest District and the *Työmies* newspaper. Wilho Boman, then a *Työmies* editor, wrote numerous articles opposing the mandate. For Boman's insurrection, the CPUSA – after receiving direct orders from Moscow – labeled him an opportunist and forced him to resign from the newspaper. He was then expelled from the CPUSA.*

Next, the CPUSA demanded mass expulsion for everyone who was wavering, but John Wiita asked the CPUSA to give the Midwest District time to adjust. Wiita had recently become the editor-in-chief of the Finnish Federation's Eastern district's *Eteenpäin* but was directed to move to Chicago before the annual meeting in August 1925. He was also charged with dissolving the Finnish Federation. Wiita did not want to move to Chicago but was soon ordered by the CPUSA to take the first train to Chicago and take charge of the dissolution. "I had no alternative but to obey the command," Wiita later recalled in his memoirs. "One day I got a telegram that the Party Central Committee 'urge you to take the first train to Chicago.' That ended my resistance. I was a member of the Central Committee, and the Communist Party had the same kind of discipline as military organizations have. You have to obey the command and be ready to go when ordered."[3]

When Wiita reached Chicago, he felt that an impending crisis was brewing between the three major institutions in the Finnish Federation's Midwest District – the Työmies Society, the CCE, and the Finnish Federation. The new orders mandated that Finns and all other nationalities meet in a central hall instead of their local ethnic halls. John Wiita remembered, "We held this to be impossible. We explained that the Comintern did not understand American conditions. Reorganization would destroy the whole CPUSA. And a part of the Finns were afraid that others [other ethnic groups] in the party would take possession of their halls, newspapers, and other properties and destroy them, as they would destroy all their cultural activities."[4]

In November 1925, the Finnish Federation held their convention in Chicago. Anticipating a divisive convention, Otto Kuusinen sent Yrjö Sirola (who traveled to America using the alias Frank Miller)

---

* Boman completely dropped out of politics and became a masseur in New York City.

from Moscow to the convention to "bring everyone in line and conform to communist discipline." During the very contentious convention and after much debate, the Finnish Federation was formally dissolved. The American Communist Finns prevailed, though, and with the approval of the communist leaders in Moscow, the Finnish Federation was to be reorganized as the Finnish Workers Federation (FWF). They remained affiliated with the CPUSA.

Over a year later, the Finnish Workers Federation was officially organized in Chicago in late January 1927. The CPUSA Central Committee appointed an editor to supply political and organizational material to the *Työmies, Eteenpäin,* and *Toveri* newspapers. Dues stamps were sold to the local Workers clubs nationwide. John Wiita was elected national secretary. Yrjö Sirola, who had returned to Moscow a few months earlier, joined Otto Kuusinen and Kullervo Manner,* the "Big Three of the Communist Party of Finland," in sending a congratulatory cablegram to the Finnish Workers Federation.[5]

John Wiita felt that the formation of the Finnish Workers Federation had a revitalizing and unifying effect on the radical, pro-Communist Finnish Movement and the Cooperative Movement. Many members of the CCE and its leaders were members of both the Finnish Workers Federation and the CPUSA.** Wiita recalled, "All of the Finnish Workers Federation members throughout the country enthusiastically greeted its new national organization, feeling that once again they were one national body, which had been temporarily separated, and that once again they had a national center that would give them help and guidance in their work for the advancement of the ideas and interest of the working class. The founding

---

* Kullervo Manner was a SDP member of the Finnish Parliament and the leader of the Red Guard during Finland's Civil War in 1918. After fleeing to Russia, he helped establish the Finnish Communist Party with Kuusinen and Sirola and became a Comintern official. After falling out of favor with Otto Kuusinen, Manner died in a gulag.

** Members of the CCE who did not belong to the CPUSA did not join the Finnish Workers Federation. Instead, they had a growing sense of unease as the Communist Finns in the CCE began veering more strongly toward the dictates coming from Moscow. John Wiita believed that the battle for the CCE began in 1925 when the Comintern demanded that the Finnish Federation be dissolved.[6]

The final convention of the Finnish Federation. Chicago, Illinois, November 28-December 3, 1925. *IHRCA Archives, Anderson Library, U of MN*

Joseph Stalin, left, and Otto Kuusinen. After Vladimir Lenin's death, Stalin demanded that the Finnish Federation dissolve. Otto Kuusinen, charged with verifying that the foreign communist parties complied with Stalin's orders, often sent Yrjö Sirola to be his American eyes and ears.
Wikimedia Commons

convention and the establishment of the Finnish Workers Federation had a tremendously unifying effect among the Finnish Workers' clubs and all their institutions."⁷

THE TAKEOVER OF THE FINN HALLS

Matti Tenhunen had been active in the CPUSA as soon as it was established in the Superior-Duluth area. He supervised the CPUSA's activities in Superior and was Superior's best-known communist. In 1927, Tenhunen also became known as "Russia's immigration agent" after he proclaimed that "Russia is the place for all workers. The Russian government will soon free all the world's laborers. The Soviet flag is an emblem of freedom for all small countries and all the oppressed."

As The Roaring Twenties continued, Tenhunen made several trips to the Soviet Union on the behest of the Comintern. In 1927, he was a CCE delegate at the International Co-op Congress in Stockholm, Sweden. Before returning to America, Tenhunen traveled to Moscow and met with Otto Kuusinen and other leaders of the Finnish Communist Party.⁸

Although the Finnish Workers Federation had a unifying effect with the Communist Finns, it increasingly polarized the Finnish communities. Battles for control of the Finn halls – the important cultural centers of the Finnish communities – destroyed friendships and family ties as the chasm between the political ideologies increased. The divisions were determined by the way each group viewed communism and Soviet Russia, with each side more unwilling to budge as time went by and even questioning the rationality of the opposing group. Communist promoters, speaking more frequently in the Finn halls, only widened the divisions and increased the discord. Matti Tenhunen and Oscar Corgan were well-known charismatic, electrifying speakers in many regional Finn halls in the Upper Midwest.

The management and control of Waino's Finnish Round Hall was determined in the summer of 1927 when members from Waino, Oulu, Maple, Iron River, and Brule cast their votes. Oral history relates that the Communist Finns took control of the hall because

A summer youth camp in 1926 at the Waino Round Hall in Waino, Wisconsin. The Young Workers League, whose parents were members of the CCE, always enjoyed the classes and recreation at the camp. The following year, only the children of the Communist Finns attended the camp.
IHRCA Archives, Anderson Library, U of MN

of two votes cast by a married couple who hadn't paid their annual membership dues. About the same time, Oulu's Finn hall also fell under the Communist Finn's control.

The loss of both halls was a bitter blow to the non-Communist Finns, most of whom had personally helped build the halls or donated the building materials. "It was like a tall black wall existed between the Finns and the Communist Finns," recalled Viola Wentela Palo, the granddaughter of August Wentala, who had built the circular addition of Waino's Round Hall. Viola remembered her mother's staunch refusal in allowing her to play or associate with the children of the Communist Finns. There was no middle ground between the two groups, and the ideological chasm divided families, friends, and neighbors.

THE BRULE CO-OP PARK

"During the past, the 'Round Hall' of the Finnish Farmer's club at Waino, Wis., came to be the center of many activities [youth camps, schools, and summer festivals]. Nevertheless, it had not been originally intended for use on a large scale as the manifold needs of the district require, lacking recreational grounds, athletic fields, etc., and the fact that the Waino Hall Association fell into the hands of a group that is now openly hostile towards the cooperative organizations has put an end to further using that hall for the district gathering and schools in the future...

"A search that has lasted for more than three years has now come to an end and the several thousands of cooperatively organized workers and farmers...are now the possessors of some 80 acres of fields and woodland retreats along the famous Brule River...."[9]

Almost immediately after losing the Waino Round Hall to the Communist Finns in 1927, a search for a location that would be ideal for a replacement hall began. Factors considered by cooperative members in Upper Michigan, northern Wisconsin, and northern Minnesota included: "It had to be centrally located but not directly in the path of public traffic; on good roads; easily reached but at the same time providing privacy for our summer schools and camps, and for those who want to seek healthful recreation there; and it had to be either on an inland lake or river."

Many potential locations were considered, but a site was finally chosen four miles north of the village of Brule on the Brule River. It was also decided to form the North Wisconsin Cooperative Park Association (NWCPA) with the park being owned and managed by the workers and farmers of the district that included Waino, Oulu, Brule, Iron River, Maple, Wentworth, Superior, and Duluth. The first officers of the NWCPA were Henry Aho, president; George E. Wentela, secretary; Toivo Tenhune (the son of Matti Tenhunen); and Guy Lansdale.

The 80 acres of land and buildings, originally owned by the Banks family of Superior, were purchased through the Lake Superior Land Company for $10,000. The Banks family had used the property as a summer residence and country club, and their lodge was put into use as a dormitory by attendees of the NWCPA's summer classes. Plans were immediately put into motion to develop areas for sporting events, picnics, summer youth courses, open air concerts and dances, and accommodating people there for swimming, recreation, and leisure during the summer months.

Viola Palo recalled: "In the beginning of the summer youth courses, the Banks' summer home was used as the dormitory with the girls sleeping in the bedrooms and the boys sleeping on the outside veranda. Later, a dormitory was built. It had a large central hall with numerous rooms on each side – one side for boys, the other side for girls – filled with bunk beds. Summer courses included learning about cooperative theory, folk dancing, heritage, and exercises."

Every year, hundreds attended the numerous festivities at the Co-op Park, and dozens of children, youth, and adults attended the summer camps. The attendees came from Wisconsin, Minnesota, and Michigan with children as young as eight eligible for the children's camp. The Co-op Park had activities for everyone.

Herbert Aho often fondly reminisced about the Co-op Park: "Dad [Henry Aho] used to work in his blacksmith shop in his white shirt while he waited for Maw [Sandra] to finish her household chores. Then we'd all walk down the Clevedon Road to the Co-op Park. There was always something going on there – dances, movies, roller skating... Basketball tournaments were held in the hall, and there was an outside ring for boxing matches. Talent shows were popular, but the big event every year was when Viola Turpeinen performed. The money raised from her one night at the Park paid for the entire year's electricity. Everyone from miles around attended the Co-op Park activities."

Merlin Miller, a cooperative member from Kansas City, Missouri, described his visit to the Co-op Park: "Here, under the tall pines and sweet-scented birches, cooperators congregate daily to relax, play together, or study... It is no exaggeration to say that this co-op camp is used daily. Several nights a week the pavilion is engaged – winter and summer – except when the big snows block the highways. Here is the recreation center for a whole countryside...

"The night we drove in, a play was in progress. The house was full, and the audience was obviously having a good time. Twice a week there are movies. Two wedding dances were scheduled for the week following our visit. Roller skating and basketball games alternate during the long winter evenings...

"The Co-op Park at Brule, Wisconsin, is more than a vacationer's paradise. It is the nerve center where more people are all-around cooperators than anywhere else in America...."[10]

Over the years, the laughter, joy, and new memories made at the Brule Co-op Park gradually replaced the bitterness caused by losing their halls to the Communist Finns.

THE GREAT DEPRESSION BEGINS

The Roaring 20s, a time of unprecedented growth in America, came to an end in 1929. During the 1920s, the American economy grew by 42 percent. By the end of the decade, nearly 60 percent of households owned radios, and there were rumors of a future radio with a moving picture that would be known as a television. Mass production enabled washing machines, refrigerators, and vacuum cleaners to become necessary appliances in homes. The car industry exploded, and the aviation industry was born. Banks flourished, and credit was easily attainable.

Republican Herbert Hoover was sworn in as the 31st President of the United States on March 4, 1929. Hoover believed that capitalism in a free-market economy could and would fix any economic downturn that might occur. In a further gesture of optimism for future prosperity, he lowered the top income-tax rate from 25 percent to 24 percent.

The economy began faltering in August, but not many were concerned. *How could the good times ever end?* No one knew that when the Dow reached a record high of 381.7 on September 3, that record would stand for over 25 years. No one knew that the true Great Depression had begun.

On October 28, 1929, stock prices fell by 13 percent. Now known as Black Monday, it was followed the next day by Black Tuesday, when stock prices plunged by an additional 12 percent. In just two days, the stock market lost $30 billion in value, which at that time was ten times more than the annual federal budget. By the end of 1929, more than 650 banks had failed.

In June 1930, Hoover signed the Smoot-Hawley Act, increasing taxes on 900 imported products in an effort to help the struggling American farmers. Instead, the Act launched a trade war,

THE CONTINUING GREAT DEPRESSION

Wanting to reduce the federal deficit, President Hoover signed the Revenue Act of 1932 and increased the top income tax rate to 63 percent. He also believed that bolstering the banks and railroads would strengthen the economy. Hoover believed his actions would restore confidence in the economy despite millions of Americans now being unemployed and forced into food lines. Instead, Hoover's actions worsened the Depression. In addition, natural disasters – 14 dust storms – severely impacted the Midwest in 1932, ravaging farmers and farm land. The national economy dropped by an additional 13 percent in 1932, and the national unemployment rate rose to over 23 percent. Hoover's inability to reverse the Great Depression was the major factor that led to his failed bid for re-election in 1932.

Shortly after his inauguration in March 1933, President Franklin Delano Roosevelt (FDR) launched his New Deal and immediately closed all American banks in order to halt any additional bank failures. Also in March, the Civilian Conservation Corps was formed and immediately hired three million workers.

In May, the Federal Farm Mortgage Act offered farm loans to millions of struggling farmers. The Federal Deposit Insurance Corp stabilized banks. The Public Works Administration added even more jobs.

In November, 48 dust storms wreaked havoc through the Great Plains. FDR created the Federal Surplus Relief Corp to feed struggling Americans with excess farm products. Yet, even with the additional federal programs, the national unemployment rate rose to nearly 25 percent.

Black Sunday, April 15, 1934, saw the worst dust storm in history. Nationwide record high temperatures scorched the land, and droughts covered 75 percent of America. But in spite of the natural disasters, the economy slowly began responding to the New Deal programs, and unemployment fell to less than 22 percent.

Continued on page 124

and international trade began collapsing. The Great Depression worsened in 1930 when a severe drought – said to be the worst in 300 years – impacted 23 southeastern states. Crop failures were followed by runs on banks as depositors rushed to withdraw whatever savings they still had. Banks on average only held 10 percent of their deposits and, by the end of 1930, another 1300 banks had failed. Still, Hoover remained opposed to providing federal aid for struggling Americans as the Depression deepened.

In the Twin Ports of Western Lake Superior, the Citizen's Alliance continued weakening the Labor Movement while the Great Depression continued. As the economy struggled, forcing industries to slow down, Citizen's Alliance promoted a reduction in wages, and 10-hour work days were the norm.[11]

Unemployment in the Midwest – and throughout America – soared. At one time, Duluth had the highest unemployment rate in America based on cities with populations over 100,000. By 1932, Duluth's unemployment rate was more than 30 percent.

During the 1920s, about 90 percent of the total tonnage shipped out of the Twin Ports was iron ore. Forty-five million tons of iron ore left the Twin Ports in 1929, but the shipped tonnage dropped by 62 percent the following year when only 28 million tons were shipped. Total iron-ore shipments worsened even more the following year when the tonnage dropped by two-thirds, or 15 million tons, of the pre-Depression total. The unemployment rate in the iron ore-related industries in the Twin Ports soared to over 40 percent.

The economic downturn also affected the copper industry on the Keweenaw Peninsula. After over 80 years of continuous operations, the Quincy Mining Company temporarily shut down. Low copper prices and very little demand slowly closed an increasing number of mines. The C & H continued their underground operations, but at an extremely reduced capacity.

In 1935, the federal government began paying farmers to plant soil-building crops that would minimize dust storms, and the Rural Electrification Act brought electricity to farms and rural areas. The Works Progress Administration hired 8.5 million Americans. In August, the Social Security Act provided income to the blind, disabled, elderly, and children living in poverty. The economy grew by nine percent, and unemployment fell to 20 percent.

The hottest year on record began in June 1936 when 20 states experienced temperatures of at least 110 degrees, and four states saw highs exceeding 120 degrees. The heat killed nearly 1,700 people, and 3,500 more drowned while trying to cool off. Yet despite the devastating weather conditions, unemployment fell below 17 percent, and the economy grew by 13 percent. In November, FDR easily coasted to a second presidential term.

The New Deal programs continued to slowly lift America out of the Great Depression, but the national debt soared. As 1937 began, the national debt was $34 billion and, in total, FDR created the largest national debt increase in history. In 1938, President Roosevelt signed the Fair Labor Standards Act that established a national minimum wage, required time-and-a-half for overtime pay, and placed restrictions on child labor. The Great Depression ended in 1939 when Adolf Hitler invaded Poland and World War II began. FDR was easily re-elected in 1940 to a historic third term.

STALIN'S FIRST FIVE-YEAR PLAN

Joseph Stalin exuberantly proclaimed that the Wall Street crash and resulting Great Depression was proof-positive that capitalism was finally and irretrievably ending. And he extolled his vision of Soviet Russia rising to unparalleled heights in the history of human development.

Communist parties worldwide became completely subordinate to the Soviet Communist Party, and the Comintern became an organ of the Communist Party of Russia during the First Five-Year Plan. Stalin had an absolute consolidation of power.

In the Soviet Union, Joseph Stalin's First Five-Year Plan had begun in October 1928. The Plan focused on rapid industrialization within the Soviet Union as well as bringing farming and logging methods into the modern era with the most modern equipment of the time. Revenue from logging, much of it generated in the Russian province of Karelia, played a major role in Stalin's Plan. Karelia in 1928 was underdeveloped as compared to other Soviet Union regions, but southern Karelia had one of the most thickly forested regions within the Soviet Union. Plus, waterways and railroads allowed for relative ease in transporting wood products to markets throughout Europe.

Problematic, too, at the beginning of Stalin's First Five-Year Plan were Karelia's old-fashioned work methods, outdated equipment, and unskilled workers within the farming and timber industries. Additionally, in order to meet the Plan's quotas, Edvard Gylling estimated that up to 50,000 skilled workers were needed in Karelia. Gylling, who still believed that Karelia was destined to be the Red Finland, helped solve the problem by requesting the recruitment of skilled professionals – who would arrive with their own tools and equipment – from America and Canada. Whenever possible, the workers would be Finnish-speaking with strong communist beliefs.

THE QUEST FOR CASH

For several years following the Bolshevik Revolution, Czar Nicholas' jewels and art collection were a reliable source of income for the leaders in Soviet Russia. The treasures of the slain czar and his family had been sold in, among other places, a Scandinavian shop until the seller suddenly disappeared with the income and remaining treasures. Then in 1927, a substantial portion of the Soviet funds were stolen from the State Bank of Moscow.[1] Neither thief was ever apprehended.

Joseph Stalin's First Five-Year Plan to industrialize the Soviet Union as quickly as possible diverted funds into his Plan from "non-essential" government departments that included the Comintern, which was soon severely defunded. The Comintern's financial crisis created a ripple effect financially throughout the Communist Parties worldwide, including the CPUSA.

9 THE BATTLE FOR THE CCE

"The chain of events that triggered the final struggle [for control of the CCE] *over the issue of political neutrality started far from Superior – in Moscow, in fact, when the Comintern veered sharply to the left in the late 1920s in preparation for the final collapse of capitalism...."*

HISTORIAN MICHAEL KARNI

THE CPUSA, WHICH HAD previously relied on the Comintern for up to two-thirds of its income, found itself deeply in debt by the middle of 1929. The Comintern and the CPUSA, both desperate for new revenue sources because of Stalin's First Five-Year Plan, were well aware of the financial success of America's upper-midwestern wholesale giant, the CCE. The link they shared with the CCE was the Työmies Society in Superior, Wisconsin, and a plan was soon implemented to acquire a portion of the CCE's profits. John Wiita, who had become the editor-in-chief of the *Työmies* newspaper in May 1928, was also the secretary of the Finnish branch of the CPUSA. Wiita, being in the most influential position, was chosen to initiate the plan.

Since its inception in 1917, non-communist and communist CCE members had harmoniously worked together in the organization with the understanding that the CPUSA would not interfere in the CCE's affairs. At the 1928 CCE annual convention, the delegates confirmed that the Upper Midwest's cooperatives strongly supported the Labor Movement but would not allow the "differences of political and economic organizations to weaken or divide the Cooperative Movement." In 1928, the non-communist and communist CCE members, numbering over 20,000 in Upper Michigan, northern Wisconsin, and northern Minnesota, set their political differences

The annual Cooperative meeting in Superior, Wisconsin. April 22-25, 1929
IHRCA, Anderson Library, U of MN

Editor-in-chief John Wiita and linotypist Sjogren at the Työmies building in Superior, Wisconsin.
IHRCA, Anderson Library, U of MN

aside and were firmly committed to the success of the wholesale organization. The same policy was reaffirmed during the annual convention in April 1929.

By the late summer of 1929, there were ominous signs of the coming Great Depression. In August, as the economy of The Roaring '20s reached its peak, feelings of unease by many Americans about the increasingly shaky economy were heralded with jubilation by the Communist Party in Moscow as the impending end of capitalism. The Moscow communists believed that the long-anticipated workers' revolution – first envisioned by Karl Marx and later by Vladimir Lenin – was near, and they needed to take action in order to be at the forefront of the coming revolution. To accomplish this, however, they needed immediate funds.

Later in the summer of 1929, Matti Tenhunen, then a CCE board member, received a letter from the CPUSA (and written by John Wiita) demanding an immediate loan of $5,000 "for the payment of the CPUSA's bills and to aid Communist Finns living in Moscow." The CPUSA also demanded one percent of all CCE annual gross income.* Tenhunen and the CCE communist board members refused the request and did not share the letter with the non-communist CCE members, realizing that any aggressive moves by the CPUSA would destroy the harmonious working relationships within the CCE.[2]

Shortly after the first letter came a second letter from the CPUSA, addressed specifically to Matti Tenhunen. The letter was also written by John Wiita. The powerful CPUSA leader's letter to Tenhunen referred to his previous letter and stated, "You know how to take care of book entries." Wiita suggested setting up a pseudo lawyer in New York City who would periodically be compensated by the one percent "contribution" from the CCE's gross revenue.[3] Although the CCE communist board members were becoming increasingly alarmed, they again kept the letter from the other members.

After Matti Tenhunen's second letter from John Wiita, the CPUSA tried a different tactic and sent a very influential member

---

* Beginning in 1928, the CCE's gross revenue exceeded $1 million annually. The CPUSA's demand for 1%, or at least $10,000 of the gross revenue, amounted to $150,860 in today's dollars.

Some members of the Cooperative Management Committee, 1928 (l to r): Oscar Corgan (Pres.), Matti Tenhunen, Eskel Ronn (Manager), and George Halonen (Educ. Dir.) *IHRCA, Anderson Library, U of MN*

Työmies building (left) and the 1st floor type-set office (below) in 1928. An elegant staircase ascended to the 2nd floor meeting area. Corgan and his family periodically lived on the 3rd floor. The basement had two tunnels and three staircases.

Both photos: IHRCA, Anderson Library, U of MN

of their Central Committee to Superior. Robert Minor's orders were to pressure the CCE into giving the CPUSA the $5,000 loan and a portion of all future income. Matti Tenhunen and George Halonen, who belonged to both the CCE board and the CPUSA, refused Minor's demands. By then, the increasingly aggressive moves by the CPUSA were rapidly sending the CCE and CPUSA relations spiraling to the breaking point.

For George Halonen's noncompliance, the CPUSA immediately expelled him from the Party and demanded he be fired as the CCE's Education Director. The CCE's communist board members flatly refused and countered by finally revealing all of the CPUSA's demands to the CCE's non-communist board members. The CPUSA considered this a declaration of war and focused their aggression on Halonen, labeling him as an opportunistic renegade. The *Työmies* newspaper joined in the attacks against Halonen, printing scathing articles about him and denouncing him as a traitor.[4]

In an effort to silence the CCE's attacks against them, the CPUSA called a meeting with the Työmies Society Board of Directors on November 28, 1929, in Superior. John Wiita and another senior CPUSA representative demanded and received total Party loyalty from the Työmies Society Board of Directors, which was then forced to declare war on the CCE policies and leadership and sever all ties with the giant wholesaler. Their decision was an extremely difficult one, primarily because the Työmies Society and CCE had enjoyed a very close relationship since the CCE's origin in 1917. Making the choice even harder was Matti Tenhunen, who was considered to be the Työmies Society's leader and was also a CCE board member in opposition of the CPUSA. In the end, all Työmies Society board members signed a declaration in support of the CPUSA. Oscar Corgan, who was the Työmies Society's business manager at the time, broke down completely and asked to resign.*[5]

---

*After Corgan's resignation, he and his family moved to Virginia, Minnesota, where Oscar managed a cooperative creamery.

Less than a month after the CPUSA's meeting in Superior, Matti Tenhunen and John Wiita were ordered to Moscow in late December 1929 by the Communist Party's "High Command."* The two longtime friends, who now found themselves on opposing sides of the CCE conflict, traveled together on the German liner *Stuttgart*. Both men avoided discussing the CCE issue and arrived in Moscow during the first days of January 1930.⁶

Once in Moscow, Tenhunen and Wiita** were separately interrogated for days by Otto Kuusinen. Kuusinen, who was one of the highest-ranking members of the Communist Party and the Comintern, demanded to know every detail about the CCE struggle. His office had a long table where he kept his notebook, occasionally making notes while pacing incessantly and sipping coffee. (Coffee, cigars, and women were said to be Kuusinen's vices.)

Otto Kuusinen, the most powerful Communist Finn in Soviet Russia.
Wikimedia Commons

When Matti Tenhunen returned to America from Moscow in January 1930, he had switched from supporting the CCE's position to now siding with CPUSA and the communists in Moscow.*** Matti Tenhunen was well known within America's Finnish community among both communists

---

* Otto Kuusinen was responsible for guiding the Comintern's principles and monitoring political and economic developments in foreign capitalist countries. Conflicts within a foreign Party were resolved in Moscow. The conflict resolution was written in Moscow, and the delegate brought it back to his country where the resolution was enacted.⁷

** While Wiita was in Moscow, he spent an evening with Leo Laukki, his former teacher at the Work Peoples' College, who was then a *Tass* newspaper correspondent. Wiita also met with his mentor and old friend, Yrjö Sirola, who was teaching at the Lenin School in Moscow.⁸

*** It was perhaps during Wiita and Tenhunen's time in Moscow that the initial demands for a portion of the CCE revenue shifted to a desire for total communist control of the CCE. (Author's note)

and non-communists. In 1930, he had lived in northwestern Wisconsin for nearly two decades. He had been instrumental in forming the CCE, the Workers Mutual Bank in Superior, and had hundreds of acquaintances within the giant CCE. He was perceived as the head of the Työmies Society, whose newspaper was read in every Finnish community in the region. To most, he was trusted and well-respected, and now he had joined with the clearly emboldened communists in Soviet Russia, who demanded the total compliance of the CCE.

In January 1930, the *Työmies* published an editorial flatly stating that the CCE leaders denied the validity of the Comintern and the Comintern's belief in the coming workers' revolution (which the communist leaders in Moscow still believed had begun with the Great Depression). Later, John Wiita lamented, "All the battle lines were drawn and both sides had mobilized all their forces and utilized their 'heavy artillery' against each other… All [meaning the FWF, CPUSA, Työmies Society, Comintern, and the Communist Party in Moscow] directed their attacks against their recent brother organization [the CCE], which had deserted the camp of its creators and friends…."[9]

In the early months of 1930, the non-communist members of the CCE began believing that the control of their cooperative network was in serious danger of being lost to the communists. Their understanding of the conflict was a result of Matti Tenhunen's son, Toivo Tenhune, who worked hard to convince the CCE membership that the communist members on their Boards of Directors must be rejected and not be allowed to attend the annual meeting.

Matti Tenhunen, shortly after returning from Moscow, joined forces with Oscar Corgan* and began a well-planned propaganda campaign. The two men traveled to Communist Finn halls and cooperative stores throughout the region, sometimes speaking passionately throughout the night, urging CCE members to elect communist delegates to the upcoming annual meeting. In Superior, they

---

* Corgan was still a cooperative manager in MN when he teamed with Tenhunen in early 1930. On October 14, 1930, a passport was issued to Corgan, after which he sailed to Europe on the *Europa*. He was listed as a Swedish national. Corgan stopped in Soviet Russia before returning to America.[10]

were joined by Kullervo Manner,* who had arrived from Moscow to help in the battle.¹¹

At times, Toivo Tenhune and the other non-communist speakers who helped him were in the same location, on the same night, as the communist campaigners, but the hard work of Tenhune's group prevailed. By the time of the annual meeting, every non-communist member of the 20,000-member CCE knew that their wholesale was in danger of falling to a hostile takeover by the communists.

Brule resident and CCE delegate Oscar Maki** traveled by train with his fellow delegates to the three-day annual meeting and later described the fist fights, shouting, and rancor that filled each day as 249 delegates battled for the future of the CCE. Many CCE members also belonged to the CPUSA and were torn between the communist and non-communist heated arguments. The fighting split friends, families, and even spouses at the meeting and within the delegates' communities.

Years before, Matti Tenhunen had strategically placed at least one communist on the board of the 130 cooperative stores within the CCE district, and the majority of the CCE's Board of Directors were communists. For the most part – thanks to the efforts of Toivo Tenhune – the majority of the delegates were non-communists by a margin of over 10 to 1. At the end of the annual meeting, the communist members and their ideologies were decisively rejected by the majority of the CCE delegates, and those members were expelled from the CCE.¹²

Later, a CCW publication*** mentioned those divisive times: "*The Communist Party fails to gain control of CCE by attempted pressure upon the directors and responsible executives, and launches a violent attack to either capture or destroy the central organization and its supporting societies... The attack fails and the struggle serves the happy end of unifying the cooperatives throughout the*

---

* Kullervo Manner had worked with Edvard Gylling, Yrjö Sirola, and Otto Kuusinen in the Finnish SDP before they escaped from Finland following the 1918 Civil War. After escaping to Russia, Manner, Sirola, and Kuusinen had organized the Finnish Communist Party. Gylling was living in Sweden at that time.

** Told to the author by Oscar Maki's daughter, Jennie.

*** The CCE changed its name to the Central Cooperative Wholesale (CCW) in 1931.

district and establishing beyond question the cooperative integrity of the CCE and its affiliated societies....

"The Year 1930: ...The three-day annual meeting, attended by 249 official delegates from 72 member societies, not only administers a complete defeat to the remaining small communist faction but also ousts from the board three directors who had joined with the communists in machinations against the CCE."[13]

A CCE meeting in January 1931 was the final battle for control of the cooperative wholesale. The CCE voted to remain politically neutral, and the few communists who still remained were expelled immediately from the organization. Matti Tenhunen, who had retained his position on the Board of Directors until the annual meeting in 1931 stated, "I shall fight on for the working principles in the cooperatives. This is my answer to the crooked and uncalled for cross-examination given me at the board meeting by some board members."[14] Tenhunen was then personally escorted from the building by his son, Toivo Tenhune.*

AFTERMATH OF THE BATTLE FOR CONTROL OF THE CCE

The CCE revised its manual to emphasize that the democratically run cooperatives were non-partisan on both religious and political issues and replaced the *Työmies* newspaper with *The Workers Cooperative Journal*.

George Halonen, who had been so severely attacked by various communist organizations as well as by articles in the *Työmies*, started *The Workers Cooperative Journal*. Two editors from the *Työmies*, Henry Koski and Kalle Aine, began working for the new CCE paper.

John Wiita, still bitter about losing control of the CCE, stated that *The Workers Cooperative Journal* was "used in the struggle against the Party [the CPUSA and the Communist Party of Russia], the Finnish Workers Federation, the Työmies Society, and against

---

*Toivo changed his last name to distance himself politically and ideologically from his father.

all their former comrades and friends." The split was the largest division within the Finnish communities since the Finnish Federation's Eastern District and their newspaper *Raivaaja* had severed ties with the Finnish Federation's Midwest and Western districts in late 1920.[15]

In May 1930, John Wiita resigned his position as the *Työmies* editor and moved to New York City to be closer to the Finnish Workers Federation's headquarters.* He found office space in Harlem near the local Communist Finn hall and CPUSA headquarters. He became the National Chairman of the FWF, which meant he was also its Central Editor, supplying material to the three daily papers.

After the Communist Finns lost their battle for control of the CCE, they formed the Workers & Farmers Cooperative United Alliance to compete with the CCE distribution center in Superior, Wisonsin, and located their offices in the Työmies building. Matti Tenhunen was instrumental in its organization, and Otto Kuusinen, along with the communist leaders in Moscow, approved of the Alliance.[16]

Communist Finn stores opened regionally with a store in Oulu being operated by the Oulu and Waino Leftist Cooperative People who pledged "to obtain goods of value to its patrons at the most advantageous prices." On March 29, 1931, during their meeting at the Communist Finn hall in Oulu, they adopted the name of Twin Town W & F Co-op Society, but a few days later (on April 3, 1931) they changed their name to the Northern Co-op Society.** All of their purchase orders to the CCE were denied.[17]

---

*The FWF voted to relocate their national headquarters from Chicago to New York City at the national convention in Detroit on March 17-19, 1929 in Detroit. Wiita led the convention.

**The building for the Northern Co-op Society's store is now part of the Oulu Cultural & Heritage Center in Oulu, WI.

The communist's hostile takeover of the CCE had failed, and the communists – both in Soviet Russia and the CPUSA – were increasingly desperate for a new revenue source. Joseph Stalin's First Five-Year Plan still needed a revenue source to buy modernized equipment and hire skilled workers who could operate that equipment. And Edvard Gylling still wanted Communist-Finn immigrants – immigrants who could increase the ethnic base in Karelia while bringing in the needed skills and machinery.

As the CCE expelled the last Communist Finns from their membership and firmly reinforced its political neutrality in Superior, Wisconsin, a new organization was being formed by the Central Committee of the Communist Party in Moscow. The new organization seemed to be a potentially perfect and lucrative solution to all of the communists' problems. If the plan succeeded, it would not only bring in the needed equipment and skilled communist-leaning manpower at no cost, but it would also bring in additional revenue needed by so many communist organizations.

The new organization was named Karelian Technical Aid (KTA), and their target group was the North American Communist Finns who, with the right recruiters, could probably be encouraged to move to Karelia. They would not need financial incentives but might even be willing to pay for the opportunity if they were told how much they were needed and wanted to help build Karelia. They were a skilled workforce, and many already owned the newest tools and equipment so badly needed in Karelia and the rest of Soviet Russia.

The North American Communist Finns, Edvard Gylling suggested to the Central Committee, should be allowed to bring their own tools and equipment duty-free in order to maximize the importation of the most modern technology simultaneously with the needed expertise. Single men would be the preferred immigrants, but families would not be discouraged. Another very important consideration was the financial support they could bring to the KTA, which would then distribute the revenue.

Matti Tenhunen was selected by the Central Committee of the Communist Party in Moscow to head the KTA, and plans for the recruitment of the North American Communist Finns began immediately.

THE WIN-WIN SOLUTION

In December 1929 when Matti Tenhunen and John Wiita were summoned to Moscow to explain the failed takeover of the CCE, Edvard Gylling was preparing to petition Stalin for permission to recruit more Communist Finns to Karelia as part of Stalin's First Five-Year Plan. Stalin acquiesced, and the Sixteenth Party Congress voted during the summer of 1930 to "expand the practice of drawing workers and specialists from abroad." Gylling could now recruit North American Communist Finn workers and expand Karelia's Finnish population.[1]

Karelian Technical Aid (KTA) was designed to bring much-needed money, skilled workers, supplies, and equipment to Soviet Russia as well as Karelia, and it was officially sanctioned by the Comintern and the Communist Party of the Soviet Union. After Matti Tenhunen was expelled from the CCE, he worked as an editor for a communist newspaper in New York City. Tenhunen then left for Soviet Russia in February 1931 where the communist leaders in Moscow ordered him to organize the KTA with its headquarters in New York City.

The North American Communist Finns had no idea that they had been caught in a maelstrom created by the powerful forces in Russia, who were aided by very charismatic, very trusted agents in North America. As the seemingly eager-to-help but pernicious influences of Karelian Fever reached the Finnish communities, they were enthusiastically embraced by thousands of Communist Finns.

The communist leaders in Moscow entrusted Matti Tenhunen with many responsibilities, and he didn't disappoint them. Tenhunen was able to satisfy both Stalin's and Gylling's "wish lists" with the North American Communist Finns.

> ### THE COMMUNIST LEADERS' MANDATES FOR IMMIGRATION TO KARELIA[2]
> - Immigrants must have a communist ideology
> - Workers must arrive with knowledge and tools
> - Equipment could be brought custom-free into the country
> - Country could sell excess equipment at a higher price
> - Immigrants must travel at their own expense
> - Reimbursement of tool or machinery expense is two rubles per each dollar spent

10 KTA: PROMOTING KARELIAN FEVER

> *"The current Five-Year Plan called not only for machines but for skilled workers and, above all, dollars to Karelia, and a campaign was launched to induce Finns to settle and 'build socialism' there. An appeal backed by glowing promises was now directed at the Finnish-American community. Karelia Fever spread like wildfire. The victims of this propaganda were promised work, good wages, and housing. Destitute Finns were not accepted, but there was a welcome for those who possessed expensive tools, factories or workshops. They were persuaded to take all their movable property with them."*
>
> AINO KUUSINEN
> *The Rings of Destiny*

THE KTA OFFICES OPENED in New York City and Toronto, Ontario, on May 1, 1931, with Matti Tenhunen managing the New York City office and John Latva hired to manage the office in Toronto. The offices handled both the recruitment and preparations for immigration to Karelia. Advertisements in the FWF newspapers and other Communist Finn newspapers began appearing as soon as the offices opened, urging those interested in moving to Karelia to seek help from the KTA. Tenhunen began an early advertisement with, "Help is needed in lumber camps, river runs, saw mills, paper factories, fishing, agriculture, and construction." He went on to say that they, the Communist Finns, were urgently needed to keep Karelia from failing. He labeled the immigrants-to-be as valiant workers who would help the first-ever country of free and equal workers get on its feet.[3]

Fishermen, farmers, loggers, and construction workers were given

APPLYING FOR IMMIGRATION TO KARELIA

The first question asked on the immigrant application was how much the applicant could contribute to the KTA. Every family was asked to contribute at least $400, but some gave thousands of dollars. Private donations from non-immigrants also funded the KTA, as well as the commissions received by the shipping lines for each passenger.[4]

There were numerous fundraisers for the KTA in the Communist Finn halls, but the largest portion of funding was received by the immigrants to Karelia. In addition to the initial donation to the KTA, they were also urged to donate as much as they could to the "Machine Fund" and were told they would need no money in Karelia. Receipts for the Machine Fund donations were signed by Kalle Aronen and, later, Oscar Corgan.

The immigrants filled in the application forms and attached three passport photos and a doctor's certificate. Next, the local Finnish Workers Federation reviewed the application. The applicant's skills and political ideologies were important considerations. Reasons for refusals included excessive drinking, failure to sell their property before migrating, or not subscribing to the radical newspapers like the *Työmies*.[5] If the applicant was accepted, the Federation's officers signed the application and sent it to the KTA offices.

The referred applications were next considered by committees in New York City and Toronto. Frequently, preference was given to those who promised a generous donation to the Machine Fund. The application received final approval by three examiners who then sent the lists to the Labor Commissariat in Petrozavodsk, Karelia. By mid July 1931, Petrozavodsk had received nearly 700 applications.

The Labor Commissariat in Petrozavodsk confirmed the lists and sent them to Moscow for the final approval. Every family who immigrated to Karelia was counted as "1," so that number included the spouse and other family members. Young single adults were given top priority, because it was easier to find housing for a single person than a family.

Upon final approval, the communist leaders in Moscow issued the visas.[6]

LETTER OF APPROVAL FOR A DISTRICT 9 COUPLE

They have done good work in the Movement recently but have no basis of making a living. Have agreed to loan the Työmies [Society] one thousand dollars when they sell their home. Recommend transfer.[7]

a very high priority. Loggers, who were in great demand in Karelia, often brought trucks, axes, and tractors with them. Their technical skills were the most valued, because they generated income from timber sales to other European countries and supplied lumber needed for housing the thousands of immigrants awaiting approval to immigrate.

Farmers and fisherman were needed to provide food for the burgeoning population. Construction workers were essential. Printers and their equipment were also needed and welcomed.

Matti Tenhunen had been known as a popular and trusted figure throughout the Finnish community for many years, and he now urged those interested in Karelia who packed the Communist Finn halls to, "Dispose of your homes, your farms, whatever you have, and donate the money to Karelia. Hold on to enough to pay for your tickets. Our task is not to let the Finnish nation die... Karelia must be a homeland of the Finns."[8]

> **IN THE FINNISH WORKERS FEDERATION NEWSPAPERS, TENHUNEN WROTE:**
> I need to help train the local Karelian labor force.
> I can't be a burden to Karelia.
> I need to pay my own passage to Karelia.
> I must buy machines and tools from Amtorg.
> [Receipts from Amtorg allowed purchasers to receive refunds once the immigrants reached Karelia at a rate of 2 rubles per each U.S. dollar spent.]
> I must buy or bring the machines and tools that I will need.[9]

Thousands of Communist Finns listened to Matti Tenhunen speak, or they read the Finnish newspapers articles – most of which were written by John Wiita – filled with glowing accounts of how much better life was in Karelia. For many, it was the lifeline they had been seeking.

Later in 1931, before the ships began carrying eager Communist Finns to their new homeland, Matti Tenhunen, along with his wife and daughter, moved to Karelia.* Tenhunen had been charged with managing the Resettlement Administration in Petrozavodsk, which began in early October 1931. Among his many duties, he was responsible for finding housing and work for the arriving immigrants while continuing to oversee the KTA activities in North America. He answered directly to Edvard Gyyling, who answered to Otto Kuusinen on behalf of the communist leaders in Moscow.[10]

Portrait of Matti Tenhunen in Isheming, Michigan, prior to immigrating to Karelia.
IHRCA, Anderson Library, U of MN

On October 3, 1931, a group of Communist Finns left America for Karelia. Their farewell letter stated: "We the undersigned, leaving behind this country of capitalist exploitation, are headed for the Soviet Union where the working-class is in power and where it is building a socialist society. We appeal to you, comrades, who are staying behind, to rally round the communist slogans, to work efficiently to overthrow capitalism and create the foundation of a republic of labor."[11]

---

* Before moving to Karelia in 1931, Matti Tenhunen signed over all his American real estate and bank accounts to his son, Toivo Tenhune, who remained in America and adamantly opposed communist policies. The communist leaders viewed Tenhunen's decision very unfavorably but chose not to act immediately.[12]

Kalle Aronen replaced Matti Tenhunen in KTA's New York City office when Tenhunen moved to Karelia.* Aronen's job of coordinating Karelian immigrants arriving from all regions of America – setting up their lodging, overseeing their purchasing, and readying them for the voyage ahead – became increasingly busy thanks to the promoting efforts of the media and radical speakers. John Wiita, as Central Editor of the FWF, continuously filled the pages of the three FWF district newspapers with articles about the opportunities in Karelia and positive letters from Karelia.

The KTA set up "Karelian Committees" in Finnish communities throughout America and Canada who coordinated the recruitment of prospective émigrés. Speakers were an important aspect of the recruitment and circulated through the Finnish communities. The more dynamic speakers whipped audiences into a frenzy in revivalist-style meetings filling the Communist Finn halls before discussing life in Karelia and how to get there.

The best known activist speaker was Oscar Corgan, who quit his manager's job in Virginia, Minnesota, and moved into the Työmies building in Superior when the KTA was organized. Corgan, as well as Kalle Aronen and John Latva in Toronto, were registered as employees of the Karelian Resettlement Administration and reported to Matti Tenhunen and the Karelian leaders. From the beginning, the KTA had to be a self-sustaining organization, and income came from a variety of sources. Their salaries were paid from commissions received, in part, by fees charged by the Swedish American Lines, the shipping company used primarily by passengers immigrating to Karelia.** The commission paid to the KTA was $11.50 per adult and $5.75 per child.[13]

Oscar Corgan, who was also the KTA's top recruiter, traveled extensively and touted the glories of Karelia, what goals were being met, and how satisfied the workers were to be doing their fair share and helping Karelia. He spoke at the Waino Round Hall, then controlled by the Communist Finns, and at the communist hall in Oulu.

---

* Matti Tenhunen's advice to Aronen before leaving was to "recruit anyone with money."[14]

** The KTA received $60,000 from the Swedish American Lines during the early 1930s.[15]

CPUSA Alarmed at Karelian Fever

From the beginning of the KTA, the CPUSA was alarmed at the fervor shown by the Communist Finns – especially in District 9, which was heavily populated by Finns living in Michigan, Wisconsin, and Minnesota. The CPUSA feared that an excessive loss of Party members and skilled workers would harm America's Communist Movement. Their concerns began less than two months after the first immigrants reached Karelia, and the following excerpts were written in a 10-week period:

From the minutes of the District Secretariat on November 30, 1931: *The situation is becoming more serious as over 50 Party members have left within the last 6 months to our knowledge, and a large number are preparing to leave in the spring.*

From the District Committee minutes on December 30, 1931: *Lost 75 to 100 members, gone to Karelia....*

From a letter to Aino Kuusinen (aka A. Morton) on January 28, 1932: *We again want to call to your attention that something drastic must be done about the Karelian migration. As far as this district is concerned, there are more than 50 Party members preparing to leave in the spring... From one small community, 15 comrades are planning to go....*

To the Party's Organization Department on February 9, 1932: *We were informed that 22 left from Brantwood* [a small community in northern Wisconsin].

Another report stated that cities were experiencing the liquidation of Party and hall activities as the Communist Finns scrambled to leave for Karelia.[16] Many people planning to leave were the most active members in their local communist parties.

(The April 6, 1931, minutes of the Oulu and Waino Leftist Cooperative People's meeting at the Oulu workers' hall mentions, *"For the opening ceremony it was announced that Oscar Corgan was coming as speaker."*)

Corgan's young daughter Mayme often accompanied her father to the meetings and remembered, "The Finn Halls were always lit up, the smell of hot coffee wafted out into the night, and the Finns showed up from miles around to hear Father speak. Outside there were cars and horses waiting, and inside there was someone to lead my father to the platform and introduce him to the crowd. A meeting would typically last for hours."

Oscar Corgan's message was consistent: "Karelia needs you. It needs strong workers who know how to chop trees and build houses and grow food. Isn't that what we Finns have been doing in the United States for the past 30 years? And wouldn't it be wonderful to do the same work in a country that needs you, a country where there is no ruling class, no rich industrialists or kings or czars to tell you what to do? Just workers toiling together for the common good."[17]

The Communist Finn halls were a lucrative source of income for the Machine Fund as well as the KTA, even if everyone listening to Oscar Corgan wasn't planning to leave America. Thousands, though, were tired of being exploited by greedy employers, or were unemployed with no hope of a job anytime soon. Some missed the family they had left in Finland and liked the thought of living in Karelia, close to the Old Country. The radical revolutionaries in the crowds were eager to live in a communist country where everyone was an equal.

Oscar Corgan told his energized audiences that the KTA would take care of everything – arrange their travel overseas, help them buy their needed tools and supplies, and make sure they had a place to stay in New York City until they departed for Karelia. Corgan also warned people that life in Karelia might be primitive for a while – like it was when areas in America and Canada were first settled with no running water or electricity. There would be plenty of work for everyone, though, and it was only a matter of time before everything was running smoothly. Corgan often spoke late into the night, well after the meeting was over, to individuals or small groups who wanted more specific information.

There were going away parties. During warm weather at outdoor farewell picnics with radical speeches and programs, friends and family members said good-bye to many they would never see again. There were tears but also much excitement for the new adventure that lay across the ocean. The Communist Finn halls hosted many of the organized activities. In 1932, Oscar Corgan spoke at the Mesaba Park* at a gathering for departing Communist Finns.[18]

By early 1932, Matti Tenhunen** realized the Resettlement Administration couldn't meet the demands of finding housing and jobs for the thousands of immigrants arriving in Petrozavodsk from North America, and Kalle Aronen left the KTA office in New York City and became Tenhunen's assistant in the Resettlement Administration. Oscar Corgan replaced Aronen in March 1932.

Matti Tenhunen and Edvard Gylling managed the influx of workers to Karelia, and there was nothing but continuously positive news in the North American communist newspapers – most of which was funneled from Otto Kuusinen in Moscow to John Wiita. Gylling was getting the Communist Finn workers that he wanted. The Resettlement Administration's Machine Fund was bringing much-needed equipment and money to Karelia and Moscow's communist organizations, and commissions from the shipping lines and stores

---

*Land for the Mesaba Co-op Park near Hibbing, MN was purchased in 1928 for $2,000 by 40 Communist Finn organizations. The 160-acre parcel included a 52-acre lake and, over the years, a pavilion and other buildings were constructed. In 1930, a 4-day celebration of the park's opening included "the well-known radical activist speaker Oscar Corgan."[19]

Activities at the park were similar to those hosted at the Co-op Park in Brule, WI. Mayme Corgan became a Young Pioneer when she attended summer camp at the Mesaba Co-op Park. Mayme's red kerchief, which she received there, signified her membership in the Young Pioneer Communists.[20]

**In August 1932, Matti Tenhunen left Karelia for America and stopped in Finland, where he was promptly arrested. Tenhunen's son, Toivo, learned of the arrest from a representative of the Swedish American Line and travelled to Moscow and sought Otto Kuusinen's help. Kuusinen arranged for Tenhunen's release through a prisoner exchange. Kuusinen emphasized to Toivo how vital his father was to the KTA. Tenhunen was released from the Finnish prison in January 1933.

in New York City were making the KTA more than self-sufficient, as it needed to be. So a letter sent from the Party's Organization Department to District 9 (which included the western Lake Superior region) did little to slow the exodus of Communist Finns: "We may advise you that the comrades across [in Soviet Russia] have once again asked us to be very firm with applicants for transfer. We cannot issue transfers to any except those who can prove to us that they have a job waiting for them there."21

Some did have concerns, though, about the countless ships traveling from the East Coast and filled with enthusiastic workers and their families. In 1932, John Wiita traveled to Petrozavodsk on business. While there, he met with Yrjö Sirola, who was then working in Karelia. The two friends talked all night about the astonishing Finnish immigration to Karelia. Both felt the Finns, with their higher standard of living, would have difficulties with the Karelian hardships. Back in America, Wiita followed up on his concerns. In the CPUSA minutes on November 19, 1932, John Wiita declared that, "It is time to speak the truth about it [Karelia]." After Wiita's statement, the Comintern ordered, in mid 1933, that Wiita be expelled from all Finnish work in the CPUSA and FWF.22

Aino Kuusinen had been ordered to America by the communist leaders in Moscow during the height of Karelian Fever and was alarmed by the misinformation that was being proliferated to the Communist Finns. In her memoirs she wrote: "I had visited many of these Finnish-Americans and had admired their secure, comfortable way of life. What could Karelia offer them? A wretched fate awaited them, and how would their children survive the food shortage? I knew only too well that people were starving and that even in Petrozavodsk, the capital, these newcomers would not get enough to eat or find decent places to live.

"I did try once or twice to warn people I knew well what a miserable place Karelia was, but my words fell on deaf ears. One of my friends simply replied, 'I am sure we can adapt to conditions there. We're going to live there and build up socialism.' One woman bought a crate full of electrical appliances and said proudly, 'I will fill up an electric kitchen there.' I thought to myself, *you'll be lucky to have a kitchen of any kind.*

"Gorin* got wind of my attempts to warn people... I received a letter from Edvard Gylling, the President of the Karelia, complaining of my conduct and requesting me to cease dissuading the Finns. He needed the immigrants and their property so as to carry out the plan, which he described in detail, to make Karelia a flourishing community."[23]

Aino Kuusinen, after receiving the warning from Gylling for not promoting the Karelian exodus and attempting to control the affairs within the Communist Finn communities, was ordered back to Moscow. She also voiced her concerns to Otto Kuusinen, who refused to listen. Getting equipment, skilled workers, and money to Karelia was all-important.

Most emigrants typically stayed in New York City for about two weeks before sailing to Karelia, and most of that time was spent in preparing for their new lives. They were encouraged to stay in specific rooming houses, which charged higher fees. Special sales were offered in specific stores where the emigrants were urged to buy supplies and tools that would be needed in Karelia. The KTA received a commission for both the lodging and sales. One émigré noted, "Aronen fussed around us...shepherding his lambs so that they could not break out of the pen...."

Emigrants were also encouraged to donate whatever they could for those left behind and still suffering the tyranny of capitalism. Most of them bought bright red handkerchiefs for waving goodbye – sold by the KTA for 75 cents.

It was an exciting time and a happy time, and the Communist Finns were eager participants who were more than ready to begin their new lives. While gathering at the port terminals, the departing

---

*Communist Party members often traveled using aliases. Kuusinen's memoir refers to Gorin as a "wily agent" and the person who employed Oscar Corgan. The author believes Gorin may have been Matti Tenhunen, who would have needed an alias if he traveled to America on business.

groups sang labor songs and waved their new red handkerchiefs. They shouted slogans against the capitalists while praising Karelia and Soviet Russia.

By the beginning of 1934, it was clear that the KTA had served its purpose. The need for new workers had dwindled, and Petrozavodsk was having trouble finding housing and bringing in enough supplies needed by the immigrants. Word was received from Karelia that no additional workers were needed, and the KTA office in New York City closed on April 2, 1934, officially ending the Karelian recruiting. On April 4, Oscar Corgan, his wife Katri, and their children Mayme, Paul, and Aino sailed for Karelia.

The Communist Finns left homes they had often built with their own hands, and the Finn halls they had helped build for everyone in the community. They left the communities where their children had played and where many of their like-minded friends, relatives, and neighbors still lived. They knew their skills and capabilities, and they knew what they needed to do to build new homes, and new Finn halls, and new communities. They had the experience, the ability, and the enthusiasm, and it wouldn't take long to build their new lives in a land where they were wanted, and they wouldn't need to strike for better working conditions and be blacklisted so they couldn't work at all. No one in their new land would persecute, scorn, or ridicule them for their political beliefs. Everyone was free and equal, and success in their new homeland – Karelia – was all but guaranteed.

A DEAFENING SILENCE

Tens of thousands of Communist Finns still remained in North America after the KTA offices closed and the last ship sailed for Karelia. Some stayed in America and Canada because, despite the ongoing Great Depression, they had a relatively good life. Some remained because family members – who may have already emigrated from Finland – refused to leave. Others did not have sufficient financial resources, and their applications for moving to Karelia had been rejected.

For those still in America and Canada, the Communist Finn newspapers were filled with reports of Karelia's continuing successes. Letters from the North American Finns in Karelia initially expressed optimism – things were improving, but slower than expected. It was plausible to believe, then, that the increasing silence from their friends and family members in Karelia was because they were busy building the country, as they had vowed to do. Writing letters took time from their work, they reasoned, plus there was probably no extra money for postage.

Most historians agree that some 10,000 Communist Finns "caught" Karelian Fever and left North America for a capitalist-free life in Karelia. When Oscar Corgan closed the New York City's KTA office and left for the Workers' Paradise, he was the seventh of the eight influential Red Finn activists who had relocated to Soviet Russia. Only John Wiita remained in America.

Karelian Fever ended with the closing of the KTA offices and, shortly after, Joseph Stalin fortified his country's borders with heavily armed guards – effectively sealing the immigrant Communist Finns from the rest of the world. The CPUSA and Finnish Workers Federation, after receiving orders from the communist leaders in Moscow, suppressed all rumors and adverse reports coming from Karelia. All personal letters were confiscated or heavily censored. And after 1938, speaking of Stalin's appalling atrocities became a punishable crime.

11 THE DOOR CLOSED

The citizens of Karelia were silenced....

WORLD WAR II

In September 1939, World War II began when Adolf Hitler's Nazi Germany invaded Poland. One by one, the European countries fell before the Nazi invasions during the following years until many believed there was no stopping Hitler.

Joseph Stalin attacked Finland's eastern border on November 30, 1939, in an attempt to acquire additional territory. The Winter War lasted less than four months with the Finns incurring 70,000 casualties. Stalin's losses were five times greater, and the Soviet Union was expelled from the League of Nations for its aggression. Hitler viewed the Winter War as a sign of the Red Army's weakness and invaded the Soviet Union in June 1941 in a campaign code-named Operation Barbarossa. Casualties in the brutal conflict totaled some 6 million and launched the Allied coalition, which included the Soviet Union, against Hitler and his Axis allies.

Japan, an Axis ally of Germany, attacked America's naval fleet at Pearl Harbor on December 7, 1941, and America immediately entered World War II as a member of the Allied Forces. After joining countries including Great Britain, Canada, Australia, and the Soviet Union, the Allies slowly began forcing Hitler and his Axis allies into retreat from the lands they had conquered and claimed as their own.

The overwhelming might of the Allies' air offenses made the outcome of World War II a foregone conclusion, but it wasn't until the European countries had endured massive destruction of their infrastructure, buildings, and economies – and Japan sustained the explosions of atomic bombs on Hiroshima and Nagasaki – that World War II came to an end in August 1945.

American President Franklin D. Roosevelt, who had led Americans through the Great Depression and World War II, died shortly before the war in Europe ended. By then, Adolf Hitler was dead, too, having committed suicide rather than be tried for the horrific war crimes and unspeakable Holocaust atrocities committed during his reign.

The Holocaust ended with Nazi Germany's unconditional surrender on May 7, 1945, but not before nearly six million European Jews had lost their lives. Historians believe that approximately three million of those who died were exterminated in the camps controlled by members of Hitler's Third Reich. Torture, starvation, and disease took many more.

World War II remains the world's deadliest military conflict. Over 60 million people died worldwide, including both military personnel and civilians, with some casualty estimates going as high as 85 million. Of this total, the country with the greatest loss of life was the Soviet Union with between 20 and 27 million casualties. Germany's death toll is estimated to be 5.7 million people. The American casualty total is some 419,400.*

---

* (en.wikipedia.org/wiki/World_War_II_casualties)

From Karelia, there was only silence....

THE COLD WAR AND IRON CURTAIN

The term "Cold War" was first used in 1945 and referred to the tense relationship between America and the Soviet Union. Even though the two countries had fought as part of the Allied Forces during World War II, America had a long history of mistrust for the communist country as well as concerns about Stalin's tyrannical rule and the rumors of murders on a massive scale. On the other hand, Stalin blamed America's late entry into the war for the tens of millions of Soviet citizens who lost their lives during World War II.

In 1947, the U.S. Congress held a series of hearings to prove that communist subversion was still active in America. To contain the threat of communist expansion, the American government instituted a policy of "patient but firm and vigilant containment" against "Russian aggressive tendencies."

By 1948, Americans were aware that Stalin probably had agents working within the government's nuclear program, but it wasn't until 1949 that Klaus Fuchs, a German-born communist, was charged with the theft of nuclear secrets. Fuchs had begun passing America's atomic bomb secrets to Moscow in 1945. He was caught and confessed after British Intelligence cracked a Russian code and was sentenced to 14 years in prison.

On June 19, 1953, the only two American civilians to be executed for espionage during the Cold War died in the electric chair. Julius Rosenberg and his wife, Ethel, were charged with passing top-secret nuclear weapon designs and other highly classified information to the Soviet Union. They had met in the Young Communist League in 1936 and married in 1939. Julius, an electrical engineer, was 35 when he died. Ethel, a former actress and singer, was 37.

The Cold War, nuclear destruction, and the spread of communism were constant fears for decades as the American government struggled to contain the spread of communism. The containment strategy more or less remained in effect until the Soviet Union's break-up decades later. The strategy was also the rationale behind a large increase in America's defense spending and the start of the decades-long Arms Race between America and the Soviet Union.

Shortly after World War II ended, Joseph Stalin politically and ideologically sealed the Soviet Union and other Eastern European communist countries from the West and other noncommunist countries. The Iron Curtain, as it was named, was first mentioned by British Prime Minister Winston Churchill during a speech in 1946 when he said, "...an Iron Curtain has descended across the continent."

Stalin wished to seal the communist countries from the West in part to conceal the atrocities he had committed as the absolute leader of the Soviet Union, and partly to prohibit the spread of democratic ideologies. Deaths attributable to Stalin vary widely, but the consensus of most historians is that some 20 million Soviet citizens perished from executions, famine, brutal work conditions, and torture during Stalin's regime. The Iron Curtain also prevented the citizens of the Soviet Union, Eastern Germany, and other communist countries from escaping to the West.

From Karelia, the silence continued....

THE "RED SCARE"

In 1950, Washington, D.C., was consumed by an anti-communist fervor known as the "Red Scare." It began in February 1950 when Wisconsin's Republican Senator Joseph McCarthy claimed, "I have here in my hand a list of two hundred and five people that were known to the Secretary of State as being members of the Communist Party and who nevertheless are still working and shaping the policy of the State Department."[1]

Without naming a single person, McCarthy also stated that 81 members of the U.S. Congress were chumming around with communists, making them "loyalty risks." McCarthy then began an anti-communist crusade and cast himself as an unrelenting patriot and protector of American values. His enemies claimed he destroyed the careers and trampled on the civil liberties of actors, artists, and politicians who he accused of being communists and anti-American.

After he was re-elected to the U.S. Senate in 1952, Joseph McCarthy became chair of the Senate's Subcommittee on Investigations and widened his hunt for communists. For the next two years he fanned the Red Scare flames, interviewing countless witnesses. He was, however, never able to substantiate any claims whatsoever.

Drew Pearson, a well-known radio host and newspaper columnist, was a victim of McCarthy's communist accusations. He lost listeners and sponsorships for his radio show before being found not guilty of all charges. Later, he published scathing articles against McCarthy and his methods of ferreting out supposed communists.

McCarthy's downfall began in October 1953 when he started investigating the "communist infiltration in the military," and President Eisenhower realized McCarthy needed to be stopped. A 36-day televised hearing in 1954 exposed McCarthy for overstepping his authority. He was condemned on the Senate floor on December 2, 1954, and stripped of his chairmanship. "McCarthyism" was named for Senator McCarthy's panic-inspiring witch hunts and the irrational fear of communism that spread through America from coast to coast.

During the 1950s, the Red Scare arrived in northwestern Wisconsin when government agents stopped at a small grocery store in Oulu, Wisconsin, and demanded a list of local communists. Shortly after, the local Communist Finns held one final meeting in a member's basement in Waino before quietly dispersing.[2]

It was now over 20 years since the last ships carrying the Communist Finns had crossed the Atlantic Ocean, bound for their new lives in Karelia. Memories of the friends and family members who had forsaken America slowly faded as the older generation in North America passed and the younger generation married, had children of their own, and forged new friendships as they dealt with their everyday lives.

∞

At the age of 74, Joseph Stalin died from a cerebral hemorrhage on March 5, 1953. The tensions caused by the Iron Curtain relaxed somewhat under Nikita Khruschev's leadership but increased once again when the Berlin Wall was built and Khruschev's terrifying statement, "We will bury you," reverberated throughout America.

From Karelia...still silence....

THE SPACE RACE

On October 4, 1957, the Soviet Union launched *Sputnik*, the world's first satellite, and the Space Race began. The launch came as an unpleasant surprise to America, which had struggled to keep up with the Soviet Union's space program. In 1958, America launched its first satellite, and President Dwight Eisenhower authorized the creation of the National Aeronautics and Space Administration (NASA). The Soviet Union remained one step ahead of America, though, when it launched its first man into space in April 1961. One month later, America successfully launched astronaut Alan Shepard into space in *Freedom 7*, a Project Mercury capsule.

The 1960s in America were marked by the continuing threat of communist infiltration into the western hemisphere, assassinations, civil rights struggles, and the Vietnam War. The Bay of Pigs invasion in 1961 and the Cuban missile crisis in 1962 confirmed that the communist threat was less than 100 miles from American soil. Millions of American students learned how to survive a nuclear attack, and nuclear shelters were provided in countless public buildings in every state.

The political and civil unrest of the 1960s contributed to the high-profile assassinations of President John Kennedy, Senator Robert Kennedy, Malcolm X, and Dr. Martin Luther King Jr. Riots, civil rights marches, demonstrations for women's rights, and anti-war protests filled the nightly news broadcasts.

America's "containment of communism" strategy that had begun after World War II was tested in Southeast Asia when North Vietnam – backed by the Soviet Union – invaded the anti-communist country of South Vietnam. What began as an American commitment to support the South Vietnamese government in the 1950s spiraled into a war lasting into the 1970s. During that time, America sent some 2,594,000 soldiers to South Vietnam. There were more than 58,000 deaths.

The USSR experienced a coup in October 1964, and Nikita Khruschev was replaced by hard-liner Leonid Brezhnev. Citizens in the Soviet Union soon feared the return of Stalin's repressive years, but Brezhnev's regime became one of economic stagnation, corruption, and inefficiency while he strengthened USSR's political standing in the Middle East and Africa.

The technological gap between America and the USSR widened during Brezhnev's 18-year reign, and tensions between the two superpowers increased. The American-Soviet Space Race effectively ended on July 20, 1969, when American astronaut Neil Armstrong became the first man in history to walk on the moon.

The American-Soviet Arms Race slowed significantly during the presidency of Richard Nixon (who also became the first American president to resign while in office). Nixon is credited with signing the Strategic Arms Limitation Treaty in 1972, which took a step toward reducing the threat of nuclear war by prohibiting the manufacture of nuclear missiles in America and the Soviet Union.

From Karelia...continued silence....

THE ERA OF *GLASNOST*

Over 50 years had now passed since the last ship filled with enthusiastic, idealistic Communist Finns sailed from North America. Tensions between America and the Soviet Union had slowly eased with the end of the Arms Race and Space Race. Still in the future was the dismantling of Germany's Berlin Wall, the break-up of the Soviet Union, and the end of communism as Karl Marx, Vladimir Lenin, and Joseph Stalin had envisioned it.

In 1985, Mikhail Gorbachev became the General Secretary of the Soviet Communist Party. Born in 1931, Gorbachev was barely a teenager during World War II and had only a faint recollection of the beginnings of the Iron Curtain and Cold War. His policies of *glasnost* (openness) and *perestroika* (restructuring) calmed America's fears that communism's ultimate goal was the complete destruction of every capitalist country in the world. Fears of nuclear war eased, too, and the hands of friendship were tentatively extended between the two super-powers.

THE DOOR SLOWLY SLID OPEN

The year after Gorbachev began leading the Communist Party down a more peaceful path, a train slowly chugged into Petrozavodsk and ground to a halt at the station. On board was a group of 33 American men and women from Duluth, Minnesota. On that early fall day in 1986, the passengers had enjoyed their scenic ride as the train passed through vast, seemingly endless far-northern forests broken by sparkling lakes and streams that reminded them of northern Minnesota. Gradually, the forests had become dotted with an increasing number of houses before revealing the outskirts of the Karelian capital.

Now the Duluthians anxiously peered out of the train's windows, hoping there would be someone, anyone, in Petrozavodsk who could understand and speak English. The City of Duluth had recently made Petrozavodsk its Sister City, and the Duluthians had been entrusted with forging ties with Petrozavodsk's citizens. Previous communication attempts had all gone unanswered, but they had ultimately decided to proceed with their plans.

As the train approached its final destination, the Duluthians noticed a small group of people excitedly waving, laughing, and smiling broadly while obviously waiting impatiently for the train to stop. As the heavy metal door slowly slid open and the travelers tentatively stepped from the train, waves of shock and surprise rippled through every single one of them. *The waiting crowd was greeting them in perfect American English!*

Who were these complete strangers, where had they come from, and what were they doing in Petrozavodsk?

Finally, the silence ended.

THE DAWN OF REALITY

When the Communist Finns defiantly sailed from the North American shores in the early 1930s, bound for Karelia, they were filled with high hopes and dreams. They were determined to help build a country filled with hard working, like-minded people who were all equal.

Upon arrival, though, many were disappointed with what they found. Some returned to the Finnish communities they had rejected, but many relocated to a different area in America or Canada to avoid further ridicule and scorn. Others returned but refused to speak of what they had witnessed. But most immigrants remained in Karelia, confident that they were helping to improve their new homeland. Those immigrants endured the full force of Joseph Stalin's Great Terror.

Most of the adult immigrants who remained in Karelia were never heard from again.

12

THE JOURNEY TO KARELIA

> "We the undersigned, leaving behind this country of capitalistic exploitation, are headed for the Soviet Union where the working class is in power and where it is building a socialistic society. We appeal to you, comrades who are staying behind, to rally around communist slogans, to work efficiently to overthrow capitalism and create the foundation of a Republic of Labor."
>
> From a Communist Finn newspaper

MOST OF THE THOUSANDS of Communist Finns bound for Karelia bought passage on the Swedish American Line (SAL) and left North America from New York City or Halifax, Canada. Their journeys across the Atlantic Ocean were usually on the *Kungsholm*, *Drottningholm*, or *Gripsholm* and ended in Goteborg, on Sweden's southwestern peninsula. From there they boarded trains and travelled across Sweden to Stockholm. Smaller ships then took them from Stockholm east over Baltic Sea to the Gulf of Finland. Their voyage ended in Leningrad.

The Communist Finns liked to wear red to show their "redness," and most of them waved to all passersby with the red kerchiefs they had purchased before they left North America. As they departed, many sent or published optimistic farewell letters or cards to the friends and relatives they left behind.

Others sent cables from the ships, expressing their rebellious emotions as they left America and Canada: "Down with capitalist exploitation! Down with capitalist wars! Long live the Soviet Union and the World Revolution!"

Another cable from a group who departed in July 1932 stated: "Expressing the opinion of our group about information based on news received from the Soviet Union and Karelia, which mainly touches upon the difficulties, obstacles, and deficiencies in Karelia, to which we are bound, we express our readiness to accept the obligations set before us by the Karelian and Soviet governments; we unanimously promise to subject ourselves to the decisions adopted by the central organs... In practical constructional labor devoted to the development of the Soviet Union, we pledge to do our best, regardless of conditions... We promise to behave in a comradely fashion with one another in work and leisure... We promise to fight for the Soviet Union and for the exploited working class of the whole world, for victory of the world revolution."[1]

"Great! Wonderful! Exciting!" were the memories of many teens on board the ships steaming east to Europe. The adults, after upending their lives, wanted their children's journey to be as pleasant as possible. Activities much like they had experienced in the Finn halls at home – including plays, dances, and games – were scheduled to keep the children occupied. Many wrote complimentary letters afterward to SAL for their excellent food and service.

In Leningrad, many of the new Soviet citizens willingly gave up their passports while waiting for the train that would take them on the final leg of their journey. Other Communist Finns suddenly realized that various customs agents had confiscated their personal possessions, tools, and equipment they needed in Karelia. Most of them never saw their possessions again.

The typical stay in Leningrad was a few days before a train took the North American immigrants on their journey of just over 200 miles. Along the way, the mostly untamed northern wilderness was occasionally broken by a small town, and one town, about two-thirds of the way to Petrozavodsk, was Olonets.

Olonets is a village in southern Karelia, and just over one mile from Olonets was the land assigned to the immigrants from Cobalt, Canada, in 1925 for their commune known as Säde, "The Ray of Light."

In October 1925, the first Cobalt residents had arrived in Karelia to secure a location for their commune. They were assigned an area that was about 650 acres of what was a virtual wasteland and 15 acres of an old overgrown field.

At first, rain water was collected for their needs and was their only water source. There were no nearby rivers or lakes for water, but the new Karelian citizens later found two small ponds on their land. The winter of 1925 and spring of 1926 were spent cutting large trees and hauling nearly 3,000 logs to the area they had chosen for Säde's future building site.

The next group of Cobalt residents, including Elis and Emma Ahokas and their daughter Vieno, prepared for their journey to Karelia in April 1926. Everyone was limited to one steamer trunk, which was filled with necessary clothing and household items. A train took them to Halifax in Nova Scotia, where their two-week journey across the Atlantic Ocean began. After spending a few days in London, the travelers journeyed across the North Sea and Baltic Sea and into the Gulf of Finland. Next, they travelled north by train from Leningrad.* Horse-drawn carts transported them on the last leg of their journey, passing a few small villages along the Olonka River. All the houses in Karelia were built of logs at that time, and most families had a sauna near the river bank.

The commune members arrived in Olonets, Karelia, on May 1, 1926. No buildings had been completed yet at Säde, so the commune members were temporarily given living quarters in the second story of a building with no furniture. There was no electricity in the building. Mattresses filled with straw were laid on the floor for sleeping. There was an outdoor privy. The commune members

---

*Petrograd was renamed Leningrad in 1924 after Vladimir Lenin's death. In 1991, Leningrad was renamed St. Petersburg.

ADVICE TO THOSE DEPARTING FOR SOVIET KARELIA

"…We bear responsibility only for donations to the MACHINE FUND. On the basis of a KTA receipt you are entitled to be reimbursed in keeping with the Soviet exchange rate. The Karelian Resettling Management is responsible for this reimbursement.

When you come to the USSR border, declare all your money to the customs officials. They will confirm your currency and there's no danger of anybody taking it away from you… At present in the Soviet Union and in Karelia you can buy goods in the foreign currency stores which are probably not available in rubles… Beware of exchanging foreign currency with anyone else as it is strictly forbidden… Selling goods to private persons is also forbidden: You have been granted customs-free entrance as you are bringing in goods only for YOUR OWN PERSONAL needs.

Comradely greetings,

The Soviet Karelian Technical Aid"[2]

walked over a mile each way every day until they finally moved to Säde later in 1926.

The 15-acre old field was plowed and seeded that first summer using a tractor they had purchased in Canada and brought with them. The tractor – a Canadian Fordson – was the first tractor ever seen in Karelia. Hay and clover were planted for the animals. Potatoes, usually the first subsistence crop, were planted for the commune members. A sauna was built and used for the first time to celebrate *Juhannus*,* the celebration of midsummer, in late June.

By early November in 1926, the Säde commune members were living on their land. A large log building housed everyone, and furniture built from the lumber they had logged filled the building. A large iron stove they had bought in Canada provided heat and was used for cooking. The Ahokas family – Elis, Emma, and Vieno – was assigned a second-floor room with a table, three stools, and two beds. The commune had also built a barn big enough for two cows and three horses – the beginning of their successful farm. The members of Säde were on their land and ready to face their first winter together.

Every day was a work day, and everyone was assigned tasks according to their skills. One of the women was a laundress and was tasked with washing and ironing everyone's clothes. Another woman watched the children, and the other women cooked, cleaned the house, and took care of the animals. The men maintained the equipment, logged, and worked the fields. There was no idle time. Everyone worked where necessary if they finished their assigned tasks.

Morning began about 6:30 when a gong announced that breakfast was ready. Everyone ate together at three long handmade tables and usually ate a breakfast of porridge, milk, and rye bread. A meat soup,

---

* Scandinavians have celebrated midsummer – when the daylight is at its peak and weeks of long days and warm weather lie ahead – since pagan times. Until the dawn of Christianity, Finns worshipped the pagan god Ukko, hoping for fertility as well as good weather and growth for their crops. In Finland as well as Finnish communities worldwide, the midsummer celebration, now a combination of pagan and Christian rituals, is known as *Juhannus*.

In the early 1900s, the northern Wisconsin communities of Waino and Oulu began *Juhannus* by thoroughly sweeping the yard with leafy birch branches. Then every family dressed in their Sunday best and met in the community's center to welcome summer with food and festivities.

milk, and rye bread was served at noon, and potatoes or casseroles with milk and bread were served at 6:00 in the evening. After the meal, the commune members usually gathered in the common room talking, reading, playing games, or listening to the radio, which was a gift from Edvard Gylling's Karelian government.

The Säde commune members raised mainly root crops – potatoes, onions, carrots, and beets – although cabbage was also grown successfully. Because of the short growing season and cool climate, there were no fruit trees in Karelia.

The Säde members believed that every ruble mattered and their time was valuable. Discipline and order were also very important. Their hard work was rewarded with a gold medal and a car in 1930, and their chairman said, "In Canada, deep underground in the mines, we often dreamed of fresh air, of the smell of freshly plowed earth, of growing and harvesting crops. Now our dreams have come true and we are very happy."

Säde was a community free of capitalist oppression, certainly "The Ray of Light," but it came to know horrors far worse than the capitalism they had left behind.

After the long train ride through the Karelian wilderness, the first impressions the immigrants had of Petrozavodsk were of shockingly harsh living conditions. The communist recruiters in America and Canada had painted visual images of a modern city with wide, paved streets. Instead, the travelers saw no high-rise buildings. Petrozavodsk in the early 1930s was a small dirty town with cobblestones on only about a quarter of the streets. There were a few streetlights but no paved sidewalks. After a rain or snow, the unpaved streets became muddy paths with deep ruts. Cows and goats freely grazed within the town, and horses provided the main transportation source. Buses and taxis were nonexistent.

The reality of Karelia didn't correspond at all with what the recruiters had promised and, after noting the stark conditions, many Communist Finns never unpacked their belongings but inquired about the next train back to Leningrad. They refused to turn over their papers required to register for employment or lodging. Many only wished to return to America or Canada as soon as possible and hoped they still had enough money and could afford the cost. They felt fortunate to have kept their passports.

The majority of the Communist Finns, however, viewed their new home with an unbending stoicism. Many of them had given their life's savings to the Machine Fund or bought the equipment they had been told they would need. They had willingly given up their passports and were now citizens of Soviet Russia. They had immigrated to help build Karelia, and they knew that with hard work, they would make a difference. Horse-drawn carts took the new immigrants from the train station to the barracks where most of them would live for a long time.

FAILURE IS NOT AN OPTION

Edvard Gylling's vision of a Red Finland in Soviet Russia continued to take shape. Enthusiastic Communist Finns brought the skills and equipment he needed to meet the goals of Joseph Stalin's First Five-Year Plan. The Resettlement Administration, headed by Matti Tenhunen, seemed to be overwhelmed by the immigrants who all needed food and shelter, but Moscow was very satisfied with the financial success of the Machine Fund. Housing was a problem that would be eased as the immigrants settled in, gradually built new homes for their families, and focused on Karelia's needs.

"We had a dream." Lawrence and Sylvia Hokkanen were doing well in Michigan during the Great Depression but believed the fervent recruiters like Oscar Corgan, who told them an even better life awaited them in Karelia. The spirits of all the immigrants were high in the first months after they arrived, and the difficulties were met with an undaunted willingness to pitch in and help the new country. It was understood that housing was of secondary concern. Working for the common good — building schools, hospitals, factories, and utility systems — were their primary goals.

The Communist Finn immigrants believed that the seemingly overwhelming hardships could be overcome only by true communists. If anyone dared complain, the attitude was, "Let those who grumble go back to Capitalist America where nobody gives a damn about you."

13

LIFE IN KARELIA

> *"The rush to Utopia ended in a colossal tragedy, as it was bound to do."*
>
> AINO KUUSINEN
> *The Rings of Destiny*

IN PETROZAVODSK, NO NEW houses had been built since World War I and caused an immediate housing shortage when hundreds of North American Finns began flooding into the city every month. Two long log barracks called the *Valiparakit* were quickly constructed. Both two-story buildings had long hallways with eight rooms on each floor. At times, up to three families were crammed into one room. Cockroaches and bedbugs were rampant.

The buildings had no insulation, but each room contained a wood stove that was used for heat and cooking. There was a kitchen on each floor but no bathrooms. A community well provided water. During the long winters when the well froze repeatedly, axes were needed to chop out the ice. Wood sheds and outhouses were built between the buildings.

Living in the *Valiparakit* was considered to be temporary, and many families were shown lots where their permanent homes were to be built. All homes in Petrozavodsk were built of logs and, in the early 1930s, only one-quarter of them had electricity. The North American Finns gradually built the single-family homes as time allowed. The first running water was supplied to Petrozavodsk in 1933 from Lake Onega Bay by wooden water pipes.*

Shortly after the Resettlement Administration was established in October 1931, Insab and Torgsin stores came into being in Karelia.

---

* The wooden water pipes were not replaced with metal pipes until 1970.

Insab stores carried a higher quality food that was only available to immigrants, and the American Finns received an allowance for the Insab stores. It was believed that Petrozavodsk had the best Insab stores. (Edvard Gylling believed that the American Finns would adjust to their new lives in Karelia more readily if they had access to a higher quality food than the Russians and Karelians normally ate.) In the early 1930s, potatoes and bread were the typical staple foods. Fresh fruit and vegetables were unavailable. Many of the new arrivals became very ill because of the severe change in their diets, and long lines were typical sights at the doctors' offices.

Torgsin stores carried food of the highest quality, but only foreign currency, gems, gold, and silver were accepted for purchases. When the American Finns first arrived in Karelia, they were encouraged to donate all the money they still had and were told they would never need money again. Later, those U.S. dollars were crucial in the Torgsin stores for much-needed commodities.

The Karelian government provided state-owned canteens for meals. A typical lunch consisted of a thin soup and locally caught fish from Lake Onega.

Lawrence and Sylvia Hokkanen moved from Michigan and arrived in 1934. Living in Petrozavodsk, they had no indoor plumbing and poor quality food. Sylvia Hokkanen stated, "Of course we didn't expect to find wealth and material comforts, but we did feel that there would be an opportunity to work for a better life with a good chance of success." Lawrence was assigned to work in a factory. Sylvia became a teacher.

Most immigrants tried to make life as positive as possible by socializing with other Communist Finns. Schools and Finn halls were built. By 1932, there were two women's and two men's baseball teams. A choir was organized, and an orchestra comprised mainly of American immigrants performed at funerals, public gatherings, and dances. Actors in the Finnish Theater provided entertainment in Petrozavodsk and traveled to other Karelian cities and logging communities. Cross-country skiing and skating were popular winter sports.

Many North American immigrants were transitioned to other locations, but the vast majority stayed in Petrozavodsk. One Michigan man and his family were placed in a remote area after arriving and had vivid recollections of their lives in Karelia:

"I traveled with my wife and children on a ship of the Swedish American Line. Accommodations were luxurious but upon crossing the Russian border, everything changed. The food was such that as Americans we were in desperate straits. In one way or another the *kasha*, or buckwheat porridge, which we ate with olive oil because there was no milk, went down. At the logging camp we lived with several others families in a pigpen that had been converted into a barracks. Our American housewives got it into satisfactory condition, considering the situation.

"Because I was a carpenter I got better wages than many of the others who had no special trade. As long as the clothes and tools we had brought from America lasted, we were able to manage somehow. We were not permitted to build houses for ourselves... For the children's sake we tried to keep a cow, but the tax on it was so high that we could not afford it.

"The Americans and Canadians put the Karelian lumber industry on its feet, setting up loading and unloading equipment such as had never before been seen in Karelia. Once, when wages were not received for a long time, the Finns had a meeting and sent in a protest. Russian party bosses appeared on the scene and announced that party actions must not be criticized and demanded that the protest be revoked.

"After two years, the choice had to be made as to whether to become a citizen of Soviet Russia or leave the country. We returned to America by way of Finland. Those who had not succeeded in hiding their money were compelled to stay in Karelia because they were unable to pay for transportation."

Many Communist Finns who built factories or plants in record time were given Certificates of Commendation and prizes. Women worked in offices as typists or bookkeepers. They also worked as cleaners and cooks.

The best jobs in Karelia, however, were in the Resettlement Administration or with the Kirja Publishing Company. Matti Tenhunen headed the Resettlement Administration, and Kalle Aronen, who had preceded Oscar Corgan in New York City's KTA office, was his assistant. Tenhunen and Aronen were paid through the Machine Fund.

Matti Tenhunen lived a very busy life in Petrozavodsk. He was able to successfully coordinate all of the Karelian Technical Aid (KTA) activities from Petrozavodsk, and he was able to also run the Foreign Department of the Resettlement Administration, although he was barely settled in Petrozavodsk before the first American Finns arrived in October 1931. He was also the head of the Karelian Labor Department, tasked with assigning jobs to the immigrants.

The Machine Fund was part of the KTA. When immigrants to Soviet Karelia donated to the Machine Fund, equipment and supplies were usually bought before they arrived in Karelia, because there were no customs fees for personal belongings, supplies, and equipment brought into the country by the immigrants. Once the equipment arrived in Petrozavodsk, it was sold by the Resettlement Administration with 50 percent added to its original cost.

The receipts for the equipment were signed in New York City by Kalle Aronen and, later, by Oscar Corgan. Upon arrival the immigrants gave the receipts to the Karelian government. The Communist Finns were then eligible for compensation on their purchases, although compensation did not always happen. The compensation rate was two rubles for every U.S. dollar paid, even though the exchange rate should have been at least five times higher.

Men brought their tools and equipment to their work location, and it immediately became the property of that location. If the men voluntarily changed jobs, they had to leave what they'd brought with them, and they weren't reimbursed.

When Matti Tunhunen sold the Machine Fund's tools, equipment, and supplies for a higher price, Edvard Gylling wanted the proceeds to be primarily used for improving the immigrants' lives. Unfortunately, only a portion of the profits filtered down to the immigrants. Equipment and tools were needed for Stalin's First Five-Year Plan. Another large portion of the proceeds went to the communist leaders in Moscow. Also, from the start of KTA until the offices closed in 1934, the Machine Fund received a total of $162,146 in money and equipment, but an estimated $20,000 "disappeared."[1]*

---

*In today's dollars, donations to the Machine Fund were approximately $3,051,000. The unaccounted-for monies would be valued at approximately $375,000 in today's dollars.

The Machine Fund ended when the KTA offices closed in 1934. The income once generated by the direct financial donations and equipment sales were gone, and the first to be impacted were the immigrants who had been promised compensation for what they had brought with them. When the American Finns formed a commission and demanded to know where their compensation had been spent, Matti Tenhunen claimed that he hadn't kept the financial records.[2]

Another amount that was never accounted for was the approximate $10,000 U.S. dollars (today's value is approximately $187,500 U.S. dollars) "earned" by the Resettlement Administration for the under-reimbursement of the American Finns for the equipment they brought with them. The reimbursement they received (or should have received) was at least five times less than the exchange rate.

The Resettlement Administration also aggressively urged the immigrants to convert their U.S. dollars into tokens. They were told the tokens could be used in the torgsin stores, but that wasn't true. Matti Tenhunen and Kalle Aronen refused to issue any refunds, saying the immigrants had made the exchange willingly. Tenhunen then warned the complainers that anyone who returned to America and criticized life in Karelia would be branded traitors and not believed.[3]

The Corgan family arrived in Petrozavodsk on April 30, 1934. They had spent several days in Stockholm, Sweden, while waiting for a boat that would carry them to Leningrad. Then, the ride to Petrozavodsk had been a long, uncomfortable 18-hour train ride from Leningrad on hard wooden benches. Everyone in the Corgan family was relieved to finally reach their new home town.

Oscar Corgan and his family were given one room in a *Valiparakit*. Living in the *Valiparakit* was supposed to be temporary, but the Corgans were one of the last families to arrive in Petrozavodsk, and it became their home for the next two years.

They were given a monthly food ration card, and they were allowed to shop at the Insab store. Katri began making their one room into a home while caring for Aino. Mayme and Paul were soon enrolled in a Finnish school, and they were able to play again with some of the friends they had known in America.

Oscar donated a printing press that he had purchased in America to the Kirja Publishing Company and began working for them as a newspaper editor. He also began taking night classes to learn Russian. On most Saturdays, he joined other Finns and worked on needed community projects in Petrozavodsk such as sidewalks, plumbing, and housing.

Shortly after the Corgans began settling into their new lives in Karelia, Oscar met with Yrjö Sirola, who warned him to take his family back to America immediately. Oscar would not consider it, though. His family was adjusting well in Petrozavodsk. They were citizens of Soviet Russia now, and they were determined to build Karelia into a thriving Russian province.

The North American Finnish immigrants did not easily integrate with the Russians and other native Karelians for many reasons. Most of the immigrants spoke Finnish and English but no Russian, so language became the first barrier. The Finns tended to stay in their own communities where Finnish was the primary language and the familiar Finnish customs remained intact.

Thanks to Edvard Gylling, the immigrants received monthly ration cards that were unavailable to the native Karelians, and the insab stores only dealt with the North American Finns. For the Karelians living with inadequate diets, the foods distributed only to the immigrants were a source of great irritation and envy. "They're taking all of our food" was another common complaint.

The cars, tractors, pianos, washing machines, sewing machines, and other supplies, tools, and equipment brought by the North American Communists were often viewed with awe by the Karelians, most of whom had never seen such things. When the North American immigrants attempted to share their skills and equipment with the Karelian natives, they were often viewed as the "extremely arrogant, know-it-all Americans," and many Karelians refused to learn any new skills.

North American Canadians were able to blend into Karelian life better than the Americans. Many of the Canadian Communist Finns were poorer and brought fewer things with them. Edvard Gylling needed skilled loggers, and a large percentage of the Canadians were sent to camps deep in the forests where everyone consumed the same food. It was also more difficult for the Canadians to form segregated Finnish communities when everyone lived and worked together.

On December 1, 1934, Leningrad's Communist Party boss, Sergei Kirov,* was assassinated. Kirov was thought to be a good man, a man of the people, but a man who was considered by many to be the rival of Joseph Stalin. Kirov's killer was never apprehended.

After the assassination, Oscar Corgan was called to Moscow in early 1935 by Yrjö Sirola. Sirola was then working for the Comintern and again urged him to take his family and leave immediately, because very bad times lay ahead. Corgan, however, refused to leave unless he could take all of the Communist Finns that he had convinced to leave America.

After three days, Corgan returned from Moscow. That night, several prominent American Communist Finns, including Matti Tenhunen and Kalle Aronen, met with Oscar and discussed what Sirola's warning might mean. After that night, the men began meeting more frequently as mysterious, ominous reports from Moscow gained in frequency. Years later, Mayme Corgan still remembered the worried, late-night conversations between her parents and their American friends.

Life in Karelia began to change for the thousands of Communist Finns who had so eagerly migrated to Karelia after being told they were needed and wanted. The Resettlement Administration ended in October 1935, and Matti Tenhunen began working with Oscar Corgan for the Kirja Publishing Company.

---

* Sergei Kirov was a Bolshevik who rose to power with Joseph Stalin. Many historians believe that Stalin used Kirov's assassination as an excuse to further control and suppress the Soviet citizens – as well as eliminate his enemies – and many also view Kirov's death as Stalin's first Great Terror execution.

Edvard Gylling's dream of Karelia becoming the Red (Communist) Finland province of the Soviet Union seemed to be working, but many Russians and Karelians believed that Karelian Fever had been too successful. A meeting of the Central Committee in Karelia in October 1935 determined that Gylling, as Karelia's leader, had aggressively and purposely pursued a policy of "Finnicization," and they believed that Gylling's goal was to actually annex Karelia to Finland. A decree was issued that specifically condemned the policy that had recruited the North American Finns, and the term "Finnish nationalist" was given to anyone they believed tried to make Karelia as "Finnish" as possible.[4]

The American Finns were now increasingly viewed with suspicion and as possible spies. Non-Finnish Karelian newspapers launched a campaign against the Finnish leaders who they labeled as "Finnish nationalists." Their campaign resulted in the Finnish language being banned from Karelia and the Leningrad regions. Finnish-language schools, newspapers, and radio stations began closing gradually as a wave of Russian nationalism swept through Karelia. Classes that had been taught in the Finnish language were forced to give final exams in Russian, and the children of the North American Finns could only fail.

Until the Finnish nationalism campaign, the North American Finns had been free to leave Karelia but, beginning in 1935, there was increased pressure on them to renounce their American or Canadian citizenships and become Soviet citizens. At that point, many immigrants could not leave because they no longer had valid American or Canadian passports. Many had voluntarily acquired Soviet citizenship or did not have the money to travel to Moscow or Leningrad to renew their foreign passports. They had received Soviet citizenship and passports instead. Sylvia Hokkanen began teaching but was told she needed a Russian passport first. By applying for the passport, she unknowingly lost her American citizenship, which she later regretted.

Slowly, the improvements made in Petrozavodsk and privileges enjoyed by the Communist Finns came to an end. There were no longer building materials, and the projects were left unfinished. The insab stores closed, and the monthly ration cards the immigrants had been receiving were banned in 1936. The torgsin stores remained open, but only to the very few who still had foreign currency, gems, gold, or silver.

Everyone was now forced to shop in the Russian stores, where there was less and less food as the months passed. Potatoes and dark bread became the primary staples, even in the capital city of Petrozavodsk.

Arrests, disappearances, and banishments began. Edvard Gylling learned that the leaders in Moscow now claimed that they had never agreed to the organization of a larger Finnish community in Karelia, and he realized that he and thousands of North American Finns were now in grave danger. A few months later, Gylling – a popular and trusted figure within the Finnish communities – was forced to leave his position as the head of Karelia. Later, the North American Finns recalled this time as the beginning of the Great Hate.

Rumors of the arrests reached the Säde commune and terrified its members. One fall day, Elis Ahokas and two other members living in Säde were suddenly arrested and removed from the commune. At a meeting immediately after the arrests, the commune voted unanimously to evict the families of those arrested, revoke their membership cards, and deny them food. The shunning of arrested Finns' families would soon become characteristic throughout Karelia.

Emma Ahokas moved to the small town of Soroka and was taken in by a mother and her daughter. The mother's husband had been arrested previously, and she found work for Emma at a saw mill.

At the time of Elis' arrest, Vieno Ahokas was in ninth grade at a Finnish school in Petrozavodsk. As soon as word of her father's arrest spread, she was shunned by her friends. No one dared to be associated with the families of those arrested, because Stalin believed the arrested and their families to be enemies of the people.

After several months, the arrested Säde men were freed and returned to the commune. When Emma returned, she no longer wanted to live in Säde where their friends had turned their backs on them. But Elis would not listen to her protests, saying that Säde was their only home. Besides, Elis wanted to show everyone that he had a clean reputation.

In January 1937, the Kirja Publishing Company transferred Oscar Corgan to Uhtua, a small, Finnish-speaking village north of Petrozavodsk that was less than 20 miles from the border with Finland. Katri, Paul, and Aino moved with Oscar, but Mayme stayed in the *Valiparakit* with a friend and the friend's mother so she could continue learning the Russian language. The Corgans were assigned a small log house in Uhtua near a river with enough land for a garden.

In Uhtua, Oscar worked in a bookstore as a representative of Kirja. Katri found work in an orphanage and planted a garden in the spring. Paul enjoyed the more rural setting and often caught fish to supplement the family's diet. Even Aino seemed happy and more content when Mayme joined them as soon as the school term ended in early June.

On her first morning in Uhtua, Mayme joined her brother as he fished for the family, and Paul soon shared his concerns. "Something's going on here," he began. "I'm not exactly sure what, but Mother and Father seem worried."

"What do you mean?"

'Some of the men are gone – the fathers of some of my friends. Someone said they were arrested," Paul confided.

"*Arrested!* What for? What have they done?"

Paul's answer sent a chill through Mayme. "I don't think they did anything wrong."

The "white nights" of summer arrived – the weeks in June and July when there was darkness for only a few hours each night. Katri's garden was successful, and the family enjoyed salads of lettuce, tomatoes, and cucumbers for the first time since they'd left America over three years before. A theatre group from Petrozavodsk entertained the Uhtua-area residents for several weeks that summer, and there were often dances in the evenings at the Finn hall.

It was during the summer in 1937 when Mayme learned that Edvard Gylling had been arrested. "Why?" she asked her father.

"Nationalism," Oscar replied after a pause. "Enemy of the people. He must have done something that we don't know about, but I thought he was a good man."

Yes, he was a good man, a good leader, Mayme thought. *He had been instrumental in bringing all of us North American Finns to Karelia. You never knew why things happened....*

Joseph Stalin's campaign against foreigners intensified through 1937, and he mistakenly believed the Finns in Karelia were organizing a force that would attempt to annex Karelia to Finland. The Finnish language was banned, allowing only Russian to be spoken in public. Finnish teachers were fired, and Finnish institutions – even the cherished Finn halls – were closed. Before long, a Politburo decree classified all of the North American Finns as suspicious.

On November 4, 1937, Oscar Corgan was arrested late in the night.

THEY DON'T ARREST INNOCENT PEOPLE

A *dvoika* – two men – led Oscar Corgan to his unknown fate after riffling through his family's papers and taking photos, birth certificates, and other important documents. They also took the family's radio, camera, and typewriter – the potential ways of receiving news and communicating – but advised Oscar to leave his gold watch with the family. As the frigid November wind howled through the open door, the terrified Corgan family watched Oscar disappear into the black night.

Mayme Corgan was going to school in Petrozavodsl when she learned about her father's disappearance and confided her fears to her friend Vieno and Vieno's father, Kalle Sevander. Kalle gently responded, "You know, Mayme, they don't arrest innocent people." Later, Kalle learned otherwise.

Thousands of people were disappearing after seemingly baseless arrests, usually leaving a struggling family without their husband and father. After an arrest, the family members were always shunned, because guilt by association had resulted in numerous additional arrests. "Why?" was the question everyone asked, but there was no clear answer. Trusting only the closest friends and family members became the norm, and speaking privately in whispers behind closed doors seemingly became the safest way of avoiding arrest.

Joseph Stalin controlled everything. He controlled the media, and he allowed the Soviet citizens to know only what he allowed them to hear and read. But Joseph Stalin wanted more control and, as he reasoned, he needed to purge the Soviet Union of everyone he deemed to be disloyal to the Soviet Union, the Communist Party, and – most importantly – to himself.

Stalin's killing rampage had begun with the assassination of Sergei Kirov. Next were the arrests and murders of Communist Party officials charged with disloyalty. Military officers followed. Then came the eradication of peasant farmers, ethnic minorities, religious leaders, singers, actors, and every other innocent Soviet citizen deemed to be an enemy of the people and Joseph Stalin.

Stalin's annihilation of thousands, then tens of thousands…hundreds of thousands of his own people is one of the darkest episodes in human history. The Communist Finns trapped within Karelia's borders knew it as the Great Hate. Others called it the Great Purge. For all who heard and survived the knock on the door in the dark night, the mysterious arrests and disappearances, or the sudden exile to labor camps and primitive outposts, it was known as the Great Terror.

14 JOSEPH STALIN'S GREAT TERROR

"Remember when I tell you how my father was dragged away from his home in the dark and cold of a bitter November night in 1937. Remember when I tell you how my brother was thrown into a labor camp, as I was, and how my mother and sister faced death in exile. Remember that these things happened again and again, thousands upon thousands of times, to families of American Finns, like mine, who had gone to Karelia with strong ideals and high hopes… If you remember nothing else, remember that…."

MAYME CORGAN SEVANDER
Survivor of Joseph Stalin's Great Terror

ENEMIES OF THE PEOPLE. Nationalists. Spies. The North American Finns, who had immigrated to Karelia after the communist recruiters in their Finn halls told them they were both needed and wanted, were now prisoners in the country that had once welcomed them, and there was no way to escape. The borders were fortified by heavily armed Russians who did not hesitate to shoot. Letters that revealed the desperate situation were thoroughly censored or destroyed. The North American Finns, most of whom couldn't speak Russian, were now silent in public lest they be labeled as spies and led away to an unknown fate. And no one knew why they were suddenly subject to repressions and persecutions. No one knew what triggered the arrests. The North American Finns lived in abject fear, and terrifying stories whispered behind closed doors spread like wildfires throughout Karelia.

In the Matrosa lumber camp, things seemed to be going well until the summer of 1937. Everyone knew that Karelian timber was vital

BEHIND THE ARRESTS

Joseph Stalin was a paranoid leader, and he believed nearly everyone was conspiring to overthrow him. Stalin used Sergei Kirov's assassination in late 1934 as his excuse – his rallying cry – to rid the Soviet Union of his enemies, even though many historians believe that Stalin himself was behind Kirov's murder.

The Great Terror began with the arrests, trials, death sentences, and executions of top-ranking party and government officials – the old Bolsheviks – who had worked closely with Lenin and Stalin. Anyone who disagreed with Stalin in any way was immediately tortured, imprisoned, or executed without a trial. Military officers whom Stalin believed might be disloyal were the next to be purged. Scholars, priests, historians, and philosophers were suddenly classified as enemies of the people and were eradicated from the Soviet society. Next came the kulaks – rich peasant farmers – who provided the Soviet Union with food and whose arrests caused a famine that killed more people. Many of the ethnic groups targeted – such as the North American Communist Finns – were not spies, or insurrectionists, or traitors bent on ousting Joseph Stalin. They were believers in a true communist society, but those who had developed the Finnish culture in Karelia had to go, including the agents who had organized the North American immigration.

The first gulag – forced labor camp – was built in northern Karelia, and gulags throughout the Soviet Union imprisoned millions of "enemies of the people" during the 1930s. Soon the gulags were overflowing with diseased, overworked, and starving prisoners, most of whom were innocent.

On July 30, 1937, the Soviet Union's NKVD (the secret police, which later became the KGB) decreed – with Joseph Stalin's approval – that anti-Soviet elements were to be eradicated from the country during the coming months. Every republic was given an arrest quota with a specific percentage of those arrested to be executed. The order detailing the operation gave *dvoikas* (two men) and *troikas* (three men) license to arrest anyone for any reason or no reason at all. They were allowed to interrogate those arrested using any means necessary. And they ensured that the sentences were carried out without a trial. The *dvoikas* and *troikas* were under orders not to accept any excuse or defense of those under arrest. The mass arrests began in 1937 and continued into the late fall of 1938.

for lumber products, paper production, and exportation. Anxiety began, though, when workers stopped appearing for work. They had been arrested the night before, but no one could verify the arrests. The remaining loggers were pushed to work harder and produce more, and they continued to believe that their co-workers would return. It was only a matter of time.[1]

A number of people were told that the men in a certain house were scheduled to be arrested the following night. The men and their families fled to a nearby island and returned to their homes a few weeks later. They all escaped arrest. Their rooms had been sealed, but they broke the seals and continued living in them.[2]

Paavo Honka was arrested but was able to have a note smuggled to his family. He wrote, "Go back to where we came from. I'll find a way to join you there." He never joined them, and his note was one of the very few sent from wherever the accused were being held.[3]

Desperate people threw themselves into Lake Onega, preferring drowning over arrest.

One night, they came for Kalle Sevander, the father of Mayme Corgan's friend. As he was led away, his last words were, "Tell Mayme I now believe that her father was innocent."

Katri Corgan's worst nightmare had come true. While the family was still living in America, she had worried about being left to care for her children without Oscar. Finnish was the only language she knew and, after Oscar's arrest, she became silent when she was in public lest she be arrested, too. Oscar Corgan's family was shunned, as were the families of everyone who had been arrested. Guilt by association was terrifying....

Mayme Corgan remained in Petrozavodsk and continued her education in the Russian school. Katri, Paul, and Aino stayed in their small home in Uhtua, and Katri managed to keep working at the orphanage. Paul and Aino walked to the orphanage after school and were given a hot meal. Most days, that was the only meal they had. Katri lamented, "It's our fault. If we hadn't come here, we'd all be happy together."

One night less than two months after Oscar's arrest, the director

REASONS FOR ARREST

Ruined crop rotation by intentionally plowing hay fields and thus destroying the farm's fodder crops.

While working at a saw mill, ruined the driving belt and put the saw mill out of operation for 15 days.

Recruited in America by Matti Tenhunen.[*] Established contact with agent Ida R. to whom he passed information about supplying Petrozavodsk with electricity. In preparation of an act of sabotage, he discovered all the weak spots in a power station. [This arrestee was actually a musician in a symphony orchestra in Petrozavodsk.]

A woman was arrested because she had maintained contact with relatives in America and praised life in capitalist countries. She was also accused of collecting information for the Finnish intelligence service.

While working in a stable, had intentionally switched the harnesses so the bigger horses got smaller harnesses, which caused sores from rubbing. Also didn't cut the horses' manes in order to limit horses' range of visibility.

Made incisions in new tires. As a result, the plan for transporting logs was disrupted.

Arrests were often made after an arrestee had been tortured – sometimes for days – before finally uttering the name of an innocent friend or acquaintance. Or a man was threatened that his wife and children would be killed if he didn't name a "fellow spy." Once the NKVD had a name, that person was arrested, and the interrogation began again.

---

[*] After Matti Tenhunen encouraged the North American Communist Finns to donate whatever they could to the KTA and Machine Fund, he signed over his personal bank accounts, his home in Superior, Wisconsin, and his farm in northwestern Wisconsin to his son, Toivo Tenhune. Because Toivo had been on the Board of Directors when the communists failed to take control of the CCE, he was considered to be an enemy of the Soviet Russia communists. Matti's transfer of his assets to his son and not the KTA was considered to be an act of treason.[4]

of the orphanage was arrested and, soon after, Katri lost her job. It wasn't long before Katri, as the wife of an "enemy of the people," was evicted from her home, and the family was forced to live in an abandoned house with shattered windows and no heat. As the Corgan family waited, hoping for Oscar's return, they weren't alone in their despair. Nearly every man in Uhtua had also been arrested.

After a few months, Katri and her children were given one day to pack what they could and leave Uhtua. (Among the few essentials they packed were two books – a dictionary and a book of classics – that had been purchased in Superior, Wisconsin.) They were trucked with other fatherless families to a primitive logging camp in northern Karelia. The Corgans' new home was a large barrack where they lived with 60 other families. The building had single-pane windows and no insulation, and a large cooking stove also provided heat. Except for the old men who had avoided arrest, everyone exiled at the logging camp had lost the adult men in their families.

As the arrests began, the North American Communist Finns didn't know that they had been specifically targeted as part of the Finnish Operation of the NKVD. They also didn't know that Karelia's original required arrest quota was 1,000 citizens with 300 of the total scheduled for execution.

In July 1937, Joseph Stalin and Nikolai Yezhov, the head of the NKVD, signed Order No. 00447, listing 268,950 Soviet citizens to be arrested. Of that total, 75,950 were First Category Arrests slated for execution in order to fill the death quotas authorized by Stalin.

Shortly after Stalin and Yeshov signed the Order, Karelian anti-Gylling government officials requested that their quota be increased, seeing the way to rid Karelia of some of the Finnish immigrants who had been favored by and given special treatment by Edvard Gylling. Many of the American Finns were labeled as First Category Arrests.

The Karelian *dvoikas* and *troikas* repeatedly requested that their quotas for arrests and executions be increased during the Great Terror in 1937 and 1938, seeking Stalin's favor and therefore avoiding their own arrests. By the end of December 1937, some 2,000 North American Finns had been arrested. Of that total, 1,640 were executed.

Later, Mayme Corgan recalled that "NKVD leader Nikolai Yezhov, followed by Genrikh Yagoda and Lavrentiy Beria, excelled in signing death sentences with one bold stroke of the pen. But the NKVD leaders were replaced in the same manner... The butchers-in-chief [Yezhov and Yagoda] shared the same fate as their victims."[5]

The arrests continued. Those who were tipped off that the *troikas* were coming for them left their homes and hid for a few days. The *troikas* seldom visited a second time – they had quotas that needed to be filled, and the people they arrested were of no consequence to any of them.

William Jukkola was told that men were being called to a lumber camp where the NKVD was waiting to take everyone away. Jukkola took food and clothing and hid in the woods for ten days. He was spared.

One morning, half the Karelian Symphony Orchestra did not show up for work. They had been arrested the night before.

A tractor factory that employed 300 American Finns lost their employees when they were ordered to report to an assembly hall. Once they were assembled, they were all arrested.

After Edvard Gylling was forced to leave his leadership position in Karelia, he became one of the thousands who suddenly disappeared. One night, 23 workers from his ski factory also disappeared.

In one small Karelian village, only male children, a 16-year-old boy, and a 60-year-old man avoided arrest. Every other male slowly disappeared.

Benjamin Koskinen was able to talk to his daughter before his execution and said, "Remember me as our family's enemy. I brought you, your sickly mother who died a premature death, and your brother whom we lost in the terror wave, to this country. I ruined everybody's life. Yes, I was an enemy to all my dearest!"[6]

In the summer of 1938, a truck roared into the yard of the Säde commune, and the NKVD arrested all of the adult males except the young and the elderly. The next day, all of the documents written in Finnish were ordered to be immediately destroyed because, "No memory of those nationalists and enemies of the people must be left." The men had been cleaning the well when they were arrested. With the men went their knowledge of equipment repair as well as the manpower needed to keep a farm operating. The women and children left behind were unable to harvest all of the crops and maintain the farm and its animals.

Years later Toivo Tuulos wrote of that day when his father, Nick, and the rest of the men were arrested and taken from Säde: "Only three [male] members of the commune were not arrested... Forever will my memory retain the terrible event. A few days remained until the harvesting. All of them were wet and dirty when the NKVD guys drove up in trucks and ordered the men to get in. About 20 laborers boarded the trucks that drove off, leaving a cloud of dust in their wake on that beautiful summer day. Never were they seen again...."

Emma Ahokas remained in Säde after her husband's arrest, and Vieno Ahokas continued her schooling in Petrozavodsk while hoping her father would soon be freed. It wasn't long, though, before the families of those arrested were evicted and expelled from the area. One day with no warning, trucks stopped at the barracks and left with everyone who still remained. They were then hauled to barges, which took them to an old limestone quarry on Olenia Island. The first to arrive on the island moved into abandoned homes. The other families were given a stall in old stables.

Anyone old enough to work was ordered to work in the limestone quarry. Many died of malnutrition and starvation. A child ate a pebble of lime and died instantly.

The horrible, terrifying days continued. The North American Finns were targeted and arrested in their homes at night, at work during the day, or in the middle of town at any time of the day or night. People quit staying at home during the night or, if they did, they laid awake, waiting for the sound of boots in the streets, then coming up the stairs or down the halls before the knock on the door. The *dvoikas* and *troikas* usually arrived at night....

Rumors flew, and stories of torture and executions after the arrests paralyzed grieving family members. Most wanted to leave their homes and hide, but where? Where could they go where their husband, their father, or their brother could find them when they returned? Some of their friends disappeared suddenly, then reappeared weeks later, frostbitten and starving. They had hidden in the vast Karelian forests or on the islands of Lake Onega. Those were stories of hope, but there were very few of them.

Some were brave enough to question authorities on the whereabouts of their loved ones, but they had to be extremely cautious lest they were arrested, too. After Oscar Corgan's arrest, Mayme Corgan wrote to the NKVD and Supreme Soviet, asking for information detailing her father's arrest. The teenager was summoned to their offices in Petrozavodsk.

The NKVD officer told Mayme that Oscar had received a ten-year prison sentence and was incarcerated in eastern Soviet Union near Vladivostok. Then in a second meeting on the same day, a military official of the Supreme Soviet claimed that her father was being detained for 15 years in the Kazakh Republic south of Karelia. When Mayme demanded the truth, the Supreme Soviet officer's chilling reply was, "You'd better watch yourself. If you were of age, we'd put you in the same place where he is."

The NKVD had confiscated nearly every radio in Karelia, and most news came from the communist newspapers that were controlled by Joseph Stalin. During the Great Terror, faith in Joseph Stalin had remained steady and unwavering for most Soviet citizens who were unaware of the truth behind the atrocities that were being committed. The Karelian Finns were sure that when Stalin was finally made aware of the terrors they were experiencing, he would stop them immediately. After all, he had welcomed them to Karelia.

Sometime in 1938, the Great Terror ended. In November 1938, Joseph Stalin declared that the country's enemies had been removed.

Stalin only then "suddenly" became aware of the NKVD atrocities when, in actuality, he had authorized the extensive obliteration of his own people. Declaring that NKVD leaders Nikolai Yeshov and Genrikh Yagoda had been "excessive" and had "violated the law," Stalin ordered their executions with hope of deflecting blame from himself. Stalin then ordered that speaking of the Great Terror was a punishable offense. Through fear and continued censorship, the Soviet citizens became silent for decades.

Katri Corgan, her children, and everyone else who had survived life in the primitive logging camp were suddenly free to move anywhere but back to Uhtua, which was too close to the Finnish border. Katri decided to live with her sister Maria,* whose husband had also been arrested and still had not returned home.

The Säde commune was renamed Papanin after all the men were arrested and the remaining commune members returned from the limestone quarry. After the loss of so many members, though, the once thriving commune slowly fell into disrepair and was abandoned. Emma Ahokas eventually moved in with her daughter Vieno, who was teaching in Petrozavodsk.

Vieno's bittersweet memories evoke the enthusiasm of the early days in Säde after a group of Canadian miners and their families relocated to Karelia and wrested a new life from the rugged wilderness: "One can't help but think about the ironies of life. Säde's buildings were burned to the ground. This devastating fire was the closing scene of the prosperous enterprise set up by very special, honest, and industrious idealists who played a major role in the development of Karelia in its early days. The fields have reverted to scrub, and the place has reverted to the same thicket that it was when we first arrived. Only memories are left, some sweet, some heartbreaking."

---

*Maria Alalauri was the eldest daughter of seven children. She married Antti Nissinen, a Red Finn, before they moved to Hancock, Michigan, in 1910. Katri and her sister Anna had followed Maria to Hancock. Later, Maria and Antti immigrated to Karelia before the Corgan family did.

Reporters for *Raivaaja*, the Finnish-language newspaper for the non-communist Finnish Americans, had heard rumors of Edvard Gylling's arrest and expressed their anxiety when no news was coming from Karelia. Later, an article in the *New York Times* confirmed their worst fears:

> ### SOVIET EX-PREMIER REPORTED SLAIN FOR PRO-FINNISH POLICY
>
> The *New York Times*
> January 4, 1939
>
> Edvard Gylling, Finnish-born former premier of the Soviet Karelian republic in northern Russia, who recently was deposed by Dictator Joseph Stalin for alleged pro-Finnish leanings, has been murdered, according to reports from Russia today.
>
> He was sentenced to "deportation" in November and, under a strong guard of Red soldiers, he started the journey first to Leningrad and later toward the dreaded Solovetsky Island prison camp in the White Sea, near the Arctic Circle.
>
> The soldiers arrived there without Gylling, and soon afterward rumors began to spread that the soldiers had killed him during the journey. Soviet authorities have neither confirmed nor denied the rumors. According to other reports, Soviet officials continue a vigorous purging of the former Gylling regime in Karelia and Moscow and are now concentrating their efforts on ousting all American communists who obtained official posts during Gylling's rule.

Afterwards, an article in *Raivaaja* mentioned: "If ever any group of people has displayed superiority and disrespect, a lack of compassion for human life, they are the Finnish American communists who recruited their spiritual comrades to Karelia."[7]

Through the Great Terror and after, the Finnish Workers Federation's American newspapers, including the *Työmies* and *Eteenpäin*, remained silent in their reporting of anything except good news and positive reports from Karelia. The Communist Party in Moscow continued to dictate what would be shared with the American Communist Finns, and most of them had no idea that thousands of their comrades who had moved to Karelia – their former friends and neighbors, and even their relatives – were now gone.

Lawrence and Sylvia Hokkanen survived the Great Terror, and they managed to leave Karelia and return to Michigan. Shortly after their return, Lawrence visited his mother and relived the terror they had endured for those agonizing months and years, the sudden disappearances of so many friends, and the ongoing heartbreak of still not knowing the whereabouts of so many who had not yet returned.

Lawrence's mother, who was still a staunch Communist Finn and a devoted reader of the communist newspapers, listened quietly to her son, looked him straight in the eyes, and firmly stated, "That never happened."

WHERE ARE THEY?

No one will ever know how many citizens of the USSR perished from starvation, torture, overwork, disease, or execution during Joseph Stalin's Great Terror. Most historians agree that the death toll was at least 700,000 with some believing the total exceeds 1,200,000.

In Karelia, the figures also vary. Of the 10,000 North American Communist Finns who immigrated to Karelia, many believe that about one-quarter perished during the Great Terror. Others maintain that, of the 9,536 Karelians arrested during the Great Terror, 85 percent were executed. Other historians state that of the Finnish American immigrants, 47 percent of the family breadwinners were arrested and executed.[1]

The numbers are staggering, but they still aren't the end of so many stories of shattering grief. After the frightening loss of their beloved family members, very few of the North American Communist Finns resumed a normal life. The wives and children remaining were often torn from their homes and exiled in a faraway land where they were forced to work in inhumane conditions while facing starvation and disease.

And always at the forefront of their minds were the haunting, tormenting questions: Where are they? When will they return? Will they ever return? After the Great Terror ended, families whose loved ones had disappeared waited for their return, unwilling to move lest their family member returned and was unable to locate them.

The evidence of the crimes against humanity that Joseph Stalin and his NKVD committed during the Great Terror was buried deeply in remote forests and in the well-hidden, secret police files until over 40 years after Stalin's death. When the unimaginable, incomprehensible facts and horrific details were finally revealed, they shook the world.

15

THE TRUTH BE TOLD

"The final result of this mass deception was an even more frightful chapter of human misery than I could have imagined."

AINO KUUSINEN, wife of Otto Kuusinen
and author of *The Rings of Destiny*

JOSEPH STALIN DIED AFTER five long, agonizing days as a result of his own policies and decisions. By early 1953, Stalin – a heavy smoker – had had several small strokes as well as a major heart attack, and his health was in a gradual decline. In the evening of February 28, 1953, he held a meeting at his *dacha* with several prominent communists including Nikita Khruschev and the head of the NKVD, Lavrentiy Beria. When the men left at 4:00 a.m., Stalin dismissed his guards and ordered that he not be disturbed.

Stalin was usually awake and requesting tea by 10:00 every morning but, on March 1st, the guards became increasingly nervous as the day wore on with no sign of their leader. The fear of disobeying Stalin's orders and being sent to a gulag, or worse, kept them from even knocking on Stalin's firmly closed door. There was no one at the *dacha* with enough authority to override Stalin's order, so they waited...and waited...and waited.

Finally, at 6:30 that evening, a light came on in Stalin's bedroom, but there was still no sound. It wasn't until 10:00 before a guard summoned the courage and opened the bedroom door with the day's mail in hand as his excuse. What he discovered was Joseph Stalin – unable to talk or move – lying on the floor in a pool of urine.

Stalin's guards believed they did not have the authority to contact any doctors and instead notified the Minister of State Security, who then notified the NKVD head, Beria. When doctors finally arrived on the morning of March 2, they found Joseph Stalin vomiting blood, partially paralyzed, and struggling to breathe. Specialists were clearly needed, but the top specialists who had been treating Stalin were at that time all imprisoned by Stalin.

More time passed as Stalin's blood pressure gradually spiraled higher. After the doctors had finally located and conferred with the incarcerated specialists, they decided applying leeches to Stalin's face and neck would best reduce his blood pressure. Two applications with eight leeches in each treatment failed, though. Stalin's condition worsened during the next few days until the evening of March 5. Recalling the time of his passing, "The death agony was terrible. He literally choked to death as we watched."[2]

After four days of national mourning, Joseph Stalin's remains joined those of Vladimir Lenin in Red Square on March 9, 1953. As his remains passed through the throngs of mourners, several hundred people were fatally trampled as the crowds pressed forward, trying to get a glimpse of their beloved leader. They were the last victims of Joseph Stalin's reign of terror.

In February 1956, nearly three years after Joseph Stalin's death and over 18 years after Stalin's Great Terror ended, Nikita Khruschev, as the First Secretary of the Communist Party, spoke before the Congress of the Soviet Union. In a shocking speech that was broadcast throughout the Soviet Union, Khruschev revealed that the Soviets had been misled by propaganda spread by Joseph Stalin's controlled media. The four-hour speech bluntly outlined the arrests, the tortures, and the executions committed on innocent Soviet citizens. In his speech, Khruschev said that, "Stalin originated the concept of 'enemy of the people.' This term made possible the usage of the cruelest repressions, violating all norms of revolutionary legality, against anyone who in any way disagreed with him...."

Khruschev clearly stated that hundreds of thousands of innocent Soviet citizens had died because of Stalin's atrocities and, for the first time, the hopeful families who had been waiting for their loved ones were finally forced to confront reality. The victims of Stalin's Great Terror would never return.[3]

Mayme Corgan was utterly stunned by the speech: "We believed Stalin was a good man, a staunch communist, a worthy successor to Lenin. We did not know that he was behind the purges. We did not know that he was slowly killing us all."

After Khruschev's speech, the Supreme Court of the USSR received an avalanche of requests for information on missing loved ones who had disappeared during the Great Terror. *How did they die? When did they die? Where were they buried?* As the death certificates were received, the causes of death listed were eerily similar. Apparently, every prisoner had supposedly died of natural causes – stomach ulcers, cancer, heart attack, dysentery, or pneumonia. There was no information listing the burial locations.

Oscar Corgan's Death

The first death certificate was issued on November 30, 1956, nineteen years after his arrest. The certificate states that Oscar died of stomach cancer on July 18, 1940. Where he died and where he was buried were not noted. Oscar's second death certificate was issued on August 16, 1991, with his cause of death listed as shot. The date of death was January 9, 1938, with no place of burial.

Elis Ahokas' Death

In 1956, Emma and Vieno Ahokas received Elis' first death certificate stating that he had died from a heart attack in a prison near Moscow. In 1992, they received a second death certificate stating that Elis had been shot on February 4, 1938. His place of burial was not listed.

Nikita Khruschev then began a period of "De-Stalinization" to reverse Joseph Stalin's policies and end what was perceived as a "cult of personality." The Soviet government began the slow process of "rehabilitating" – clearing of all charges – those who had been arrested and executed during Stalin's Great Terror. After the accused had been rehabilitated, the survivors were eligible to receive a *tapporahat* (compensation for the murder) of one month's salary. Many survivors, however, considered it beneath their dignity to collect the paltry sum for the irreparable loss of their beloved family member.[4]

SANDARMOKH'S FIRST EXECUTIONS

On October 27, 1937, three barges were scheduled to have been deliberately sunk in the White Sea, drowning everyone on board. On the barges were 1,111 prisoners from the Special Prison in Solovki.* For decades, there was no reason to dispute the facts of the tragedy.

In 1996, Veniamin Ioffe, the co-chair of Memorial's branch in St. Petersburg, discovered files in the NKVD archives that became a history-changing event. In the documents were the Solovki prisoners listed as First Category Arrests – prisoners scheduled for execution – and not the victims of drowning as had been previously believed. Subsequent documents revealed that NKVD Captain Mikhail Matveyev reported that he had executed 1,111 prisoners at a place now known as Sandarmokh. The prisoners were executed between October 27 and November 3 in 1937. Matveyev reported that he had fulfilled his orders on November 10, 1937, thus completing the scheduled execution quota.

SANDARMOKH'S FIRST CHIEF EXECUTIONER

Born in 1892, Mikhail Matveyev joined the Bolsheviks in 1917 and was soon serving as an executioner for Cheka – the forerunner of the NKVD. On November 28, 1936, he received the Order of the Red Banner, given to executioners of those perceived to be enemies of the people.

Matveyev was sent to Sandarmokh to organize the first killings at the mass-execution site. His first victims were the 1,111 First Category Arrests from Solovki prison. Matveyev's preferred method of killing was forcing the victims to lie face down in a large pit and shooting a single bullet into their skulls. For his good work against the "counter-revolution," he received a commemorative gift – a set of gramophone records and a radiogram – on December 20, 1937.

Mikhail Matveyev was the first of three chief executioners at Sandarmokh and died of natural causes in 1971. The two executioners who succeeded him were both arrested in 1938 – when Sandarmokh's executions were completed – and were shot for "exceeding their authorization."

---

* Solovki was the first permanent concentration camp established by Vladimir Lenin in 1923. It was the model from which the entire Soviet gulag system developed and was made famous by Aleksandr Solzhenitsyn's *The Gulag Archipelago*.

The details of Joseph Stalin's orders for the mass executions committed during the Great Terror remained a dark, closely guarded secret buried deeply in the files of the NKVD for 60 years, but demands for the truth about human rights' infringements and the atrocities committed by Joseph Stalin and the NKVD had their beginning in 1973. That year, Aleksandr Solzhenitsyn's* historical novel, *The Gulag Archipelago*, chronicled the details of the gulag system – Solovki prison in particular – and the personal stories of those incarcerated. The novel outraged citizens worldwide.

Memorial** was founded in Russia in the late 1980s during an unusual period of *glasnost* (openness). In 1989, it was officially recognized by Mikhail Gorbachev, then the leader of the USSR. Memorial (International) was organized for the purpose of discovering the truth pertaining to Stalin's atrocities and perpetuating the memories of Stalin's Great Terror victims. Once it received its official recognition, Memorial began searching for clues to the past in earnest, hoping to finally bring closure to the thousands of citizens whose questions about their still-missing family members remained unanswered.

The existence of a mass-execution site north of Petrozavodsk near the town of Medvezhyegorsk was uncovered in 1996 after secret NKVD files were ordered to be opened. Documents discovered within the NKVD files pertained to prisoners of Solovki prison, and what they revealed was staggering. Previously, the widely held belief was that the prisoners had drowned in the White Sea while in transit, but the documents revealed them as actually being executed in an area near the north shore of Lake Onega in Karelia.

---

* Aleksandr Solzhenitsyn, born in 1918, was an outspoken critic of communism and the atrocities committed by Joseph Stalin. His inflammatory historical novels were published outside USSR after being banned in the country. In 1971, he survived an attempt to poison him and was stripped of his Soviet citizenship after the publication of *The Gulag Archipelago*. He moved back to Russia in 1994 after the USSR was dissolved.

** Memorial's successes in discovering the execution sites of Sandarmokh and Krasny Bor caused it to fall into disfavor as Russia's openness ended in the early years of the 21st century. Please see additional information in the Epilogue.

Yury Dmitriev was an amateur historian and a member of Memorial's Karelian branch. For years, he had been scouring the thick forests around Petrozavodsk, searching for the burial sites from Stalin's Great Terror that were rumored to be there. After Veniamin Ioffe's stunning discovery in the NKVD secret files, Dmitriev teamed up with Ioffe and Irina Flige, another member of St. Petersburg's Memorial. Based on clues found in the files, they focused their search in the area near the northern shores of Lake Onega. What Yury Dmitriev discovered on July 1, 1997, was described by the London *Times* as "one of the most grisly discoveries of post-communist Russia."[5]

The burial site is now known as Sandarmokh, and it is one of Joseph Stalin's most hideous secrets. Sandarmokh was an execution and burial site for thousands of Karelians who were rubber-stamped by the NKVD *dvoikas* and *troikas* for execution without a trial.

A large stone marks the entrance to the Sandarmokh execution site.
The inscription reads: "People! Do not kill one another."
Wikimedia Commons

The lists were then given to the execution squad leaders, who lined up the prisoners along deep burial pits. The prisoners, stripped to their underwear, then kneeled while they waited for the single shot to pierce their skulls. After tumbling into the pit, an occasional killing shot was needed.

The Sandarmokh execution site was used between October 1937 and December 1938, and some historians believe that half of the Karelians who disappeared during the Great Terror are buried among the 9,000 there. Yury Dmitriev and Veniamin Ioffe have thus far identified the remains of over 5,000 of those who were executed at Sandarmokh. Between 50 and 60 corpses lay jumbled together in each pit, and 236 pits have been carefully excavated.

Hundreds of North American Finns from America and Canada were murdered by the execution squads and are buried at Sandarmokh. The victims come from all walks of life – forestry workers, musicians, teachers, carpenters, and even housewives. One young victim who has been identified was born in Minnesota and was executed when she was 20 or 21 years old. According to the NKVD files, Helen Hill was sentenced to death for praising the life in capitalist countries and encouraging a spirit of emigration among her co-workers by mentioning her plans for escaping to Finland.

In one burial pit are the remains of two Finnish men who had arrived in Michigan as idealistic 18-year-olds, eager to begin their adult lives in America. Their lives took them to Superior, Wisconsin, where they first met during the Labor Movement, and they had both fought hard for the rights of workers. Their radical activism then carried them into the Communist Movement, and their talents as fiery, influential speakers had sent thousands of Communist Finns to Karelia. Now the two friends – Oscar Corgan and Matti Tenhunen – lie together for all eternity.

KRASNY BOR FOREST

For decades, the residents living near Petrozavodsk had known that mass executions had taken place somewhere in the nearby woods. After many years of searching, a father and son – Ivan and Sergey Chugunkovs – found depressions in the deep woods that they believed indicated mass burials.

A few weeks after the discovery of Sandarmokh, Ivan and Sergey Chugunkov led Yury Dmitriev into the Krasny Bor Forest only 12 miles from Petrozavodsk. Dmitriev verified that the depressions were, indeed, another secret NKVD execution site. Dmitriev's excavations of the site began in October 1997. Like Sandarmokh, the victims lay in jumbled stacks, each with one or two bullet holes in their skulls. Numerous vodka bottles – emptied to dull the senses during the brutal murders – were strewn throughout the remains in the execution pits.

During the Great Terror, the First Category Arrest quotas were required to be filled before or during the times when the executions were scheduled in the area. In the Krasny Bor Forest, the executions took place at two different times. From August 9 to September 15, 1937, Travin's execution platoon was present in the area. The following year, from September 26 to October 2, 1938, Goldberg's execution platoon fulfilled his orders.

The Krasny Bor Forest was the killing site of 1,193 victims including 580 Finns and 432 Karelians. Dmitriev has thoroughly investigated the site and identified all of the victims listed in the execution reports of the NKVD archives for Karelia.

Yury Dmitriev designed a monument for the site that was unveiled on October 30, 2006. In the languages of Finnish, Karelian, Russian, and Vespian are inscribed, "Blessed are those who mourn, for they shall be comforted."(Matthew 5:4)*

YURY DMITRIEV

Yury Dmitriev was born on January 28, 1956, and spent his first year in an orphanage before being adopted by an army officer and his wife. He became fascinated with the mass executions during his 30s after seeing the first mass graves of the Great Terror. He has been the chairman of Memorial's Karelian branch since 2014.

He is best known for his part in discovering and investigating Sandarmokh and Krasny Bor Forest, at one point confiding to his daughter: "I do not know who I was in a past life, but I understand the meaning of my life now, and I know that I must do this."

---

* Source: State Centre for the Protection and Management of the Historic and Cultural Monuments of the Ministry of Culture, the Republic of Karelia

What Happened to the Influential Red Finn Activists?

JOHN WIITA WAS THE only influential activist who didn't live in Soviet Russia, and he was the only one who did not belong to the Communist Party when he died. The other seven Communist Finns ended their lives in Soviet Russia after achieving prominence in at least two other countries.

Five of the eight belonged to the Second International before leaving Finland, where most of them served in the Finnish Parliament. All eight men were active members in the Labor Movement, and they made very significant contributions to the Communist Movement.

Perhaps the best known of the eight men, though, was Yrjö Sirola. His multiple skills took him to high-profile positions in Finland, America, and Soviet Russia. Edvard Gylling became Karelia's leader, and Otto Kuusinen reached the highest echelon in the Moscow leadership, but Sirola was overall the most influential through decades in time and in multiple countries.

There were other prominent Finnish men who lived during the early 1900s, but the skills and talents of these men had an unquestionable effect on thousands of North American Finns.

OSCAR CORGAN
After his arrest on November 4, 1937, Oscar Corgan's family never saw or heard from him again. He is listed in the NKVD records as being shot on January 9, 1938. His remains lie at Sandarmokh in Karelia.

EDVARD GYLLING
Edvard Gylling was forced to step down as the head of Karelia in 1935. Accused of being a nationalist – an enemy of the people – he was arrested in 1937. Dates of his death vary, but it was most likely June 14, 1938. His place of burial is unknown. He was rehabilitated – cleared of all charges against him – on July 16, 1955.

OTTO KUUSINEN

Otto Kuusinen survived the Great Terror as one of Joseph Stalin's most trusted associates. Beginning as a close confidante of Vladimir Lenin, he remained arguably the highest ranking and most influential Finn in Soviet Russia.

In 1940, Kuusinen became the head of Karelia – the position previously held by his friend since childhood, Edvard Gylling. According to Aino Kuusinen, his last secret mission was negotiating with Mao Tse-tung to reconcile the broken relations between China and the Soviet Union.

When Otto Kuusinen realized he was terminally ill, he asked to be allowed to visit Finland for one last time. His request was denied. Kuusinen died in Moscow on May 17, 1964.

His ashes were buried in the Kremlin wall – the first Finnish person to be buried there.

Otto Kuusinen's second wife, Aino Kuusinen, spent many years in the gulags after returning from America and became very embittered by her husband, Otto's, lack of interest in her dire situation. Aino later escaped from Soviet Russia and lived for the remainder of her life in various Western countries. Her tell-all book, *The Rings of Destiny*, was published posthumously, as she wished. She died on September 1, 1970.

LEO LAUKKI

After his 1918 guilty verdict for attempting to overthrow the American government, the IWW posted his bail, and Leo Laukki fled to Soviet Russia. He joined the Finnish Communist Party and, in 1921, was elected to its national committee. Laukki taught at the Western Minorities University in Leningrad and worked for the newspaper *Trud*. After Otto Kuusinen accused him of being an enemy of the people, he was executed by firing squad. His date of death is listed as September 15, 1938. His place of burial is unknown.

SANTERI NUORTEVA

After fleeing America and Canada, and rather than being deported from England back to America, Santeri Nuorteva moved to Soviet Russia. His command of multiple languages made him valuable to the communist leaders in Moscow, and Nuorteva was soon the head of the American Division of Foreign Affairs. Later, he worked as a journalist and was the chairman of Karelia's Central Committee. The time and place of death vary, but he is believed to have been executed during the Great Terror.

YRJÖ SIROLA

Yrjö Sirola was a Comintern representative to the CPUSA from 1925 to 1927, and he used the alias Frank Miller while he was in America. In 1930, Sirola became Karelia's Commissioner of Public Education in Moscow. Yrjö Sirola was a powerful Finnish leader in Moscow, second only to Otto Kuusinen. On November 18, 1936, he died of a stroke in Moscow.

MATTI TENHUNEN

"The last I heard from my father was in April of 1936," Toivo Tenhune stated.
Milwaukee Journal, April 27, 1941

In 1936, shortly after a trip to America, Russian officials attempted to arrest Matti Tenhunen. He escaped to Finland and was held in Helsinki for attempting to reach America through Sweden without a passport. Tenhunen was taken back to Russia where he was tried on two charges – escaping without a passport and defrauding the Russians of $35,000 in colonization fees. He was also accused of being an enemy of the people. His date of death is listed in the NKVD records as December 12, 1937. He is buried at Sandarmokh in Karelia.

JOHN WIITA

John Wiita was expelled from the CPUSA after his negative comments regarding Karelian Fever. He moved to Connecticut in 1945 and became a realtor. Wiita died in Connecticut in 1981.

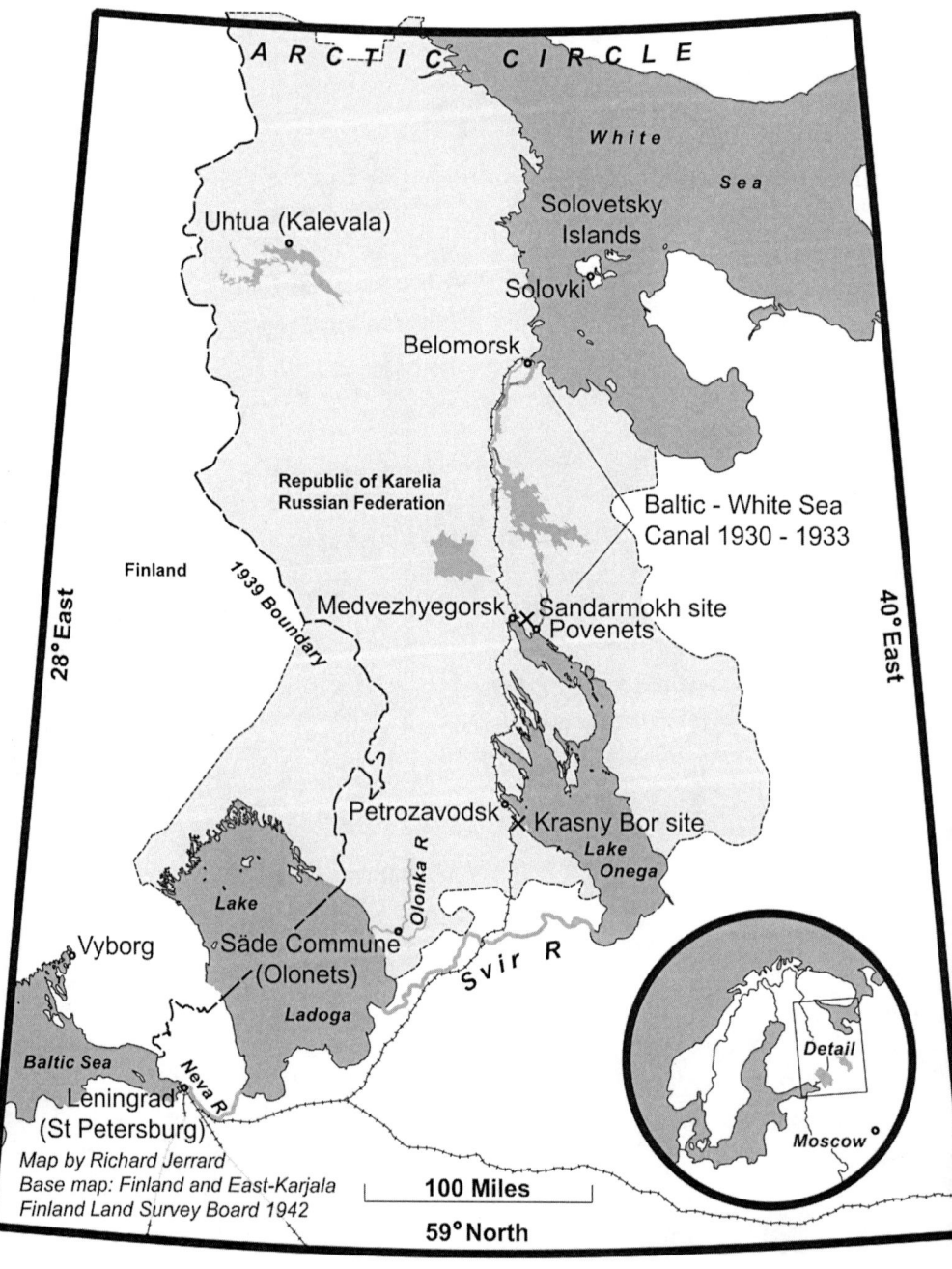

Epilogue

"Ghosts from the past will re-enter the stage in new disguise."
— Daniel Singer

MAYME CORGAN SEVANDER LEARNED that Petrozavodsk had been chosen by the citizens in Duluth, Minnesota, to be their Sister City when she had stopped by the government building in the capital city and happened to see the letter of introduction. Excitedly, she demanded, "Have you answered this request? You must write back!" But there wasn't time to reply before the Duluthians' scheduled arrival.

Sevander was instrumental in rapidly organizing the dozens of former Americans who welcomed the Duluthians to Petrozavodsk in 1986. In *They Took My Father*, she reminisced that, "We waited for the train to stop so that we could greet them, welcome them, show them the city we had helped build...and tell them our history, how we came to be here, and why we came so long ago." During the Duluthians' visit, they attended a dance, a concert, and were invited into the homes of the former Americans. The amazing, serendipitous story was a joyful ending to a painful past.

But...the story wasn't quite over.

In 1986, the surviving citizens of Stalin's Great Terror all realized that their loved ones had perished, but it was still over ten years before the members of Memorial discovered the mass burial sites at Sandarmokh and the Krasny Bor Forest, bringing the final closure to thousands of families.

∞

Memorial's success has been an embarrassment to the Russian leadership since the gruesome discoveries at Sandarmokh and the Krasny Bor Forest. The human rights society, credited with uncovering the indisputable truth of Joseph Stalin's atrocities as well as remembering the Great Terror's victims, has endured increasing pressure from Moscow to cease all activities since the discoveries. Yury Dmitriev, who is probably the most famous member of Memorial, has also become a prime target.

The first attempt to close Memorial's Human Rights Centre in

Moscow occurred in 1914 when it was declared a "foreign agent." The following year, "foreign agent" status was designated to Memorial's Research and Information Centre in St. Petersburg. The attempt to close Memorial was made by the Minister of Justice, who applied to the Russian Supreme Court. The Supreme Court rejected the application.

During ongoing conflicts in Chechnya, Memorial's office was frequently raided. At one point, journalist Anna Politkovskaya was murdered, and Memorial activist Natalia Estemirova was kidnapped and subsequently murdered when she investigated Politkovskaya's death. Over fear of additional violence, Memorial's Grozny office closed.

Yury Dmitriev was first jailed on child pornography charges in 2016, charges he vehemently denied.

Memorial was again accused of violating the Russian Federal Agent Act and was labeled a foreign agent on October 4, 2016. In 2018, masked arsonists set fire to Memorial's North Caucasus office. On April 27, 2020, the *New York Times* reported that the Russian media had been actively demonizing Memorial, calling it a "Western-backed nest of depraved traitors."

Also in 2020, nearly two dozen men broke into Memorial's offices and began harassing the members during a gathering. After the police were called, the police blocked Memorial's members from leaving for hours, forcing every member to produce passports, contact information, and employment information. After that incident, the European Court of Human Right received a complaint from Memorial International for harassment of the organization by Moscow.

In November 2021, the Russian Prosecutor's Office submitted a lawsuit to the Supreme Court, requesting again that Memorial International be closed for violating the Russian Foreign Agent Act. The next month, on December 28, 2021, the Supreme Court of Russia ordered Memorial International to close because of violations of the Foreign Agent Act. On the same day, the European Court of Human Rights ruled against Russia's Supreme Court, halting Memorial's forced dissolution pending further litigation.

Yury Dmitriev has been in and out of prison several times since his first incarceration in 2016. On December 27, 2021, he was sentenced to a total imprisonment of 15 years for child pornography.

WITH THANKS

One late summer day, I placed both elbows on my desk, stared out the window, and decided it was time to begin writing *The Communist Chasm*. That was a great resolution, but I had no clue how I wanted to begin the book, and there was no one around who could listen to my ideas. As time passed and my book developed, I was able to share my thoughts with several people who read part or all of my manuscript and provided some great ideas to improve the story and keep me focused. I appreciate everyone's input but wish to specially thank Pat DelVecchio, Steve Fortney, Duane Lahti, John Luthens, Janine Seis, and Flint Whitlock for their help and suggestions.

The Covid pandemic then came along and changed our world, making it impossible to access the research centers. When they opened again – even on a limited basis – archivists Aimee Brown at the Kathryn A. Martin Library at UMD in Duluth, Minnesota, and Joanna Chopp at the Finnish American Heritage Center in Hancock, Michigan, went out of their way to be helpful and accommodating. I remember them both with happy smiles and gratitude.

Rich Jerrard designed the maps for my book with a fine attention to detail. Thank you for an excellent job, Rich! And I am always grateful to my husband Scott for his critical opinions on a picture or story and for his tolerance in accompanying me on my adventures.

I could never complete a book without the creativity of my friends, Jackie Pechin and Larry Verkeyn. Your special finishing touches both inside and outside the book makes it a work of art.

My name might be on the cover of this book, but the input and encouragement of many others are part of it, too. You all have my heartfelt gratitude.

Source Notes

1: The Late 1800s: Migrants & Mines

1: Ross, Carl, *The Finn Factor in American Labor, Culture and Society.* Parta Printers, Inc., New York Mills, MN, 1982, p. 78.

2: Wisherd, Nan, *Echoes from the Past.* Cable Publishing, Brule, WI, 2006, p. 104.

3: Lankton, Larry, *Cradle to Grave: Life, Work, and Death at the Lake Superior Copper Mines.* Oxford University Press, New York, 1991, p. 70.

4: Wisherd, *Echoes*, p. 91.

5: Ibid, p. 115.

6: Hudelson, Richard and Carl Ross, *By the Ore Docks: A Working People's History of Duluth.* University of Minnesota Press, Minneapolis, MN, 2006, p. 35.

7: Wisherd, *Echoes*, p. 120.

2: Land Ownership & Labor Struggles

1: Työmies Society, "For the Common Good." Superior, WI, 1977, p. 72.

2: en.wikipedia.org/wiki/Hanna_Mine_Disasters

3: en.wikipedia.org/wiki/Western_Federation_of_Miners

4: Wiita, John, "Tyovaen Opisto - Working People's College." Unpublished, IHRCA, Anderson Library, U of MN, n.d., pp. 1-2.

5: Ibid, p. 14.

3: The Evolving Towns & Organizations

4: Where Were the Activists in 1916?

1: Hudelson, Richard and Carl Ross, *By the Ore Docks: A Working People's History of Duluth.* University of Minnesota Press, Minneapolis, MN, 2006, pp. 70-71.

5: The Year 1917 – A Time of Change

1: Zenithcity.com/archive/legendary-tales/duluths-red-scare-the-wobblies/2/

2: en.wikipedia.org/wiki/Co-operative_Central_Exchange

3: Ross, Carl, *The Finn Factor in American Labor, Culture and Society.* Parta Printers, Inc., New York Mills, MN, 1982, p. 143.

6: The 1917 Aftermath

1: Kostiainen, Auvo, "Santeri Nuorteva and the Origins of Soviet-American Relations." IHRCA, Anderson Library, U of MN, n.d.

2: www.roosevelt.nl/santeri-nuorteve-american-wanderings-finnish-socialist

3: Hudelson, Richard and Carl Ross, *By the Ore Docks: A Working People's History of Duluth.* University of Minnesota Press, Minneapolis, MN, 2006, p. 134.

4: en.wikipedia.org/wiki/Red_Scare

5: Kuusinen, Aino, *The Rings of Destiny: Inside Soviet Russia from Lenin to Breshnev.* William Morrow and Co., New York, 1974, p. 20.

6: Ross, Carl, *The Finn Factor in American Labor, Culture and Society.* Parta Printers, Inc., New York Mills, MN, 1982, p. 154.

7: Ibid, pp. 163-164.

7: The Roaring '20s

1: Baron, Nick, *Soviet Karelia: Politics, Planning and Terror in Stalin's Russia, 1920-1939*. Routledge, London, 2007, p. 64.

2: Golubev, Alexey and Irina Takala, *The Search for a Socialist El Dorado: Finnish Immigration to Soviet Karelia from the United States and Canada in the 1930s*. Michigan State University Press, East Lansing, MI, 2014, pp. 7-17.

3: Kuusinen, Aino, *The Rings of Destiny: Inside Soviet Russia from Lenin to Breshnev*. William Morrow and Co., New York, 1974, pp. 34-43.

4: Ibid, pp. 78-80.

8: Joseph Stalin's Dictates

1: en.wikipedia.org/wiki/Comintern_International

2: Ross, Carl, *The Finn Factor in American Labor, Culture and Society*. Parta Printers, Inc., New York Mills, MN, 1982, p. 184.

3: Wiita, John, "Crisis in the Finnish-American Left, 1925-1930." Unpublished, IHRCA, Anderson Library, U of MN, n.d.

4: Ibid.

5: Ibid.

6: Ibid, p. 29.

7: Ibid, p. 12.

8: *The Milwaukee Journal*, "Finns Return to the U.S. Displeased with Karelia." 4/27/1941.

9: *The Cooperative Pyramid Builder*, Vol. VI, #1. "A Co-operative Park in Wisconsin." 1/1931.

10: *The Cooperative Builder*, 8/5/39.

11: Hudelson, Richard and Carl Ross, *By the Ore Docks: A Working People's History of Duluth*. University of Minnesota Press, Minneapolis, MN, 2006, p. 1395.

9: The Battle for the CCE

1: Kuusinen, Aino, *The Rings of Destiny: Inside Soviet Russia from Lenin to Breshnev*. William Morrow and Co., New York, 1974, pp. 69-72.

2: Ross, Carl, *The Finn Factor in American Labor, Culture and Society*. Parta Printers, Inc., New York Mills, MN, 1982, p. 187.

3: Wiita, John, "Crisis in the Finnish-American Left, 1925-1930." Unpublished, IHRCA, Anderson Library, U of MN, n.d., p. 16.

4: Ibid, p. 24.

5: Ibid, p. 25.

6: Ibid, p. 27.

7: Kuusinen, Aino, *The Rings of Destiny: Inside Soviet Russia from Lenin to Breshnev*. William Morrow and Co., New York, 1974, p. 39.

8: Wiita, John, "Memories of Yrjö Sirola" and "Memories of Leo Laukki." Unpublished, IHRCA, Anderson Library, U of MN, n.d.

9: Wiita, John, "Crisis in the Finnish-American Left, 1925-1930." Unpublished, IHRCA, Anderson Library, U of MN, n.d., p. 22.

10: Sevander, Mayme and Laurie Hertzel, *They Took My Father: Finnish Americans in Stalin's Russia*. University of Minnesota Press, Minneapolis, MN, 2004, p. 22.

11: Wiita, John, "Crisis in the Finnish-American Left, 1925-1930." Unpublished, IHRCA, Anderson Library, U of MN, n.d., p. 26.

12: Ibid, p. 25.

13: *Työmies* 25th Anniversary Edition, "Terror against Labor." n.d.

14: *Workers and Farmers Cooperative Bulletin*, 1/1931.

15: Wiita, John, "Crisis in the Finnish-American Left, 1925-1930." Unpublished, IHRCA, Anderson Library, U of MN, n.d., p. 29.

16: Ibid, p. 28.

17: Ibid.

10: KTA: Promoting Karelian Fever

1: Golubev, Alexey and Irina Takala, *The Search for a Socialist El Dorado: Finnish Immigration to Soviet Karelia from the United States and Canada in the 1930s*. Michigan State University Press, East Lansing, MI, 2014, p. 28.

2: Sevander, Mayme, *Of Soviet Bondage: Sequel to Red Exodus*. Distributed by Brooks Anderson, Duluth, MN, 1996, p. 5.

3: Golubev, ibid, pp. 28-29.

4: Golubev, ibid, p. 29.

5: Sevander, ibid, p. 9.

6: Golubev, ibid, p. 28.

7: Ibid.

8: Pogorelskin, Alexis, "Matti Tenhunen and the Recruitment of North American Finns to Karelia: New Questions." n.d.

9: Sevander, ibid, p. 5.

10: *Journal of Finnish Studies: Victims and Survivors of Karelia*, Vol 15, No. 1 & 2. Guest editors Markku Kangaspuro and Samira Saramo, Houston, TX, 11/2011, p. 106.

11: Golubev, ibid, p. 28.

12: Sevander, Mayme, *Red Exodus: Finnish-American Emigration to Russia*. OSCAT in cooperation with Atlas Games. Distributed by Duluth International Peace Center, Duluth, MN, 1993, pp. 43-44.

13: Golubev, ibid, p. 29.

14: Pogorelskin, ibid.

15: Pogorelskin, Alexis, "Communism and the Co-ops: Recruiting and Financing the Finnish-American Migration to Karelia." *Karelian Exodus: Finnish Communities in North America and Soviet Karelia during the Depression Era*, Vol. 8, No. 1. Aspasia Books, Inc., Beaverton, Ontario, Canada, 8/2004.

16: Golubev, ibid.

17: Sevander, Mayme and Laurie Hertzel, *They Took My Father: Finnish Americans in Stalin's Russia*. University of Minnesota Press, Minneapolis, MN, 2004, p. 19.

18: Sevander, *Red Exodus*, ibid, p. 44.

19: en.wikipedia.org/wiki/Mesaba_Cooperative_Park.

20: Sevander and Hertzel, ibid, p. 78.

21: Pogorelskin, ibid.

22: Wiita, John, Unpublished autobiography. IHRCA, Anderson Library, U of MN, n.d., p. 22.

23: Kuusinen, Aino, *The Rings of Destiny: Inside Soviet Russia from Lenin to Breshnev*. William Morrow and Co., New York, 1974, pp. 44-45.

11: The Door Closed

1: www.biography.com/people/joseph-mccarthy-9390801

2: Lind, Norma, interview with author, n.d.

12: The Journey to Karelia

1: Sevander, Mayme, *Of Soviet Bondage: Sequel to Red Exodus*. Distributed by Brooks Anderson, Duluth, MN, 1996, pp. 18-19.

2: Ibid, p. 12.

13: Life in Karelia

1: Golubev, Alexey and Irina Takala, *The Search for a Socialist El Dorado: Finnish Immigration to Soviet Karelia from the United States and Canada in the 1930s*. Michigan State University Press, East Lansing, MI, 2014, p. 29.

2: Pogorelskin, Alexis, "Matti Tenhunen and the Recruitment of North American Finns to Karelia: New Questions." n.d.

3: Pogorelskin, Alexis, "Communism and the Co-ops: Recruiting and Financing the Finnish-American Migration to Karelia." *Karelian Exodus: Finnish Communities in North America and Soviet Karelia during the Depression Era*, Vol. 8, No. 1. Aspasia Books, Inc., Beaverton, Ontario, Canada, 8/2004.

4: Sevander, Mayme, *Red Exodus: Finnish-American Emigration to Russia*. OSCAT in cooperation with Atlas Games. Distributed by Duluth International Peace Center, Duluth, MN, 1993, p. 101.

14: Stalin's Great Terror

1: Sevander, Mayme, *Red Exodus: Finnish-American Emigration to Russia*. OSCAT in cooperation with Atlas Games. Distributed by Duluth International Peace Center, Duluth, MN, 1993, p. 101.

2: Ibid, p. 105.

3: Ibid, p. 106.

4: Pogorelskin, Alexis, "Matti Tenhunen and the Recruitment of North American Finns to Karelia: New Questions." n.d.

5: Sevander, Mayme, *Of Soviet Bondage: Sequel to Red Exodus*. Distributed by Brooks Anderson, Duluth, MN, 1996, p. 44.

6: Ibid, *Red Exodus*, p. 124.

7: Ibid, pp. 35-36.

15: The Truth be Told

1: Sevander, Mayme, *Red Exodus: Finnish-American Emigration to Russia*. OSCAT in cooperation with Atlas Games. Distributed by Duluth International Peace Center, Duluth, MN, 1993, p. 19.

2: Wilde, Robert, "Joseph Stalin's Death." ThoughtCo, September 8, 2021, thoughtco.com/how-did-stalin-die-1221206.

3: Sevander, Mayme and Laurie Hertzel, *They Took My Father: Finnish Americans in Stalin's Russia*. University of Minnesota Press, Minneapolis, MN, 2004, pp. 172-173.

4: Ibid, *Red Exodus*, p. 123.

5: *The Weekly Standard*, "Stalin's American Victims," Peter Day, 1/4/1999.

BIBLIOGRAPHY

AUTHOR INTERVIEWS/UNPUBLISHED MATERIAL/MISC

Centre for the Protection and Management of the Historic and Cultural Monuments of the Ministry of Culture, the Republic of Karelia, Russia.

Keweenaw National Historical Park, Calumet, Michigan.

"Historical Sketches of the Town of Oulu, Bayfield County, Wisconsin: 1889-1956." Sunnyside Homemaker's Club, n.d.

Lahti, Duane and Arnold Johnson. Email regarding early stores in Oulu and Iron River, 2/26/21.

Lind, Norma. Interview with author, n.d.

"The Merritt Family and the Mesabi Iron Range." The Minnesota Historical Society.

Report on IWW or Bolshevik Activities in the District of Massachusetts to William E. Allen, Acting Chief of the Bureau of Investigation in Washington by Boston BoI Informant J.S. Peterson, Feb. 13, 1919. DoJ, BoI Investigative Files, NARA collection M-1085, reel 923, file 167630.

Työmies Society. "For the Common Good." Superior, WI, 1977.

Wiita, John. "Crisis in the Finnish-American Left, 1925-1930." Unpublished, IHRCA, Anderson Library, U of MN, n.d.

_____ "Memories of Leo Laukki." Unpublished, IHRCA, Anderson Library, U of MN, n.d.

_____ "Memories of Yrjö Sirola." Unpublished, IHRCA, Anderson Library, U of MN, n.d.

_____ Unpublished autobiography. IHRCA, Anderson Library, U of MN, n.d.

_____ "Tyovaen Opisto - Working People's College." Unpublished, IHRCA, Anderson Library, U of MN, n.d.

MAGAZINES/NEWSPAPERS/WEB ARTICLES

The Cooperative Builder. 8/5/1939.

The Cooperative Pyramid Builder, Vol. VI, #1. "A Co-operative Park in Wisconsin." 1/1931.

The Duluth News Tribune. "Co-operative Buying May Broaden Scope." 8/26/1917.

Higgins, Andrew. "He found One of Stalin's Mass Graves. Now He's in Jail." *New York Times*, 4/27/2020.

Journal of Finnish Studies: Victims and Survivors of Karelia, Vol 15, No. 1 & 2. Guest editors Markku Kangaspuro and Samira Saramo, Houston, TX, 11/2011.

Kostiainen, Auvo. "Contacts Between the Finnish Labour Movements in the United States and Canada." IHRCA, Anderson Library, U of MN, n.d.

_____ "Santeri Nuorteva and the Origins of Soviet-American Relations." IHRCA, Anderson Library, U of MN, n.d.

_____ "Turbulent Times: The Last Years of Santeri Nuorteva in America, 1918-1920." IHRCA, Anderson Library, U of MN, n.d.

"Lenin's Famous Letter to the American Workers." Transcribed by Einde O'Callaghan, *Labor Action*, Vol. IX, No. 5, 1/29/1945.

The Milwaukee Journal. "Finns Return to the U.S. Displeased with Karelia." 4/27/1941.

Pogorelskin, Alexis. "Matti Tenhunen and the Recruitment of North American Finns to Karelia: New Questions." n.d.

Sandburg, Carl. "Finn Rebel Hid Weeks and then Makes Escape." *The Evening News*, Harrisburg, Pennsylvania, 3/4/1919.

Siitonen, Harry. "The Finnish-American Labor Movement – An Historical Outline." finnlabor.net.

Takala, Irina. "From the Firing Pan into the Fire: North American Finns in Soviet Karelia." n.d.

"They wanted to Believe." *News-Herald*, Ashabula, OH. News-herald.com/news/they-wanted-to-believe/article, 7/29/2008.

The Weekly Standard. "Stalin's American Victims." Peter Day, 1/4/1999.

Työmies 25th Anniversary Edition. "Terror against Labor." n.d.

Weidenhamer, Emily. "Disillusionment on the Grandest of Scales: Finnish-Americans in the Soviet Union, 1917-1939." geohistory.today/finnish-americans-ussr-disillusionment/.

Wilde, Robert. "Joseph Stalin's Death." ThoughtCo, September 8, 2021, thoughtco.com/how-did-stalin-die-1221206.

Wirtanen, Donald. Translation of the Työmies Society mission from July 20, 1903. *Finnish-American Reporter*, 1/1991.

Workers and Farmers Cooperative Bulletin. 1/1931.

"Workmen will have New Bank." Unk. publication, 10/16/1917.

Books

Ahola, David. "The Karelian Fever Episode of the 1930s." *A Journal of Finnish American History and Culture. Vol. 5*. Michael Karni, editor.

Baron, Nick. *Soviet Karelia: Politics, Planning and Terror in Stalin's Russia, 1920-1939*. Routledge, London, 2007.

Golubev, Alexey and Irina Takala. *The Search for a Socialist El Dorado: Finnish Immigration to Soviet Karelia from the United States and Canada in the 1930s*. Michigan State University Press, East Lansing, MI, 2014.

Hudelson, Richard and Carl Ross. *By the Ore Docks: A Working People's History of Duluth*. University of Minnesota Press, Minneapolis, MN, 2006.

Kuromiya, Hiroaki. *The Voices of the Dead: Stalin's Great Terror in the 1930s*. Yale University Press, New Haven, CT, 2007.

Kuusinen, Aino. *The Rings of Destiny: Inside Soviet Russia from Lenin to Breshnev*. William Morrow and Co., New York, 1974.

Lankton, Larry. *Cradle to Grave: Life, Work, and Death at the Lake Superior Copper Mines*. Oxford University Press, New York, 1991.

Morley, Jefferson. *The Ghost: The Secret Life of CIA Spymaster James Jesus Angleton*. St. Martin's Press, New York, 2017.

Pelto, Matti. "Memories from the Minnesota Iron Ore Mines." *A Journal of Finnish American History and Culture, Vol. 5*. Michael Karni, editor.

Pogorelskin, Alexis. "Communism and the Co-ops: Recruiting and Financing the Finnish-American Migration to Karelia." *Karelian Exodus: Finnish Communities in North America and Soviet Karelia during the Depression Era*, Vol. 8, No. 1. Aspasia Books, Inc., Beaverton, Ontario, Canada, 8/2004.

Ross, Carl. *The Finn Factor in American Labor, Culture and Society*. Parta Printers, Inc., New York Mills, MN, 1982.

Sevander, Mayme. *Of Soviet Bondage: Sequel to Red Exodus*. Distributed by Brooks Anderson, Duluth, MN, 1996.

_____ *Red Exodus: Finnish-American Emigration to Russia*. OSCAT in cooperation with Atlas Games. Distributed by Duluth International Peace Center, Duluth, MN, 1993.

_____ and Laurie Hertzel. *They Took My Father: Finnish Americans in Stalin's Russia*. University of Minnesota Press, Minneapolis, MN, 2004.

Snyder, Timothy. *Bloodlands: Europe between Hitler and Stalin*. Basic Books, New York, 2010.

Tzouliadis, Tim. *The Forsaken: An American Tragedy in Stalin's Russia*. Penguin Press, New York, 2008.

Wisherd, Nan. *Echoes from the Past*. Cable Publishing, Brule, WI, 2006.

Zlobina, Vieno. *Their Ideals were Crushed: A Daughter's Story of the Säde Commune in Soviet Karelia*. Migration Institute of Finland, Turku, Finland, 2017.

WEBSITES

Authorscorner.info/kuusin.htm

BBC.com/news/world-europe, "Soviet Union Timeline"

CNN.com/WORLD, "Pictorial Essay: Death Trenches Bear Witness to Stalin's Purges," July 17, 1997

en.wikipedia.org/wiki/Calumet_and_Hecla_Mining_Company

en.wikipedia.org/wiki/Carl_Sandburg

en.wikipedia.org/wiki/Citizens_Alliance

en.wikipedia.org/wiki/Cold_War

en.wikipedia.org/wiki/Comintern_International

en.wikipedia.org/wiki/Communist_Party_USA

en.wikipedia.org/wiki/Co-operative_Central_Exchange

en.wikipedia.org/wiki/Copper_Country_Strike_of_1913-14

en.wikipedia.org/wiki/Edvard_Gyling

en.wikipedia.org/wiki/Eteenpain

en.wikipedia.org/wiki/Finnish_Socialist_Federation

en.wikipedia.org/wiki/first_five-year_plan

en.wikipedia.org/wiki/Great_Purge

en.wikipedia.org/wiki/Hanna_Mine_Disasters

en.wikipedia.org/wiki/History_of_Finland

en.wikipedia.org/wiki/index.php?title=Sveaborg_rebellion&oldid=862161367

en.wikipedia.org/wiki/Industrial_Workers_of_the_World

en.wikipedia.org/wiki/Industrialisti

en.wikipedia.org/wiki/Iron_Curtain

en.wikipedia.org/wiki/Joseph_Stalin

en.wikipedia.org/wiki/Julius_and_Ethel_Rosenberg

en.wikipedia.org/wiki/Karelian_Autonomous_Soviet_Socialist_Republic

en.wikipedia.org/wiki/mass_killings_under_communist_regimes

en.wikipedia.org/wiki/Mesaba_Cooperative_Park

en.wikipedia.org/wiki/Oliver_Iron_Mining_Company

en.wikipedia.org/wiki/Otto_Wille_Kuusinen

en.wikipedia.org/wiki/Red_Guards_(Finland)

en.wikipedia.org/wiki/Red_Scare

en.wikipedia.org/wiki/Russian_Soviet_Federative_Socialist_Republic

en.wikipedia.org/wiki/Sandarmokh

en.wikipedia.org/wiki/Santeri_Nuorteva

en.wikipedia.org/wiki/Soviet_Union

en.wikipedia.org/wiki/Työmies

en.wikipedia.org/wiki/Vladimir_Lenin

en.wikipedia.org/wiki/Western_Federation_of_Miners

en.wikipedia.org/wiki/Work_Peoples_College

en.wikipedia.org/wiki/World_War_II_Casualties

en.wikipedia.org/wiki/Yury_Dmitriev

en.wikipedia.org/wiki/Zimmermann_Telegram

geohistory.today/finnish-american-ussr-disillusionment/

History.com/Cold War History

history.com/this-day-in-history/marx-publishes-manifesto

loffke.net/norh-americas-finns-caught-karelia-fever

sites.rootsweb.com/~wiprice/Brantwd_Finns_in_Russia.htm

Trivia-Library.com

www.biography.com/people/joseph-mccarthy-9390801

www.britannica.com/biography/vladimir-lenin

www.britannica.com/place/united-states/the-red-scare/ref613188

www.britannica.com/Second_International/ref290596

www.coldwar.org/articles/50s/senatorjosephmccarthy.asp

www.d.umn.edu/~apogorel/Karelia/Gylling.html

www.findagrave.com ID 32345469 accessed November 5, 2018

www.historymuseum.ca/blog/history-of-cobalt-ontario

www.marxists.org/history/international/index/htm

www.newworldencyclopedia.org/entry/Finnish_Civil_War

www.peacehost.net/FinnLabor/Memoirs37.htm

www.roosevelt.nl/santeri-nuorteve-american-wanderings-finnish-socialist

www.wired.com/2011/10/red-spy-steals-a-bomb-secrets/

Zenithcity.com/archive/legendary-tales/duluths-red-scare-the-wobblies/2/

INDEX

Captions: Bold, italicized
Footnotes: Italicized

A

Aho, Alexandra Laulaja, 38, 120
Aho, Henry, 37-38, 119, 120
Aho, Herbert, 120
Ahokas, Elis, 110, 111, 167, 169, 181, 199
Ahokas, Emma, 110, 111, 167, 169, 181, 182, 191, 193
Ahokas, Vieno, 110, 167, 169, 181-182, 191, 193
Akin, Sabrie, 32
Alalauri, Maria, 193
Aronen, Kalle, 140, 143, 146, 148, 175, 176, 177, 179

B

Banks family, 119
Bauer, Bruno, 14
Beria, Lavrentiy, 190, 197
Bolshevik Revolution, 7, 9, 83, 85-86, 92, 126
Bolsheviks or Bolshevists, 41, 42, 84, 85, 86, 92, 99, 186
Boman, Wilho, 94, 98, *98*, 103, 114, *114*
Brule Co-op Park, 119-121
Brule Co-op Store, 6, *81*, **102**

C

Calumet & Hecla Mining Co. (C & H), 19-20, *21*, **22**, 24, 55, 123
Capello, Dolores, 20

Carnegie, Andrew, 29
Cheka, 107, *107*
Cherry (MN) Co-op, **102**
Chester, Albert, 25
Chugunkovs, Ivan and Sergey, 204
Citizens' Alliance, 46, 59, 123
Cold War, 154
Comintern (Communist International), 4, 10, 11, *15*, 97, 99, 109, 113, 117, 126, 127, 179, 207
Communist Manifesto, The, 15
Communist Movement, 1, 3, 4, 5, 8-9, 11, 42, 96-97, 101, 104, 203, 205
Communist Party of the U.S.A. (CPUSA), 9, 92, 101, 103, 113, 114, 115, *115*, 117, 126, 127, 129, *129*, 131, 132, 134, 135, 137, 143, 147, 150, 207
Congdon, Chester, 29
Cooke, Jay, 25
Cooperative Central Exchange (CCE), 80-83, **82**, 114, *115*, 127, **128**, 129, *129*, 131, 132, 133, 134, *134*, 135, 137, 188
Cooperative Movement, 11, 127
Copper Country Strike of 1913, 59-61, 68
Corgan, Aino, 149, 178, 182, 187, 189
Corgan, Katri, 149, 178, 182, 187, 189, 193
Corgan, Mayme – see Sevander, Mayme Corgan
Corgan, Oscar, 6, 10, 13, 14, 70, 74, *81*, **102**, 117, **130**, 131, *131*, 133-134, *133*, 140, 143, 145-146, *146*, 149, 150, 172, 175, 176, 177-178, 179, 180, 182, 183, 184, 187, 199, 203, 205

220

Corgan, Paul, 149, 178, 182, 187, 189

Czar of Russia, 6, 11, 12, 43, 45, 83

D

Debs, Eugene, 92

Dmitriev, Yury, 202, 203, 204, 209, 210

Duluth & Iron Range Railway Co., 26, 27

Duluth, Missabe & Northern Railway Co., 29, 61

DSS & A Railroad, 80

Dvoika, 184, 186, 189, 192, 202

E

Engels, Friedrich, 16

Erich, Rafael, 100

Estemirova, Natalia, 210

Eteenpäin (newspaper), 103, 115, 195

Exchange Finnish Cooperative Training School, 81, **82**

F

Ferdinand, Franz, Archduke of Austria, and wife Sophie, 68

Field, Marshall, 27

Finnish Federation, 9-10, 50, 51, 54, 56, 59, 62, 66, 67, 68, 69, 74, 79, 81, 83, 101, 103, 110, 113, 114, 115, **116**

Finnish Socialist Workers' Republic (FSWR), 89, 90

Finnish Workers Federation (FWF), 115, *115*, 117, 135, 136, *136*, 139, 140, 143, 147, 150

First Category Arrests, 189, 200, 204

First Five-Year Plan (Stalin's), 125, 126, 127, 137, 138, 139, 172, 176

First International, 4, 15, *15*, 16

Flige, Irina, 202

Flynn, Elizabeth Gurley, 72

G

General Strike of 1905 (Finland), 7, 12, 44

Glasnost, 160, 201

Gorbachev, Mikhail, 160, 161, 201

Great Hate – see Great Terror

Great Terror, 1, 164, 179, 184, 185, 189, 192, 193, 195, 196, 198, 199, 201, 202, 203, 204, 206, 207, 209

Gulag Archipelago, The, **200**, 201

Gulags, *115*, 186, **200**, 206

Gyyling, Edvard, 6, 7, 9, 12, 13, 30, 70, 71, 87, 89, 90, **90**, 91, 93-95, 100-101, 105, 110, 125, *134*, 137, 138, 142, 146, 148, 170, 172, 174, 176, 178, 179, 180, 181, 182, 183, 189, 190, 194, 205

H

Halonen, Alex, 53

Halonen, George, 81, 105, **130**, 131, 135

Harju, Matt, 33, 38, 39

Haywood, Big Bill, 45

Hendrickson, Martin, 47

Hill, Helen, 203

Hokkanen, Lawrence and Sylvia, 172, 174, 180, 195

Holmes, Oliver Wendell, 98

Honka, Paavo, 187

Hoover, Herbert, 121, 122, 123

Hulbert, Edwin, 19

I

Industrial Workers of the World (IWW, "Wobblies"), 9, 45-46, 67, 68, *68*, 69, 72, 78, 91, 94, 206

Industrialisti (newspaper), 68

Insab stores, 173, 174, 178, 181

International Workingmen's Association – see First International

Ioffe, Veniamin, 200, 202, 203

Iron Curtain, 154

IWW – see Industrial Workers of the World

J

Jaakola, Matt, 65

Johnson, Fred, 39

Johnson, Jennie Maki, *134*

Johnson, Nestor, 63

Johnson, N.P. (Nils Peter), 23, 27, 35-36, 38, 65

Jones, W.B., 74

Juhannus Juhla (Mid-summer Festival), 35, 169, *169*

Jukkola, William, 190

K

Kangas, John, 39

Karelian Fever, 1, 4, 139, 143, 147, 150, 207

Karelian Resettlement Administration – see Resettlement Administration

Karelian Technical Aid (KTA), 137, 138, 139, 140, 142, 143, *143*, 145, 146, *146*, 147, 148, 149, 150, 168, 175, 176, 177, *188*

Karni, Michael G., *47*, 127

KGB – see NKVD

Khruschev, Nikita, 197, 198, 199

Kirja Publishing Co., 175, 178, 180, 182

Kirov, Sergei, 179, *179*, 184, 185

Kissanen, Aku, 51, *51*

Kopplin, Fred and son Harry, 39

Kortesmaa, Henry, 65-66

Koski, Herman, 39

Koskinen, Benjamin, 190

Kosonen, Vihtori, 47

Krasny Bor Forest, *201*, 204, 209

Kuusinen, Aino Sarola, 100, 108-109, 139, 143, 147-148, 173, 197, 206

Kuusinen, Otto, 6, 7, 12, 13, 30, 44, *44*, 45, 70, 71, 87, 88, 89, 90, 99, 100, 108, 109, 113, 114, 115, *115*, *116*, 117, 132, *132*, *132*, *134*, 136, 142, *146*, 147, 148, 205, 206, 207

L

Labor Movement, 4, 5, 8, 9, 10, 11, 13, 30, 41, 44, 45, 46, 50, 53, 56, 72, 74, 78, 101, 104, 123, 203, 205

Labor World (newspaper), 32

Landsdale, Guy, 119

Latva, John, 139, 143

Laukki, Leo, 6, 12-13, 44, *44*, 50, 53, *54*, 66-67, 68, 70, 72, 79, 91, *132*, 206

Lauri, Andrew, 39

Lenin, Vladimir, 7, 12, *15*, 41-43, *54*, 74, 83, 84, 85-86, 88, 89, 90, 91, 99, 100-101, 105-106, 107-108, 109, *167*, 186, 198, 200, 206

Lenin's Letter to America's Workers, 92

Lindqvist, Leo – see Laukki, Leo

M

Machine Fund – see Resettlement Administration

Maki, Oscar, 38-39, *39*, 134

Man car (mining), **22**

Manner, Kullervo, 90, 115, *115*, 134

Martens, Ludwig, 96

Maryland, Henry, 39
Marx, Karl, 4, 5, 9, 14-17, *16*
Matveyev, Mikhail, 200
McCormick, Cyrus, 27
McDougall, Alexander, 29
Memorial (Society), 200, 201, *201*, 202, 204, 209-110
Menshevik, 41, 84
Merritt, John, 16
Mesaba Co-op Park, 146, *146*
Miller, Frank – see Sirola, Yrjö
Mines and mining companies
    Calumet & Hecla Mining Co. (C & H), 19-20, *21*, *22*
    Minnesota Iron Mining Co., 26
    Mountain Iron Co., 28
    Oliver Mining Co., 29, 57
    Osceola Mining Co., 23, *23*
    Quincy Mining Co., 123
    Union Pacific Coal Co., *39*
Minnesota Iron Mining Co., 26
Minor, Robert, 131
Moratzski, Joseph, 74
Morecum. Elisha, 27
Morgan, J.P., 98
Morton, A. – see Kuusinen, Aino Sarola
Mountain Iron Co., 28
Murros, Kaapo, 51

N

Nicholas II – see Czar of Russia
Nissinen, Antti, *193*
NKVD (People's Commissariat of Internal Affairs), *107*, 186, 188, 189, 191, 192, 193, 196, 200, 201, 202, 203, 205, 207

Northern Co-op Society, 136, *136*
Northern Pacific Railroad, 30, 80
Nummevuori, John, 81
Nuorteva, Santeri, 6, 12, 30, 45, *51*, 67, *67*, 70, 74, 89, 90, 92, 94, 96-97, *96*, 98, *98*, 206-207
Nyberg, Alexander – see Nuorteva, Santori

O

Oja, John, 33
Oliver, Henry, 29
Oliver Mining Co., 29, 31, 57, 61
Osceola Mining Co., 23, *23*
Oulu & Waino Leftist Cooperative People, 136, 145
Oulu Co-op Creamery, 65, 66
Oulu Finn Hall, 63, 64, 118, 145
Oulu Warren School, 65

P

Palmer, Alexander, 98
Palmer Raids, 98-99
Palo, Viola, 120
Paull, Irene, 35
Pelto, Matti, 58
People's Commissariat of Internal Affairs – see NKVD
Politkovskaya, Anna, 210
Pravda (newspaper), 84
Prince, Edward, 26
Provisional Government (Russian), 85, 86
Pudas homestead, *40*
Puro, Henry – see Wiita, John

Q

Quincy Mining Co., 123

R

Raivaaja (newspaper), 8, 10, 50, *67*, 79, 89, 94, 103, 194

Red Finns, 7, 9, 86, 89, 90, 91, 101

Red Guard (Finnish), 7, 44, 90, 93, 115

Red Guard (Russian), 85, 86

Red Scare, 97, 156

Reivo, William, 79

Resettlement Administration (Karelia), 142, 146, 147, 172, 173, 175, 176, 177

Rockefeller, John D., 27, 29, 30, 98

Ronn, Eskel, **130**

Roosevelt, Franklin Delano (FDR), 122, 124

Ross, Carl, 50, 101

Russian Ark, 99

Russian Revolution of 1905 – see General Strike of 1905

S

Säde commune, 111, 166, 167, 169-170, 181, 191, 193

Sandarmokh, 200, *201*, 202, **202**, 203, 204, 207, 209

Sandburg, Carl, 93, *93*, 96

SDP (Finland), 7, 8, 10, 12, 13, 30, 44, 45, *67*, 71, 86-87, *115*, *134*

Second International, 4, 7, 11, *15*, 30, 41, 43, 47, 62, 74, 205

Seeberville Affair, 60

Sevander, Kalle, 184, 187

Sevander, Mayme Corgan, 6, *81*, 145, *146*, 149, 178, 179, 182, 183, 184, 185, 187, 190, 192, 199, 209

Sevander, Vieno, 184

Seven Iron Men, 28-29

Silvola, Charles, 39

Sirola, Yrjö, 6, 7, 12, 13, 30, 45, **52**, 54, *54*, 55, 67, *67*, 70, 71, 87, 88, 89, 90, 99, 108, 114, 115, **116**, *132*, *134*, 147, 178, 179, 205, 207

Solovki prison, 200, *200*, 201

Solzhenitszyn, Aleksandr, *200*, 201, *201*

Soviet Karelia Relief Committee, 105, 110

Space Race, 158

Stalin, Joseph, 14, *15*, 84, 89, 99, 104, 107, 108, 109, 112, 113, **116**, 125, 138, 150, 179, *179*, 183, 184, 185, 189, 192, 193, 194, 196, 197-198, 201, *201*, 202, 206

Stone, George, 25, 26, 27

Strikes
  Copper Country Strike of 1913, 59-61, 68
  Great Steel Strike of 1919, 98
  Mesabi Range Strike of 1907, 57, 59
  Mesabi Range Strike of 1916, 72
  Ore Dock Workers Strike, Twin Ports, 61

Stuntz, George, 25, 27

Swanson, Charles, 74

Swedish American Lines (SAL), 143, *143*, *146*, 165, 166, 175

T

Tainio, Taavi, 50-51

Tanner, Antero F., 47

Tenhunen, Matti, 4, 10, 13, 14, 70, 74, 80, 83, 105, 117, 129, **130**, 131, 132-133, *132*, 134, 135, 136, 137, 138, 139, 140, 142, **142**, *142*, 143, *143*, 146, *146*, 172, 175, 176, 177, 179, 188, *188*, 203, 207

Tenhune, Toivo, 119, 133, 134, 135, 142, *146*, *188*, 207

Third International – see Comintern

Tokoi, Oskari, 89

Torgsin store, 173, 174

Toveri (newspaper), 10, 51, 67, *67*, 79, 103, 115

Tower, Charlemagne, 25, 26, 27

Troika, 186, 189, 190, 192, 202

Trotsky, Leon, 85

Tse-tung, Mao, 206

Turpeinen, Viola, 120

Tuulos, Toivo, 191

Tuura, John, 37

Tuura, Lydia, 33

Twin Town W & F Co-op Society, 136

Työmies (newspaper), 8, 10, 13, 47, 50, 51, 60, 67, 68, 74, 79, 81, 103, 105, 113, 115, 127, *130*, 131, 133, 136, 195

Työmies Publishing Company (Työmies Society), 68, 114, *130*, 131, 133, 135

U-V

United Farmers Store Co., 37

United States Steel (USS), 31, 35, 57, 59, 61, 72, 98

Upton, Anthony, 90-91

USAT *Buford*, 99

Valiparakit, 173, 177, 182

Viapori Military Revolt, 12, 44

W

Waino-Oulu Telephone Association, 65

Waino Pioneer Chapel, *36*

Waino Round Hall, 38, 63, 117-118, *118*, 119, 145

Wentela, August, 37

Wentela, George E., 119

Wentela, Mary Koski, *36*

Western Federation of Miners (WFM), 9, 45, 46, 55, 57, 59-60, 61

Western Union Telegrams, 73

Westfield, Duane, 37

White Finns, 7, 86, 89, 90

White Guards, 93, 95

Wiita, John, 10, 13, 14, *51*, 54, 67, 68, 70, 74, 79, 114, 115, 127, **128**, 129, 131, 132, *132*, 133, 135, 136, 138, 140-141, 142, **142**, 143, 147, 150, 205, 207

Wilson, Woodrow, 77, 78, 92

Wirtanen, Donald, 47

Wobblies – see Industrial Workers of the World

Work People's College, 8, 10, 12, **52**, 53-55, 67, 68

Workers & Farmers Cooperative United Alliance, 136

Workers' Paradise, 1, 6, 8, 10, 110, 150

Workers' Republic of Finland, 7

World War I, 68-69, 76, 83, 97

World War II, 150

X-Y-Z

Yagoda, Genrikh, 190, 193

Yezhov, Nikolai, 189, 190, 193

Zimmermann Telegram, 77-78